Knowledge and Freedom in the Work of Luis Villoro

Also Available from Bloomsbury:

American Philosophies by Erin McKenna and Scott L. Pratt
The Philosophies of America Reader edited by Kim Díaz and
Mathew A. Foust
Emilio Uranga's Analysis of Mexican Being by Emilio Uranga
Mexican Philosophy for the 21st Century by Carlos Alberto Sánchez

Knowledge and Freedom in the Work of Luis Villoro

Emancipatory Intelligence

Carlos Montemayor

BLOOMSBURY ACADEMIC

LONDON · NEW YORK · OXFORD · NEW DELHI · SYDNEY

BLOOMSBURY ACADEMIC
Bloomsbury Publishing Plc, 50 Bedford Square, London, WC1B 3DP, UK
Bloomsbury Publishing Inc, 1359 Broadway, New York, NY 10018, USA
Bloomsbury Publishing Ireland, 29 Earlsfort Terrace, Dublin 2, D02 AY28, Ireland

BLOOMSBURY, BLOOMSBURY ACADEMIC and the Diana logo are
trademarks of Bloomsbury Publishing Plc

First published in Great Britain 2026

To my uncle, Carlos Antonio Montemayor Aceves

Contents

Contents

Figures

Foreword

Intellectual inquiry, the discovery of truth and the dissemination of knowledge have always had the potential to enhance human freedom, both political and social. Pursuing the truth is integral to any pursuit of liberation from oppression, manipulation, and abuse. Few public intellectuals, and even fewer academic philosophers, have lived their lives as fully in accordance with these principles as Luis Villoro. He was a public intellectual and political activist who faced considerable danger throughout his life, and he did so with an exceptional mixture of aplomb and reasonableness. He fought for justice without falling into the resentment and cynicism produced by ideological dogmatism. His example as an engaged intellectual is much needed today, a lesson in how to avoid ethical paralysis, political indifference, along with epistemic pessimism or skepticism.

We live in difficult times. The public sphere, at the national and international levels, has been undercut by polarization, the collective distraction caused by social media, and the attention economy. Participants in the attention economy project their most cherished opinions as loudly as possible, asserting their opinions for the sake of gaining popularity or to silence those who oppose them. In many instances, these performances are framed algorithmically, commercially monitored in order to enhance and cash in on their appeal. There is an urgent need to reshape the way we communicate. Defending and rebuilding the public sphere means trying as much as possible to cooperate with others, becoming less opinionated, and fostering practices of genuine attention and cooperation. Solidarity should be at the center of this effort, and Villoro's work can serve as inspiration for us in achieving this goal.

Villoro's work can help us imagine a new political and social narrative, focused on reasonableness rather than the rationality behind strategic reasoning. He thereby provides a new way of conceiving the relation between knowledge and politics, one that develops an emancipatory kind of intelligence to enhance social cooperation and engagement. He also offers a conception of human reason that reflects this commitment. For Villoro, an emancipatory intelligence entails a renewed account of how reasonableness should inform other kinds of rationality that depend on it for their justification, including technological, instrumental, and strategic rationality.

The concerns with knowledge, freedom, and social collaboration that preoccupied Villoro were also major concerns of the American pragmatists. This book argues that Villoro's work is best understood as a continuation of the pragmatist tradition, expanding it, with innovative insights, into a new conception of epistemic and ethical emancipation. He did so in a way that engaged the entirety of the American continent, with its rich philosophical and cultural traditions, as well as the diversity of its indigenous peoples. Villoro's work offers a pragmatism for the Americas as a whole, as Gregory Fernando Pappas has suggested.

I hope that this book on the work of one of the most politically active philosophers and intellectuals of the Americas can help inspire social activists and public intellectuals to forge a new kind of public engagement. However, like Villoro's own life, his work should also inspire academics, beginning with philosophers who work on Latin American philosophy, pragmatism, and many areas of contemporary philosophy, particularly epistemology, ethics, political philosophy, and philosophy of language. Academics in other fields, interested in how our theory of knowledge relates to ethics and politics, and on how this relation should inform social theory and political activism will find valuable insights in this book.

Political disappointment has caused a strange mixture of social indifference and social media theatricality. Instead of empty hope and encapsulated anger, we should work to create solidarity and through it, social transformation. Abstract theories and billionaires' utopias cannot heal fractured democracies. Rather, healing them requires the production of engaged and attentive, as well as reasonable, public spheres. It requires individuals to leave their comfort zones and meet the unknown or the "other." Villoro's social epistemology exemplifies one of the best ways to create this solidarity.

Acknowledgments

I would like to thank Gullermo Hurtado for his helpful insights on Luis Villoro's work and career. Guillermo's comments on the project and his support throughout its execution were crucial at various stages of writing. I am very grateful to Margarita M. Valdés for her patient and generous engagement in conversations we had about Wittgenstein and Villoro. My deep appreciation and gratitude to my friends Alejandra Cuestas and Miguel Villoro, they were constant companions in this journey. I am indebted to my friend and collaborator Ángeles Eraña for many conversations on the anchoring role of attention and for sharing her knowledge of the Ejército Zapatista de Liberación Nacional with me. Thanks to Pedro Stepanenko, Moisés Vaca, Manuel Vargas, and Carlos Sánchez for encouragement and feedback. Thanks to Alice Nakhimovsky for having been a wonderful editor. To Colleen Coalter and Aimee Brown at Bloomsbury, my gratitude for their constant support and flexibility. I also thank the organizers, as well as the participants, of the commemorative colloquium "Luis Villoro, one hundred years after his birth," which took place at the Instituto de Investigaciones Filosóficas of Universidad Nacional Autónoma de México, in November 2022. I am grateful to the Villoro archive at this Institute, particularly to Verónica Carmona and Miguel Gama for all their help while I was working at the archive. My greatest debt is to Victoria Frede-Montemayor, and to Berenice Montemayor and Berenice Romo de Vivar for their support.

Introduction

Genuine philosophy is radical and disruptive, a point that Luis Villoro elucidates in various texts. In one of them, on Edmund Husserl's phenomenology, Villoro argues that radical science is foundational because it does not depend on a specific set of disciplinary standards for its justification. Knowledge, more generally, should be a component of our quest for freedom, as part of its foundational character and independence from strategic interests. Villoro's work articulates this idea of radicalness, of philosophy as disruptive reasoning, by integrating the philosophical "sub-areas" of epistemology, ethics, and political philosophy, which makes his philosophy a thorough theory of reason and social cooperation.

This book offers the first comprehensive investigation of Villoro's philosophical work, most of which has not been translated into English. It is structured around commitments that Villoro held throughout his active political life and academic publications. The first chapter, "From the Cubicle to Zapatista Territory," surveys Villoro's trajectory. What initially seemed like inconsistencies of ideas or even of character, it shows, are in fact aspects of a deeply consistent and rigorous approach to justice, knowledge, and freedom. For example, Chapter 1 demonstrates that Villoro's earliest academic interests were already aligned with a commitment to engaging with indigenous Mexico, and that his involvement with the Ejército Zapatista de Liberación Nacional, later in his life, is fully consistent with this early commitment.

The second chapter, "The Practice of Non-exclusion: A Linguistic Analogy," articulates Villoro's general commitment to the integration of a theory of knowledge with a principle of non-exclusion to prevent forms of epistemic injustice and silencing, and their negative ethical and social consequences. This chapter begins to explore Villoro's views on reasonable communication, ethics, and social epistemology, through a linguistic analogy concerning the meta-ethical and meta-epistemological problem of how to develop, in concrete circumstances, conditions for the full and responsible exercise of our epistemic and moral capacities. Some of the illustrations of epistemic injustice and silencing in this chapter concern indigenous peoples, whom Villoro very much had in mind.

The third chapter, "Truth, Knowledge, and Freedom," centers on Villoro's analysis of reason. At its core is a commitment to distinguish proper from improper reasoning, to delineate the bounds of reason in concrete and historically-shaped situations of asymmetry and communicational pressures—a commitment that is strongly guided by a pragmatic approach. The chapter unpacks this commitment through Villoro's engagement with the work of Ludwig Wittgenstein, which was one of the main sources of inspiration for Villoro's well-known notion of the "figure of the world." One of the main texts by Villoro discussed in this chapter is his paper on Wittgenstein's *Tractatus Logico-Philosophicus*. The scope of Ludwig Wittgenstein's influence on Villoro's philosophical outlook is one of the surprises of the book. Not only does Villoro engage with Wittgenstein substantially, but his own pragmatic views are very consistent with his engagement with Wittgenstein. This was a fortunate discovery I made while working at Luis Villoro's archives housed at the Universidad Nacional Autónoma de México. Wittgenstein's investigations on the foundations of mathematics and language are relevant to Villoro's distinction between reasonable and unreasonable rationality and to Villoro's interest in the topic of the limits of reason. These themes resurface throughout the book, showing Villoro's commitment to the principle that we should never put instrumental reason above reason itself.

Chapter 4, "Reforming Intelligence," argues that to fully understand Villoro's approach to reason, we must understand his commitments to non-exclusion and reasonable communication as commitments to attend to the needs and realities of others. Such attention transforms our political and social landscapes by reducing the role of ideology and by increasing the participation of individuals and communities at all levels of society. All key intellectual duties that philosophy should promote, as its own fundamental duty, involve this *attentional anchoring of reason*. A contribution of this chapter is to show how the dilemma of ideology might be escaped, specifically, doxastic or strictly belief-based forms of rationalism that create the dilemma, in order to truly reform intelligence. Norms of attention, then, are fundamental to become less opinionated in order to become more attentive. The ideological kind of rationality, pervasive in strictly belief-based systems, explains why there can be an *invariance of structures of oppression across opposing ideologies.*

The first four chapters are devoted to Villoro's overall philosophical project as a theory of the limits of reason and of reasonableness, highlighting its originality and grounding character. This takes us into an investigation of what Villoro conceived as the normative bridge between ethics and epistemology. Chapters 5 and 6 are about Villoro's engagement with analytic philosophy. Chapter 5, "Pragmatism, Attentive Engagement, and Contemporary Epistemology," argues that Villoro's most celebrated work on analytic philosophy, *Creer, Saber, Conocer,* his book on knowledge, is best interpreted as a pragmatist view of belief and knowledge that seeks to bring together epistemic achievements with ethical principles. It presents Villoro's pragmatic view of belief and knowledge in light of the grounding function of attention, discussed in earlier chapters. The chapter argues that, while Villoro's social epistemology stands on its own, there is more coherence between his work on analytic epistemology and his political philosophy than has been previously acknowledged.

Chapter 6, "The Figure and Mind of the World: Ideology and Collective Memory," introduces Villoro's innovative distinction between the gnoseological and sociological conceptions of ideology. It also presents a framework to introduce the contemporary notions of epistemic charge and force, extending Villoro's work to recent work in social epistemology. Here, Villoro's engagement with the work of John

Rawls is relevant, explaining why it is justified to interpret Villoro as offering a non-idealist capability view of ethics in relation to epistemology. Examining Villoro's insightful and original account of ideology in light of contemporary epistemology shows how the distinction between what is rational and what is reasonable operates in the contexts of ethics and political theory, as well as its salience to contemporary debates in philosophy of language and to theories about how collective memory shapes the sociological aspects of ideology.

Chapter 7, "True Revolutions: A Bureaucracy of Intimacy," concludes the book with a summary of Villoro's approach to philosophy: the radicalness of philosophical thinking and its political implications. It discusses Villoro's engagement with social justice movements and introduces the idea of a "bureaucracy of intimacy," based on Villoro's notion of the anchoring function of reason on attention. It restates Villoro's assessment that much of the problem with our current thinking on rationality is that it simply demarcates the rational from the irrational: it would further need to distinguish the rational and unreasonable from the rational and reasonable. Without that distinction, there is no way to effectively combat ideology because the invariance of structures of oppression across opposing ideologies depends on unreasonable rationality.

This concluding chapter also emphasizes how rigor and clarity should be cultivated to fight against ideologies. Instead of structuring social hierarchization and strategic rationality, communities of attention and cooperation must reinvigorate our efforts to transform the world in a way that all benefit. In Villoro's characterization of disruptive thinking, epistemic charge and energy are needed, and he understands the latter as a kind of *cultural energy* characteristic of scientific and social revolutions. By contrast, many of us now spend our energy in ways that might count as rational, but which are in fact unreasonable, because they enfeeble and isolate us. The energy and resources that we use to compete against and attack each other should be put in the service of revolutionary thinking that enhances cooperation and peace. This is, according to Villoro, a demand of reason. Our energy arsenals should not threaten our existence, and our sciences should not be part of a commercialized arms race.

Symmetry and engagement in our relations brings out the best in us. When we genuinely communicate and cooperate, we develop our moral and epistemic competences. Communal efforts can reenergize our minds. Villoro's social epistemology and ethics are a remedy against epistemic skepticism and cynicism; against the temptation to "look inward" to justify ourselves, instead moving energetically "outwards" toward liberation and social transformation. For Villoro, there is personal involvement in how we are guided through reasonableness: we become more committed to participation and cooperation, and this enriches our lives by eliminating cynicism, dogmatism, and ideological thinking. Acting according to this principle creates a sense of epistemic solidarity and ethical trust.

Villoro reminds us that philosophy itself, when detached from the concrete needs and interests of humanity, becomes ideological. Anchoring reason in social contexts and specific realities is part of what makes philosophy disruptive and radical. While Villoro had a period where he devoted most of his energy to analytic philosophy, particularly epistemology and ethics, he never stopped thinking about politics, and in his latest academic stage it is politics, multiculturalism, and Zapatismo, that take center stage. The overall narrative arc of the book reflects this development.

History is one of the realities on which reason must be anchored. Denying or ignoring historical injustices may be justifiable according to some rules of rationality, but it is always unreasonable. For Villoro, once these injustices are clearly identified, one should proceed *negatively*: they should not be defined abstractly according to the axioms of a universal theory. Rather, to achieve justice and equality, one must pay precise attention to that which is unjust and unfair. Only by beginning with injustice in this negative path toward ethics and epistemology, by paying attention to what is unjust, can it be eliminated. Once that has been accomplished, new ideas and forms of life can eliminate resurging forms of ideological injustice, ameliorating the public sphere. This, again, is a demand of *reason* on our communicative and political practices.

The radicalness of philosophy entails rootedness and engagement. Although Villoro's ideas offer new ways of understanding traditional philosophical debates about knowledge, language, and justice across philosophical traditions, his thoughts and motivations were deeply embedded in Mexico, its history, and its future. Even so, his focus on analytic philosophy makes him one of the main exponents of this tradition in Latin America. This creates a rich tapestry of innovative and socially-rooted ideas that will surely inspire contemporary philosophers and political theorists.

Countries across the world are enmeshed in a moment of political crisis, characterized by confusion and a lack of trust. Inundating viewers with information, images, and other stimuli, social and news media demand constant attention, even as they create a general state of distraction, producing new forms of isolation and loneliness. Given the crisis of attention, Villoro's emphasis on the anchoring function of reason in concrete realities is very relevant, inviting us to concentrate differently and better, not only on injustice, but on each other. Perhaps, he may help us get out of our crisis.

Finally, a note on the translations from Villoro's work in Spanish: unless I explicitly state the name of the translator, all translations from Spanish are mine.

1

From the Cubicle to Zapatista Territory

Indigenous Mexico

Juan Villoro's moving account of his father's life was written in 2023. It starts with a photo of Luis Villoro as a young philosophy professor and ends with another photo in which he is sitting next to Subcomandante Marcos, the charismatic, knowledgeable leader and public voice of Mexico's Ejército Zapatista de Liberación Nacional (EZLN). In the first picture, taken around 1956, the handsome young professor sits at a desk, writing attentively. He is wearing a suit jacket and behind him is a bookshelf packed with books. In the second picture, taken in San Cristóbal de las Casas, Chiapas, in 2009, an old Villoro is holding an award in his name from the EZLN, framed in canvas. He is talking to Subcomandante Marcos, who appears in his usual green cap and black balaclava. How did the young professor end up in the company of rebels from Mexico's famous indigenous movement?

Given how academia works, one would expect that something went wrong between these two pictures. Something perhaps very wrong. The philosophy professor turned rogue; he joined a rebellious militia and abandoned his long, prestigious career at Mexico's flagship university, the Universidad Nacional Autónoma de México (UNAM). Maybe he lost hope and decided to abandon his practice of rigorous thinking and prolific writing for the dangers and uncertainties of a guerrilla comrade. This interpretation could not be further from the truth. The truth is indeed the opposite. Villoro was interested in what the EZLN was doing from very early in his career.

Villoro's brilliant first book, *Los grandes momentos del indigenismo en México* (The great moments of indigenism in Mexico, hereafter

"Grandes Momentos"), written in 1950 when he was 28, covers the very same set of issues that concerned the EZLN in its fight against historical injustices perpetrated by the Mexican government against indigenous communities. To Villoro, the arc of his prestigious career was always consistent with his support of the EZLN. His political activism and engagement with social causes was in its entirety consistent with his remarkable career.

Conceptions of indigenous peoples in the colonial Americas were always oppressive and often led to incredible cruelty. In the United States to this day, indigenous groups are perceived as some kind of foreign visitors from the past that don't quite belong to American culture. The shameful history of how indigenous groups were treated in Canada and the United States has largely been ignored. Narratives of the grand expansion into the west and the "taming of the frontier" prevent a collective reckoning for those crimes. Reservations are the legacy of a political conception that sees the indigenous world as alien to what the United States stands for. Indigenous peoples are not much better off in Mexico or other parts of Latin America. However, as Villoro illustrates in *Grandes Momentos*, there were transitional moments at different historical stages in which indigenous groups progressively gained a political and cultural recognition that defined Mexican culture and identity. The same holds true for other parts of Latin America, but it is clearly not the case either in the United States or Canada.

Unlike the United States, Mexico mythologized these "foreigners in their own ancestral land" as the founders of the primordial Mexican nation and as a crucial component of "mestizaje" (being of mixed Spanish and indigenous ancestry; a term that Gloria Anzaldúa uses in her philosophical appreciation of Mexican–American identity). But this mythologization of the indigenous world as the primordial root of Mexican culture was not accomplished in a single conceptual step.

An essential aspect of all the conceptions of Mexican indigenous groups is a juxtaposition between "us" and "them," a point clearly articulated by Ángeles Eraña in her preface to the fourth edition of *Grandes Momentos*. Even when the narrative says that there is some of "them" in us, "we" are never the same as "them." "They" depend on "us" for their meaning. The result is a fractured society that puts them in a hermeneutically asymmetric and unjust situation.

Grandes Momentos offers a lucid examination of three configurations of indigenous Mexico that correspond to watershed events in Mexican history. Villoro would eventually argue, in a book he published in 1998 and in other texts afterwards, that what is needed is a *pluralistic state*, rather than the homogenous nation of Mexican "citizens" he advanced in the third and final conception of the "indigenous other" in *Grandes Momentos*. Conceptions of indigenous communities as inferior or alien to mainstream culture produced appalling consequences during the colonial period. *Grandes Momentos* is Villoro's first intellectual step toward a full understanding of how the genuine inclusion of indigenous people would lead to the pluralistic state that Mexicans still hope to achieve.

The first conception of indigenous Mexico described in *Grandes Momentos* is the most devastating one, exemplifying the deep divorce between faith and morality that justified crimes and genocide. Ironically, it was in the name of Catholicism that the unconditional assimilation/ elimination of the "indigenous other" was imposed on the original habitants of the American continent. In the best of cases, indigenous people were considered "naturals" or childlike wild creatures of the new lands. Some instances of genuine care and protection emerged from within the morally committed representatives of the Catholic faith, as the remarkable example of Bartolomé de las Casas illustrates. But for the most part, besides conquering and evangelizing, the colonizers held a general belief that indigenous people had to be saved from their own savagery through the physical elimination of all traces of their sinful existence and the destruction of their culture. The implementation of the colonial conception led, at their worst, to wanton violence and destruction. One example among many collective-memory traumas perpetrated in the name of faith was the destruction of a vast number of Mayan codices by Diego de Landa, who said outright that these invaluable documents contained nothing but superstition and diabolic lies. Ancestral knowledge from the Mayan culture, including astronomical observations, was annihilated. In this first moment, the only way the Spanish conquerors of the American continent could conceptualize the otherness of indigenous Mexico was to utilize canonical European methods of social integration, including conversion to Catholicism.

According to Villoro, this first encounter with indigenous Mexico, conducted through the lens of the colonial conception, gave way to a second one. The rationalist and secularist movement that emerged from the wars of independence and reformation during the eighteenth and nineteenth centuries led to a reconfiguration of what it was to be Mexican. In this new conception, the indigenous world was a source of autonomy and pride, rather than wildness and sin. To Europe, the "criollos" (people of Spanish descent who were born in the colonies) could offer a different identity that rejected colonial subjugation. Mexicans are, under this conception, no longer colonial appendages of Spain. They have a sense of purpose, which integrates the indigenous world as an important element of the identity and independence of Mexico. Yet this integration is rather formal and abstract. The indigenous world is now conceived of as the proud *past* from which the foundations of the new, mix-raced, Mexican state emerged. It thus remains at a "safe" and considerable distance from current affairs.

The third conception of indigenous Mexico moves beyond the second one's integrative but abstract understanding. It allows us to see the indigenous world as both enigmatic and close to us. It corresponds historically to the great archaeological findings and correlative social excitement that, as Villoro says, allowed Mexicans as a whole to identify with a positive and nearby aspect of indigenous Mexico. It embodies the full acceptance of the *mestizo* (people of mixed Spanish and indigenous roots) as the galvanizing element of Mexican culture and politics. But this new idea arose within a moment of nationalism, based on the ideology of a hegemonic state. The third conception portrays "contemporary indigenous Mexico" as a scattered, heterogenous, and oppressed group, with the mestizo playing a role in that group's systematic exclusion and oppression. Nonetheless, the third movement fostered, with national enthusiasm, the hope for mutual recognition.

These conceptions had substantial and concrete political consequences. Villoro clearly sees the role of ideologies, or systems of belief that end in oppression, as the key social function that makes possible large-scale discrimination and exclusion. In the three great moments of indigenism in Mexico, denial, abstract inclusion, and inward recognition were all compatible with different forms of exclusion. The practices behind these forms of exclusion are based on rational justifications: saving the souls of the naturals; integrating the indigenous groups as citizens of the state; recognizing them as part of *our* culture. Villoro's social epistemology calls this *unreasonable* rationality. These practices *seemed* rational to their practitioners, at the time of their execution, but they all led to systematic exclusion and oppression.

As we saw earlier, *Grandes Momentos* was published in 1950. Villoro later revised his thought concerning how the indigenous world is integrated and understood in Mexico, mostly by emphasizing the importance of the pluralistic state in his engagement with the EZLN. While he distances himself from the conceptualist and theoretical attitude of *Grandes Momentos* in the preface to the third edition of this important book, it nonetheless constitutes the first stage of his thought about indigenous identity and culture in Mexico. It sets the tone for many of his philosophical inquiries, which we will examine in what follows.

While Villoro underwent major changes in intellectual orientation, his interest in indigenous peoples and culture remained constant. In the course of his productive trajectory, he would use different philosophical ideas to articulate different visions of how to address the problem. But there is enormous continuity in his effort to understand and engage with indigenous Mexico. Going back to the photos of the young philosophy professor and the elder member and advisor of the Zapatista army, we can say that nothing went wrong between them.

The question of Mexican identity:
the Hiperión group

Mexican identity and culture constituted a constant preoccupation for Villoro. While studying philosophy at UNAM, he familiarized himself with existentialist and phenomenological approaches to Mexican identity, and then joined an influential association of intellectuals called the Hiperión group. Under the guidance of Villoro's mentor, José Gaos, this group of leading intellectuals met and collaborated to create a genuinely Mexican philosophy. The group included Emilio Uranga, Ricardo Guerra, Jorge Portilla, Joaquín Sánchez McGregor, Salvador Reyes Nevárez, Fausto Vega, and Leopoldo Zea. Gaos (1900–69) had a clear and permanent influence on Villoro and on the other members of Hiperión. A Spanish refugee who became a "teacher of teachers" in Mexico, as Aurelia Valero calls him in her 2015 biography, Gaos translated major philosophical works into Spanish and inspired a generation of Mexican philosophers. Gaos was a member of the Madrid School, a student of José Ortega y Gasset. His interest in the work of Martin Heidegger and Edmund Husserl would have a decisive impact on the members of Hiperión (Gaos translated Heidegger's *Being and Time*, and Husserl's *Logical Investigations*). Villoro himself wrote an entire book on Husserl, and studied Ortega y Gasset's epistemology, particularly his notion of "belief" which we will examine in Chapter 5.

The "Hiperiones" concerned themselves with investigating the essence of what it is to be Mexican, the nature of *Mexicanness*, through the phenomenological lens they learned from Gaos. They were considered "Mexican existentialists." Their investigations focused on bridging and integrating the emerging field of Mexican philosophy, based on the crucial work of José Vasconcelos and Samuel Ramos, with the main philosophical trends of the time in Europe, chiefly existentialism, as represented by Jean-Paul Sartre, Heidegger, and Ortega y Gasset. They were original and interesting thinkers, and the group as a whole was very consequential for Mexican culture and politics. I will comment briefly on Uranga (1921–88) and Portilla

(1918–63), because of their role in centering the issue of Mexicanness on existentialist questions by using key Mexican terms concerning experiences that are difficult to classify. Their analysis of these terms, including words from the Aztec language, Nahuatl, became an important source of inspiration for other thinkers.

One of Uranga's major contributions to Mexican philosophy was his use of the Aztec word *nepantla,* translated as "in the middle" or "in between." In his book, *Análisis del ser mexicano* (An analysis of Mexican being, 1952), Uranga proposes that *nepantla* captures an existential component of the human condition as experienced specifically by Mexicans. He defines this ontological condition of Mexicanness as the coexistence of two opposites that Mexicans cannot fully reject or adopt, namely their indigenous and European roots. The Mexican condition is one of *oscillation without reconciliation,* pendulating between these two origins. This oscillating character of being Mexican is deeply related to the "accidentality" of Mexicans, their characteristic "lack of substance." This notion of not having enough "substance" resonates with some of Villoro's later ideas, particularly his emphasis on anchoring reason on what is concrete in order to avoid ideology. But Uranga's examination of *nepantla* became influential in ways that go well beyond whatever effect they had on Villoro's thought. Negative existential aspects of Mexicanness originate from the accidentality caused by experiencing *nepantla,* including the experience of *zozobra,* a vague but constant experience of uncertainty and anxiety. Gloria Anzaldúa (2015) uses the notion of *nepantla* as a central concept in her feminist and queer approach to Mexican–American identity, situated in "the borderland," and she applies it specifically to the condition of Chicanas and "in between" thinkers, whom she calls "nepantleras."

Uranga, like Villoro, became heavily involved in politics, but his trajectory was starkly different: he became one of the main intellectuals behind the official agenda of the Partido Revolucionario Institucional. This party-regime—in the words of Mario Vargas Llosa, Mexico's "perfect dictatorship"—controlled the country with an iron fist for more than half of the last century. According to the writer Juan Villoro

(2023, 93), Uranga was close to certain unnamable politicians, for whom he wrote speeches. Uranga denigrated old friends and died in total isolation in 1988. But in spite of all this, and in particular, despite the dramatic differences in their political opinions, Villoro and Uranga remained friends, as Juan Villoro documents in his book (ibid.). Their friendship, built on their common philosophical experiences and interests as "Hiperiones," proved stronger than these considerable differences.

Portilla also focused on key notions from Mexican culture and folklore to inform his phenomenological approach to Mexicanness. He examined a word that has unique connotations in Mexico, and which is quite difficult to translate: the term "relajo." His analysis of this notion appeared posthumously in 1966, in his remarkable book *Fenomenología del relajo* (The phenomenology of "relajo"). A word that has the same root as the English "relax" and "relaxation," "relajo" has connotations in Mexico that cannot be captured by these English words, although there is a clear connection among all of them. Fortunately, however unique the term, it can now be appreciated by anglophone readers, thanks to the work of Carlos Sánchez and Francisco Gallegos.

Sánchez's *The Suspension of Seriousness* (2012), which includes a translation of *Fenomenología del relajo*, provides a comprehensive examination of Portilla's thought, emphasizing the social and political consequences of "relajo." In particular, Sánchez argues that Portilla's views offer a framework for changing the processes underlying our blind acceptance of values and opens the door for a re-examination of how our current political situation of polarization and uncertainty requires that we change them. This diversion of attention has a rippling effect in the social fabric—a phenomenological method that Sánchez traces back to Husserl's eidetic reduction and Heidegger's critique of modernity. Sánchez and Gallegos (2020) extend the analysis offered in *The Suspension of Seriousness,* including new translations of essays by Portilla. This new exegesis of Portilla also focuses on attentive and sensitive attunement to the world and a socially oriented phenomenology of concrete cultural realities, appealing to Heidegger's phenomenology and to political conflicts, historic and contemporary, including cartel violence and narco-culture in Mexico. Portilla's focus on attentional reorientation as a means of restoring culture also resonates with Villoro's later work, including his social epistemology, as we will see later on.

Villoro, working with Víctor Flores Olea and the philosopher Alejandro Rossi, Villoro's close friend, collected and edited the papers that would become *Fenomenología del relajo*. Portilla died at age 45. In an obituary published in 1966, these three thinkers write that the purpose of the Hiperiones was to situate philosophy in concrete reality. As I explain later, this is also a fundamental goal of Villoro's social epistemology. Philosophy, they continue, should "go out to the streets" and meet life in all its complexity and accidentality. They saw Portilla as a lucid exponent of this proposal, a man who was constantly engaged in the painful task of questioning daily life in its immediacy and particularity. Described as a "man of crisis," Portilla is portrayed as someone who lived through the social and spiritual conflicts of his time with a personally committed philosophy. Of *Fenomenología del relajo*, Juan Villoro (2023, 93–4) says that it offers the best account of Mexicans' devotion to World Cup soccer—an example that captures many aspects of Mexican life. With no obvious gain, and in the face of constant negative results, Mexicans go through personal sacrifice to attend the games. They turn the excitement of the crowd into its own spectacle, independently of what happens on the field. Their situatedness in "relajo" is what matters—a kind of meta-theater in which the important outcome is how much fun the crowd has, regardless of the score.

Uranga and Portilla are two members of Hiperión who are finally getting the attention they deserve in the anglophone world. Manuel Vargas (2020) introduced and analyzed Uranga's notion of "accidentality" in a recent paper, and Carlos Sánchez translated Uranga's book on the analysis of being Mexican. Portilla's work is available in English through the work of Sánchez and Gallegos. The emphasis of the Hiperiones on situatedness and lived experience provides fertile ground for new approaches in contemporary philosophy. Robert Sanchez and Carlos

Sánchez (2017) published an excellent anthology of Mexican philosophy in the twentieth century. Fortunately, a lot more is being written now and there will likely be a lot more to come, part of the current effort to diversify the canon and incorporate the vast world of philosophy in the Americas that came into being not only before the twentieth century, but even before the existence of the United States. For example, and just focusing on Mexico, consider the work of Bernardino de Sahagún and Bartolomé de las Casas around 1500, and Sor Juana Inés de la Cruz in the 1600s. The Royal and Pontifical University of Mexico, the predecessor of UNAM where the Hiperiones started their group, was founded in 1551. This was 69 years before the Mayflower sailed.

As was characteristic of its time, the Hiperión group was male-centered. The powerful intellectuals who founded it kept it closed from women who were producing work of enormous value for its project, chiefly the writer and philosopher Rosario Castellanos. While many leading women intellectuals were excluded, the case of Castellanos, as Fanny del Río (2023) shows, was particularly outrageous. Castellanos was married to the Hiperión Ricardo Guerra and was close friends with other group members. Her influential "Mujer que sabe latín" (The woman who knows Latin) was dedicated to Villoro. Her feminist philosophy would have enormously enriched Hiperión's mission of creating a philosophy situated in concrete reality. And yet the Hiperiones did not welcome her.

In 1950, the year *Grandes Momentos* appeared, Castellanos published her dissertation *Sobre cultura femenina* (On female culture). As del Río shows, Castellanos's text is a landmark in Mexican feminist philosophy, closely following Simone de Beauvoir's *The Second Sex* (1949). How this achievement alone did not qualify her for membership in Hiperión is perplexing. Shortly after, Castellanos started distancing herself from the sterile style of writing considered appropriate for "professional" philosophy. She wrote novels, plays, and poetry, following the path taken by Iris Murdoch and Simone de Beauvoir. Her liminal presence at the "doorstep" of philosophy, as del Río puts it, brings new meaning to Uranga's examination of "nepantla." For women in Mexico, as del Río writes, accidentality is substance, as their existence is one of *permanent nepantla*. They are "in between" members of academia, subject to all kinds of exclusion. More generally, women are "in between" the rational and the temperamental—between abstract thought and situated emotion. Never fully seen or recognized, their philosophical contributions remain liminal and unsubstantial. Commenting on Castellanos' novel *Rito de iniciación* (The initiation ritual), del Río writes:

> One of los hiperiones, Luis Villoro, once wrote that the goal of a philosophical reflection should not be to formulate answers, but to formulate new questions. If that is the case, this novel and most of Rosario Castellanos's writings are indeed philosophical reflections regarding identity, otherness, self-discovery, cultural emancipation, colonialism, and sexism, and the only explanation as to why she is not counted among Mexico's most influential philosophical minds of the twentieth century is that, as I have shown, then as much as now, our categories of what counts as philosophy, and of what matters in philosophy, are still gender-biased, exclusionary, prejudiced, sterile, and inoperative.
>
> (2023, 101)

Villoro's philosophy is capacious enough to consider Castellanos' literary work as deeply philosophical—given Villoro's epistemic and ethical commitments, he ought to consider Castellanos' work as philosophical. But here, unlike in most of the other aspects of Villoro's life, we find a clear gap between thought and action. While Villoro's own epistemological ideas demanded that Hiperión embrace Castellanos, still she was not accepted.

Castellanos' case illustrates the disconnection between ideas and practice within Hiperión. In order to establish a firm relation between our thoughts and our actions, we must pay attention to what is salient and concrete—a central theme of the following chapters. This is very important if we are to expand epistemology into a theory of *reasonable rationality* that repels unreasonable applications of rationality. Villoro's social epistemology requires this expansion, based on attention capacities, for its full development. Ironically, it was Castellanos herself who exemplified *nepantla* most concretely, by being Hiperión's own liminal and "unofficial" woman member. Although none of the Hiperiones paid enough attention to it, her work enriched the experiential component of philosophy that they valued so much. Castellanos' case is a notable reminder that strong biases within a concrete political milieu can blind even those who carefully reflect on how to eliminate them. This is the danger of ideology.

The unity of thought and action

As the case of Castellanos shows, Villoro and his colleagues could have been more consistent within their goal of creating a philosophy that is realistic, inclusive and—in the specific case of Villoro—that leads to liberation. But Villoro is, all things considered, one of the most consistent thinkers of recent times, not merely in the abstract sense of logical consistency, but in the sense that matters personally: the consistency between thought and action, or between one's commitments and one's life. Philosophy was a way of life for Villoro, but not because he decided to live in a barrel or spend his time submerged in books. Villoro was constantly *vigilant* about what he thought to be the right course of action, and he followed through.

A major source of consistency in Villoro's life was his conviction that philosophy should never be pursued as an intellectual exercise for the purpose of abstract reasoning, or for its own sake, as if it were a kind of conjectural game. He explicitly writes about this issue throughout his career. He saw philosophy as requiring a connection to the social world, to change and improve reality. His commitment to understanding and engaging with indigenous Mexico started very early with a personal experience that marked him. As Juan Villoro documents, (2023, 121) after arriving from Europe, Villoro joined his mother and family at their hacienda in San Luis Potosí, Mexico. The peasants of the hacienda lined up to welcome the young son of the owner and they kissed his hand.

According to Juan Villoro, this was the most opprobrious moment in his father's life. What kind of demented organization would call for a poor old man to humiliate himself like that before a privileged youngster who had just arrived from Europe? (2023, 122).

This memory stayed with Villoro throughout his life, and he conveyed it to his children, in all its detail and with enormous shame. He took a similar personal approach to everything that he considered important and was never in the mood for self-aggrandizement or for blurring important distinctions in any context. Juan Villoro reports a game that he and his siblings played with his father during a meal, in which they had to pick the most emblematic person of the twentieth century. Juan recalls that he chose John Lennon, and his brother Miguel offered Albert Einstein. Because their father seemed reluctant to participate in the game, and thinking that if he did, he would pick a philosopher, they started going through the names of various candidates. Annoyed, Villoro said, "Of course not! No recent philosopher has been that important." After a pause, he added that in the twentieth century, no one was as significant as Gandhi. He said that he would be ashamed of them if they didn't agree. Villoro then asked, "Do you know what is to be an example?" "We are not judging a concept or an idea," he added, "we are evaluating the weight of a whole life." (145–6)

Juan Villoro gives the details of this conversation in the middle of a discussion of how Villoro saw his relation to indigenous Zapatista communities in Chiapas. Luis Villoro explained his choice further. "Gandhi demolished an empire with a fistful of salt," he said—a reference to the peaceful Salt March of 1930. What started as a game had become a personal reflection on what it would mean to be an exemplary human being in the twentieth century. Who really deserved such a categorization, if anyone? Exalted, with his children watching him carefully, he concluded with a degree of satisfaction: "Gandhi, the person of the century is Gandhi." (2023, 153) The game turned serious because the *question* was serious. One must always be attentive to what is important. Expressions like "the best person of the century" should not be used lightly, unless we want to stop meaning what we say, divorcing our interests from our assertions. It is fine to be playful. But one should not take a stance of indifference to what matters, as if everything is just "relajo."

A kiss on the hand from an old peasant to an undeserving youth. A fistful of salt at the end of a peaceful march, embodying resistance and bravery against imperialism. True commitment, like genuine greatness, is not dependent on popularity contests. On the contrary, both are characterized by simplicity. We don't need surveys and comprehensive statistical analyses to understand that the kiss was opprobrious and the fistful of salt, an act of greatness. A poll or a scientific account ranking Gandhi among other "great hits" of the twentieth century would obfuscate this simplicity. In fact, it is obfuscation and inattention to what is important—through social media distraction, entertainment, polarization—that has turned our societies into collections of individuals who are indifferent but nonetheless opinionated. We have become addicted to popularity, at the cost of what is deserving of our attention.

The standard of "weighing a whole life" rather than just concepts or ideas is critical here. John Lennon was one of the most important musicians (and pacifists) of the twentieth century, but he did nothing comparable to dismantling the British Empire. Albert Einstein transformed the twentieth century with his ideas and also his actions, including the creation of the Manhattan Project and the development of militarized nuclear research. As an exemplar of commitment towards peace in the world, Gandhi did a lot more than Einstein, and he stood firmly by his conviction that peace was the only way to political transformation. Integrity matters when it comes to greatness. Villoro stated in that conversation that when it came to the integrity of someone who is also great, Gandhi stood above everyone else. Without falling into self-aggrandizement, Villoro tried as best as he could to apply a high standard of integrity to himself.

Interestingly, the mere idea that a philosopher could be on the list of most important people of the twentieth century offended Villoro. Many philosophers could have made the list, including some Villoro himself had worked on—the German phenomenologists; the French existentialists (Albert Camus and Sartre received Nobel prizes, Sartre declined); Ortega y Gasset. He obviously had nothing against these philosophers as thinkers. The repulsion came from thinking that their ideas alone sufficed to put them next to Gandhi. Great ideas and accolades are certainly important, but satisfying a standard of integrity in thought and action is an entirely different matter.

Philosophy and intellectual commitment

As Villoro shows in *Grandes Momentos*, oppression is frequently justified through collective epistemologies of domination. Each moment described in the book reflects an epistemology in which inner consistency requires annihilation, exclusion, or assimilation without proper recognition of the indigenous "other." These ideologies are rational, yet oppressive. They are rational because they are based on fully consistent *systems of beliefs* that provide reasons and justifications for their coherence and evidential support. It is through a system of beliefs that the old peasant became convinced he needed to humiliate himself before the young owner of the hacienda. Villoro experienced the reality of becoming Mexican with amazement, with its merits and its sins. He felt personally and deeply the importance of addressing these disturbing realities, particularly the oppression of indigenous people. From very early on, he would inform his philosophical views with this personal commitment.

In his prologue to the anthology of Villoro's work, *La Razón Disruptiva* (Disruptive Reason; 2023), Guillermo Hurtado confronts the problem of describing the vast scope and diversity of Villoro's oeuvre. This is indeed a considerable challenge, if one approaches the work of Villoro through common strategies. As Hurtado says, a chronological approach gives the reader the impression that there are no major themes unifying Villoro's work (2023, 9). Villoro wrote about specific philosophers (e.g., Sartre, Husserl, and Ortega y Gasset);

historical events (the conquest of Mexico, the Mexican Revolution, the Renaissance); and political ideas such as democracy and pluralism (which he also presented in a variety of venues, like magazines and newspapers). A chronological approach produces a cacophony of themes, a collage that cannot capture the unity of Villoro's thought.

An account of Villoro's work presented in stages faces similar difficulties. We could start with an existentialist stage (roughly the transition between the end of the 1940s to the beginning of the 1950s); then turn to a phenomenological stage (1950–60); a Marxist stage (1950–70); an analytic stage (1960–80); a multicultural stage (1980–90); and a Zapatista stage (1990 to his death; Hurtado, 2023, 9). An approach like this is interesting, but misses the main thematic axes of his work. Instead, Hurtado proposes four major axes across time, which constitute the major sections of his excellent anthology. The first section, on "the other and others," focuses on religious and existential experiences; the sacred; and indigenous identity in Mexico. Section two, on Villoro's epistemology, covers knowledge, rationality, and truth. In section three, on power and ideas, we find Villoro's views on political philosophy; and finally, in section four—on community, democracy, and justice—we encounter Villoro's account of the pluralistic state and his proposal for a negative route to justice (the *via negativa*), which can be interpreted as a non-ideal approach to ethics. Villoro's negative route, as I shall argue in this book, is a particularly important axis of his work.

Even under the categorization provided by these four axes, Villoro's work may seem too encompassing or "unfocused" by today's ultra-specialized academic standards. Yet it might be erroneous to think that our ultra-specialized approach to philosophy is better than the way philosophy was done as recently as the beginning of the last century, and for most of its history. Our specialized silos of ultra-specialized "philosophy of *x*" may merely amount to a comforting strategy that allows us to compare ourselves with the hard sciences. In any case, independently of this issue, it is wrong to think of Villoro's work as incoherent or unfocused. Quite the contrary. The kind of integrity Villoro had in his life is reflected in his work. In this book, I focus on how Villoro's social epistemology informs most of his writings across time.

As we saw earlier, *Grandes Momentos* can be interpreted as a characterization of epistemologies of domination. This raises the issue of how to relate epistemology to ethics, or *knowledge to freedom*. Delineating the bounds of reason is a central task of philosophy, and it concerns both epistemology and ethics.[1] Immanuel Kant argued that this task is foundational to all possible investigations about truth and justification. Reasoning is a practice that includes scientific explanation, moral development, and aesthetic judgment. It shapes our political and legal institutions and is, therefore, the basis for the creation of a fair society. The way in which our capacities for reasoning should be guided concerns the limits of reason—not all reasoning is adequate. Villoro examined this foundational question deeply in the entirety of his work.

Kantians address the question of how we ought to reason through an examination of the fundamental conditions for rationality in each realm of thought and for any given thinker. By contrast, Villoro focuses on the question of what reason is for: to account for our motives by relying on the fragile nature of our capacities for communication and cooperation in a fluid and politically warped realm of action. This is how Villoro understands the personal commitment to good reasoning and engagement that is characteristic of genuine philosophy. Starting with Chapter 3, this book argues that Villoro's analysis of the bounds of reason was inspired by the work of Ludwig Wittgenstein, and that Villoro's analysis of the limits of reason reveals a considerable degree of unity and cohesiveness regarding various themes in his work, including his political philosophy. Part of the cohesiveness of Villoro's work is explained by the pragmatic orientation that he acquired from Wittgenstein and some of Wittgenstein's contemporaries.

Genuine philosophy, unlike all epistemologies of domination, has a disruptive nature. Knowledge should guide us in our fight against

---

[1] The material in the next five paragraphs is briefly discussed in my review of Guillermo Hurtado's compilation of Villoro's work at *Notre Dame Philosophical Reviews*.

oppression and ideology, and this social function of knowledge cannot possibly be reduced to mere academic speculation. Knowledge leads to concrete actions. Otherwise, one cannot fully explain the relation between knowledge and freedom. The ethical dimension of this relation entails a personal commitment to the rational disruption of various forms of oppression and epistemic injustice. Reason-guidance must make possible the integration of knowledge, participative democracy, and liberation, in opposition to manipulation and violence. In fact, Villoro argues that when reasoning prevents this integration, such reasoning should be considered either manipulative or mere abstract play—not genuine knowledge, and certainly not philosophy.

Transformative and liberational reasoning radically differs from what Villoro calls "unreasonable" rationality. To delineate the proper bounds of reason, it is essential to draw and examine this distinction. Much of our reasoning goes toward maintaining the status quo and manipulating one another. Genuine knowledge transforms and disrupts these unreasonable practices, not for the sake of spreading chaos, but to enrich and further liberate humanity. The philosopher of science Thomas Kuhn described the very essence of scientific reasoning as disruptive. The Hegelian and Marxist traditions define the progress of rationality as essentially disruptive. But Villoro's perspective on this matter is unique. We are neither progressing steadily towards eternal peace nor towards absolute truth. To find the truth, one must engage intersubjectively with as many perspectives as possible, both to guarantee that others are not excluded, and because we lack an ultimate exemplar of justice, peace, and truth. We therefore need a *negative* route to justice. We start not with an ideal of justice, but with the crude realities of exclusion and discrimination, poverty and oppression. The elimination of these realities is the path to justice.

These ideas concerning the relation between epistemology and ethics are a major source of unity, guidance, and focus in Villoro's work, from his early texts onwards, at each of the stages described above. This is why he always showed a strong interest in the relation between politics and phenomenology, from his writings on the Hiperión group and the

Mexican Revolution through his analysis of the work of Husserl and Ortega y Gasset. For example, he argues that when modern science moves away from its philosophical and social foundations it dehumanizes knowledge and eliminates personal concerns. This had also been the plea of Edmund Husserl. Knowledge, according to Villoro, is not an end in itself: it responds to our need to make the world more meaningful, and it also makes our actions more efficient and inclusive of others. Villoro's interpretation of Husserl through this pragmatic principle leads him to claim that radical science, as opposed to naïve science, is always *wise*. Wisdom does not depend, like the knowledge of the specialized sciences, on anything else for its justification. Wisdom is foundational; it concerns the philosophical foundations of science including the foundations of mathematics, and it unites knowledge with liberation.

A similar pragmatic approach can be found in Villoro's historical investigations, including his book on modernity and the Renaissance (Villoro, 1992). The Renaissance is, for Villoro, a paradigmatic example of disruptive reason, grounded in epistemic and ethical commitments. Villoro says that the Renaissance provided a delineation or "figure" of the world—a way of conceiving our position in the natural and social order, a conception that we must renew and expand. The term "figure" is used by Wittgenstein to describe the transcendental nature of value, which we will examine further on. The Renaissance widened our geographic and cosmological horizons; it created new basic sentiments about what it is to be human, thereby generating the need for new political ideals. But Villoro warns us that our science has become dehumanized, and that the promise of liberation through knowledge remains unfulfilled. A non-militarized and ethically brave scientific community is needed to secure this liberation. The Renaissance's focus on the arts and humanities as guides towards inquiry should be renewed as part of our effort. Unveiling the truth and expanding the boundaries of freedom through knowledge requires a new science that is not an alien appendage to the daily realities of most humans. The exclusion of most people from the production of knowledge should be a matter of great epistemic and moral concern.

Thus, remarkably, Villoro's life trajectory correlates with his philosophical thought. This striking coherence does not entail a complete continuity from the beginning. Villoro did become more and more concerned about political issues as time went by. Still, Villoro's intellectual and political life had a rare degree of consistency, making his support of the EZLN by no means inconsistent with the earliest stages of his career. This consistency is quite important to understand his philosophical contributions.

Political activism

Villoro's political activism was a significant source of coherence in his life. The journalist Luis Hernández Navarro says in his prologue to *La Alternativa* (The Alternative), a book that includes Villoro's correspondence with Subcomandante Marcos, that throughout his life, Villoro was an intellectual devoted to the transformation of Mexico (Hernández Navarro, 2015, 10). Regarding Villoro's dialogue with Subcomandante Marcos, Hernández Navarro sees it as the continuation of a dialogue with the indigenous world that started theoretically with *Grandes Momentos*, (Hernández Navarro, 2015, 8). Revolution and insurgence are indeed ways of fleshing out what started as dialogical explorations. But only a few politically engaged explorations can have such consequences. The nature of revolution is a central theme in Villoro's political philosophy.

Hiperión was also very political. The philosophy of Mexicanness had become important for the national orientation of Mexican politics, promoted by the university-trained politicians who were replacing the old revolutionary generals. These new leaders were seeking national unity in the "mestizo" and the "genuinely Mexican" aspects of culture as the foundations of a new nation. Given the brevity of its public existence, from 1948 to 1952, it is significant that the Hiperiones included in their ranks thinkers who saw their intellectual agenda in explicitly political terms. As we saw earlier, Uranga was very close to political power, and remained so until his death. While this was not the case with Villoro, we must consider Hernández Navarro's understanding of *Grandes Momentos* as an initial dialogue that planted the seeds for a continuous conversation culminating in Villoro's engagement with Zapatismo. Intellectually, Villoro set a political program for *Mexico*, in which he uncovered a concealed ideological agenda that was preventing the proper recognition of indigenous groups (Hernández Navarro, 2015, 14). In this sense, Villoro materialized the meaning behind the name "Hiperión," the Titan son of Gaia (earth, or the concrete and particular) and Uranus (the sky, or the universal), by unifying his intellectual agenda with his engagement with the EZLN.

Villoro wrote a comprehensive article on the purpose of Hiperión (Villoro, 1949), and then, immediately after its dissolution in 1952, he published a book about the Mexican Revolution and the history of ideas that guided it (*El proceso ideológico de la revolución de independencia*, or The ideological process of the revolution of independence, Villoro, 1953). It is important to keep in mind that these three early texts by Villoro are about indigenous Mexico; a group of intellectuals devoted to the study of Mexican identity; and the process that led to Mexican independence. His book on the Mexican Revolution concerns the collective "change in mentality" of the revolutionary "criollos" who, no longer colonial subjects, now faced their future as leaders of a new nation. Centered on Miguel Hidalgo y Costilla, the criollo and Catholic priest who was the leader of the revolution, Villoro's account is less concerned with the actual processes that led to the revolution and more on the changes in mentality that criollos needed to undergo as revolutionaries, based partly on their *moral* considerations. The moral aspects of political engagement, including revolutions, permeates Villoro's social epistemology, as we will examine in the concluding chapters.

Villoro's early interests in Mexican politics and identity turned into action in the 1960s. He participated in the student and civic movement of 1968 and was elected his department's representative to the Coalition of Teachers (Hernández Navarro, 2015, 11). In his description of the student movement, Villoro argues that the conformism, cowardness, and selfishness of the previous generations had suddenly disappeared, replaced by enthusiasm fueled by the possibility of politically liberating the country. In Villoro's understanding, the students, unlike their political leaders and oppressors, were *speaking frankly*, with demands deeply rooted in a moral standpoint that stood firmly against governmental corruption and lies (ibid). The energy of real political engagement is another phenomenon that Villoro's social epistemology and political philosophy seek to articulate and define.

The student movement was violently repressed, and many participants were killed in the Tlatelolco massacre of October 2, 1968. Juan Villoro (2023, 70–1) narrates how his father, in horror and amazement, was concerned about having escaped incarceration despite his very visible participation—many of his comrades had been imprisoned, like Eli de Gortari and Heberto Castillo who did time in the notorious Lecumberri Jail. With Heberto Castillo and Demetrio Vallejo, Villoro helped create, in 1974, the leftist *Partido Mexicano de los Trabajadores* (The Mexican Workers Party). Rooted in the student movement of 1968, this party opened a rare opportunity to challenge the hegemonic and corrupt *Partido Revolucionario Institucional*. To support the Workers Party, Castillo and Villoro came up with all sorts of initiatives, including the creation of a taquería. Juan Villoro dedicates an entire chapter of his memoir to the "taquería revolucionaria." Making notes about his expenses in a copy of Karl Marx's *Capital*, Villoro announced in front of his family that he was ready to donate their patrimony to the workers' cause (2023, 129). Unlike Uranga, who supported and inspired the political strategies of the *Partido Revolucionario Institucional*, Villoro helped create and then supported a leftist party, whose founding members were incarcerated for their participation in the student movement.

Consistent with his approach to the Mexican Revolution, Villoro said that socialism is not merely a theory of society and history, but also assumes a set of values, guided by a moral compass, in which human liberation takes the place of ideologies and state systems that seek to alienate and oppress humanity (Hernández Navarro, 2015, 15). In his analysis of the 1973 Chilean coup against Salvador Allende, Villoro concluded that in Latin America, revolution is not a dream of exalted heroes, but the only escape from the unending violence to which Latin Americans are subjected (ibid.).

However, despite his thorough knowledge of Marxist doctrine and sympathy for its moral orientation, Villoro was not a Marxist. His resistance to ideological thought that oppressed and controlled humanity included ideological forms of Marxism. This is in line with his criticism of capitalism. In his response to the first letter Subcomandante Marcos wrote to him at the start of their exchange, Villoro affirms that what is urgent in Mexico is to put ethics and justice at the center of social life. He goes on to assert that capitalism has become a global structure of domination and a politically oppressive way of thinking (Villoro, 2015, 86). Capitalism, under such an epistemic categorization, could be understood as a meta-narrative of various epistemologies of domination, which justify racism, classism, misogyny, and oppressive behaviors promoted solely for the sake of profit.

There is a lot more to say about the rich life of Luis Villoro Toranzo, but we shall shift gears at this point. This is a book about Villoro's philosophical insights, particularly his social epistemology. But given the unity of Villoro's thought and action, his political commitment and his personal approach to philosophy, it won't be surprising to find out that the aspects of his life discussed in this chapter reflect the commitments behind his philosophical proposals. One of the unique features of Villoro's social epistemology is the importance of understanding the entire corpus of his work. The next chapter analyzes one of the underlying principles of his ethics and epistemology: a fundamental principle of non-exclusion.

References

Anzaldúa, G. (2015), *Light in the Dark, Luz en lo Oscuro: Rewriting Identity, Spirituality, Reality, edited by A. Keating*, Duke University Press.

Del Río, F. (2023), Rosario Castellanos at Philosophy's Doorstep, *Journal of Mexican Philosophy*, 2(1): 82–101.

Eraña, A. (2022), Prólogo a *Los Grandes Momentos del Indigenismo en México*, 3rd edition, México: Fondo de Cultura Económica (pp. 7–17).

Flores Olea, V., Rossi, A., and Villoro, L. (1966), Jorge Portilla, *Revista de la Universidad de México*, April Issue.

Hernández Navarro, L. (2015), 'Prólogo: Don Luis', In L. Villoro, (ed.), *La Alternativa: Perspectivas y Posibilidades de Cambio*, México: Fondo de Cultura Económica (pp. 7–18).

Portilla, J. (1984), *Fenomenología del Relajo*, México: Fondo de Cultura Económica.

Sánchez, C. A. (2021), *Emilio Uranga's Analysis of Mexican Being. A Translation and Critical Introduction*, New York: Bloomsbury Academic.

Sánchez, C. A. and Gallegos, F. (2020), *The Disintegration of Community: On Jorge Portilla's Social and Political Philosophy*, New York: SUNY Press.

Sánchez, C. A. and Sanchez, R. E. (eds.) (2017), *Mexican Philosophy in the 20th Century: Essential Readings*, New York: Oxford University Press.

Uranga, E. (1952), *Análisis del ser del mexicano*, México: Porrúa y Obregón.

Valero, A. (2015), *José Gaos en México: una biografía intelectual, 1938-1969*, México: El Colegio de México.

Vargas, M. (2020), The philosophy of accidentality, *Journal of the American Philosophical Association*, 6(4): 391–409.

Villoro, J. (2023), *La Figura del Mundo: El Orden Secreto de las Cosas*, Barcelona: Penguin Random House.

Villoro, L. (1949), Génesis y proyecto del existencialismo en México, *Filosofía y Letras*, 18(36): 65–74.

Villoro, L. (1950), *Los Grandes Momentos del Indigenismo en México*, México: El Colegio de México.

Villoro, L. (1992), *El Pensamiento Moderno. Filosofía del Renacimiento*, México: El Colegio de México.

Villoro, L. (ed.) (2015), *La Alternativa: Perspectivas y Posibilidades de Cambio*, México: Fondo de Cultura Económica.

Villoro, L. (2023), *La Razón Disruptiva, Antología compilada por Guillermo Hurtado*, Mexico: Penguin Random House.

2

The Practice of Non-exclusion:
A Linguistic Analogy

The concreteness and situatedness of non-exclusion

Many instances of rationality in our daily life perpetuate domination and exclusion. This may sound puzzling at first, particularly if, like Villoro, one commits to the principle that rationality is a source of freedom and autonomy. But not all forms of rationality are liberating and justified. Once we understand the issue of scope—that rationality is a practice that can be adequate or inadequate—it becomes evident that many cases of rationality are oppressive. Consider, for instance, the legal systems that implemented slavery. Legal transactions performed under the conditions of the slave trade in the United States involved lawyers who practiced according to rational principles, like basing one's beliefs on evidence and not contradicting oneself. But this is a very rough characterization of rationality that must be refined to really get at the relation between freedom and reason. Villoro makes the argument that there is a difference between *reasonable and unreasonable rationality.*

Unreasonable rationality is *rational,* because one provides reasons for one's harmful views by assessing evidence and by following principles of rationality. The legal system of slavery in the United States was not irrational, but it was deeply unreasonable. Reasonable rationality unites knowledge with ethics, by associating genuine knowledge with freedom. This unity is behind Villoro's account of non-exclusion. Rule-following and inferential reasoning can be used ideologically—unreasonably—in order to maintain the status quo and sustain systems of oppression. In fact, we use rationality like this all the time to manipulate one another. An analysis of the difference between reasonable and unreasonable rationality is crucial in our time of political polarization. Appealing to reason to arrive at a conclusion that benefits us while harming someone else happens all the time on social media, in the courts, and within financial institutions. When, in common exploitative interactions like these, we assert to ourselves and others that we are rational because we are applying a rule or a principle, we are engaging in a kind of "rationalization" of social practices that are clearly oppressive and unethical.

How to challenge these unreasonable yet rational epistemic tendencies? Epistemic justification should be accompanied by pragmatic and ethical guidance for it to be genuinely reasonable. Recent externalist and internalist views of justification have emphasized this issue (Srinivasan, 2020; Johnson King, 2022), although we will see further on how externalism is more amenable to some of Villoro's pragmatic proposals. Reasonable rationality requires the disruption of rational practices of oppression, and this depends on a deep and conceptual relation between epistemology and ethics. This unity between knowledge and the good life is captured by a principle of non-exclusion that informs Villoro's social epistemology.

This chapter defends what I call the *Central Normative Proposal* of Luis Villoro.[1] The Central Normative Proposal is based on an interpretation of the principle of non-exclusion in ethics and epistemology inspired by Villoro's negative route to justice. The core argument is based on a linguistic analogy that demonstrates the importance of *reasonable communication* for non-exclusion in epistemology, which is assumed in various theses of Villoro. A consequence of this analogy for non-exclusion in ethics is that Villoro grounds what is reasonable on the concrete possibilities of mutual understanding in social interactions, starting with an understanding of asymmetries and injustices that are obfuscated or covered up by a strictly contractualist analysis of such social situations, based on strictly

---

[1]   The remainder of this chapter is based on Montemayor (2023a).

egalitarian principles. Villoro's criticism is compatible with some egalitarian views, but it assumes a radically different point of departure. Although some of his theses are compatible with egalitarian notions, given that his point of departure is asymmetries of power, his proposal should be understood on the basis of our cognitive capacities to understand and appreciate these asymmetries. For this reason, our chapter concludes with an analysis of the notion of reasonableness. In my interpretation, Villoro defines reasonableness in terms of our capacities for attention, which are not reducible to beliefs or systems of beliefs. In this way, Villoro's Central Normative Proposal depends on the convergence of truth and the dignity of people in communities where asymmetries exist. These asymmetries must be eliminated through concrete efforts to improve our communication practices.

Let us begin our analysis of Villoro's Central Normative Proposal with a question: what conceptual role does non-exclusion play in Villoro's epistemology, and how does it illuminate the concepts of epistemic justification and knowledge? The principle of non-exclusion is a crucial and recurrent theme in Villoro's work. I examine this principle through his Central Normative Proposal, which postulates that non-exclusion should be pursued simultaneously in both the epistemic and ethical domains, because there is an *intrinsic relation* between knowledge and freedom. For contemporary debates, this proposal affirms that epistemic injustice and violence are rational but unreasonable means for silencing and oppressing individuals and communities, and carry grave ethical consequences. The Central Normative Proposal thus establishes a necessary condition for rationality to be reasonable. With this proposal in hand, one can show that there is a conceptual relation between knowledge and freedom, which I illustrate with a linguistic analogy developed in the next section. This relation, based on non-exclusion, is essential to understand how Villoro's social epistemology informs his work on ethics and multiculturalism. Villoro writes in his major work on epistemology:

> We have arrived at a conception of belief and knowledge as dispositions that fulfill a practical function, both individual and social. By

abstraction one can separate them from the goals selected, but in concrete cases our beliefs are always in close relation to desires and interests. Because of this, in dealing with the function that beliefs and knowledge perform in concrete life, the theory of knowledge should be coupled with a theory of the precepts that regulate our actions according to ends. This is why epistemology has an intimate relation with ethics.

(Villoro, 1982|2008, 269)

Concrete epistemic societies play a crucial role for Villoro in the distribution, accumulation, and construction of knowledge, which together determines how individuals understand and classify their cognitive abilities, and therefore shapes their freedom to think and to act in general. This emphasis on our abilities to understand and to reasonably accommodate others, in order to impede their exclusion, justifies the linguistic analogy defended here. With respect to the normative dimension of such capacities, Villoro emphatically reaffirms the relation between epistemic and ethical duties, highlighting the importance of tolerance:

Truth is supposed to be a good, and therefore, we should seek the truth. This duty should not be exclusively individual, we can generalize it. Don't we have the obligation to procure access to the truth for everyone? This would imply the duty to share our knowledge and to help others to achieve knowledge. *To this duty one could justifiably add that of tolerance,* that is, the duty to respect the beliefs of others even if we don't share them [. . .] The duty to disseminate truth for everyone should not eliminate the duty to tolerate. *Both duties are present in any situation in which we communicate our beliefs and knowledge.* Education, indoctrination, and the processes of culturing entire peoples present ethical problems concerning the transmission of knowledge.

(1982|2008, 269–270; the emphasis is mine)

The mutual dependence between knowledge and freedom is conditioned by concrete social situations, most of which are asymmetric, some deeply and systematically so. Reasonable communication is a critical weapon against exclusion. As I clarify below, the type of reasonable recognition performed in the transmission of knowledge is a fundamental aspect of our linguistic practices. Our capacity to communicate reasonably should not be arbitrarily modulated by elites or simply assumed as part of an ideal theory. This confronts us with a methodological and empirical question. Villoro's methodological recommendation to begin with injustice implies attending to the epistemic and social positioning of other people, in their concrete particularity. This is the starting point of contemporary "non ideal" theories in epistemology (Srinivasan, 2020) and ethics (Mills, 2005).

Mills (2005) presented objections to ideal theories like Robert Nozick's or John Rawls's, for not explicitly addressing historical injustices, among other problems. I won't settle this dispute between ideal and non-ideal theories in this chapter, in which I will aim to be neutral, partly because Villoro favorably discusses key ideas from Rawls, particularly in Villoro's political philosophy. In Chapters 6 and 7, I examine this issue thoroughly, arguing that Villoro defends a version of the capability approach. For now, my goal is to explain the Central Normative Proposal by focusing on the empirical and methodological issues concerning our practices for non-exclusion in communication exchanges. Although Villoro would sympathize with contemporary criticisms of ideal theories because they do not start from concrete injustices, the most original feature of his criticism is how non-exclusion implies communicative labor, based on our epistemic capacities and the manner in which we distribute knowledge. Such labor is in principle compatible, and might even be essential, to understand egalitarian or contractual views and, therefore, could be logically independent from contemporary criticisms of ideal theories.

To appreciate the importance of the linguistic analogy presented below, it is crucial to emphasize that, for Villoro, reasonable communication cannot be simply based on norms and conventions. In "On the principle of injustice: exclusion (Octavas Conferencias Aranguren, 1999)," Villoro says:

> The justification for the idea of pursuing justice by means of the will to disrupt a situation perceived as unjust [...] would proceed in two

stages. First, a characterization of injustice based on a principle of exclusion. This could be defined as the situation of non-belonging to a given civil association. [. . .] The perception of exclusion would lead us to determine both the requirements for belonging to a civil association and the exigencies specified by the human condition. Second, an analysis of the main forms of exclusion and their modalities. From this analysis one could deduce the principles of a theory of justice that originates from rejecting a concrete situation of real exclusion, regardless of whether it is the result of consensus.

(Villoro 1999|2022, 65)

Concrete situations of communicative exclusion silence the oppressed. This happens in processes of the generation and distribution of knowledge, but also—and this is fundamental for Villoro—in ordinary conversations that take place in mundane contexts. Daily life is full of situations of asymmetry where some groups are constantly ignored or oppressed into submission by dominant ones. Interesting current research focuses on epistemic bubbles, epistemic bias, the violation of Gricean maxims, and other communicative practices that create exclusion in social media (some of this research is discussed in Chapter 6). All of this is relevant for the interpretation of Villoro I propose here. However, for Villoro, in order to avoid the systematic exclusion of some individuals and groups, it is not enough to appeal to the norms that govern language (or to any rules, for that matter). Participants in communication exchanges must accommodate and adjust to the concrete asymmetries of specific sociopolitical contexts. They need to be *attentive* to the context and social position of those who are silenced in order to ameliorate systematic asymmetries to the extent and parameters of what is reasonable.

In philosophy of language, the cognitive abilities of attending and accommodating to conversational cooperation have been characterized in terms of a *principle of charity*, according to which speakers, despite having evidence of linguistic infelicities, charitably reconstruct and interpret what speakers mean to communicate. But communicational charity is more vast and fundamental than this kind of reconstruction or accommodation. For Donald Davidson, as we are about to see, the principle of charity is essential to any theory of meaning. In this first approximation of non-exclusion in communication I will clarify how exactly we should interpret the notion of charity or its political equivalent, "mercy." I shall argue that attention is the key epistemic capacity to fully understand Villoro's notion of *reasonable rationality*, because attention is necessary for guiding and modulating the type of charitable accommodation required to prevent communicative exclusion. This linguistic analogy is the first stage of a broader argument, articulated in the following chapters, that shows how attention is essential for Villoro's social epistemology and political philosophy.

A linguistic analogy

The analogy between moral and linguistic rules has a large and prestigious tradition in the history of philosophy. John Rawls, whose work Villoro discusses at length in his political philosophy, proposed in *A Theory of Justice* (1971) that our capacity for representing moral principles is similar to our capacity to represent grammatical rules (a meta-ethical thesis that requires empirical verification).[2] John Mikhail (2011) develops this thesis by appealing to Noam Chomsky's theory of universal grammar. According to this proposal, our capacities to learn and understand communicative norms do not depend on social conventions or empirical data provided by sensorial information. Our capacities to generate and learn linguistic norms, at least in the context of syntax and grammar, depend on innate abilities, which are the result of a process of evolution. The linguistic analogy proposes that our

---

[2]   As I argue below, there are comparisons, made by Villoro himself, between the work of the late Rawls and the work of Jürgen Habermas. Habermas's interest in rationality and communication was more focused and systematic than Rawls's, but the comparison is justified. Villoro, in contrast to these authors, bases his theory on the foundations of his social epistemology, in a way that I find clearer and more convincing. For details see Chapter 6.

capacities for learning, recognizing, and generating moral norms have a similar innate basis, analogous to our linguistic capacities, which allow us to quickly identify and learn them, quite early in our educational development.

It should be clarified that, for this view, although the capacity for grammar is universal and innate, languages exhibit considerable diversity and variation. Humanity is endowed with an innate capacity to generate and learn grammatical rules that allow for the enormous variety of languages in history, spoken and archivally documented. The fact that the cognitive basis is innate and shared among humans does not entail that languages must be homogenous or even very similar. On the contrary, the innate basis for syntax provides a fundamental structure for any child to learn any language, but its contribution is minimal. From this shared structure emerges the semantic and pragmatic richness of all languages. Similarly, the fact that there is a "moral syntax" does not entail that moral and ethical systems, contemporary and historical, need to be homogenous. The thesis of a moral syntax is thus compatible with the great heterogeneity of moral systems registered by history and anthropology.

The proposal for a universal moral grammar offers a plausible case for how moral rules can play a fundamental guiding role in legal epistemology (Mikhail 2011; Montemayor 2008). However, the linguistic analogy, in its most general form, does not depend on nativism about the mind. One could make the case that moral rules are similar to linguistic rules on the basis of alternative views about the epistemology of language. For instance, non-nativist views about language learning are based on *conventional* rules, rather than structures based on mental states.[3] According to this version of the linguistic analogy, conventional rules guarantee, through socially instituted processes of learning, that the epistemic coordination among speakers concerning the rules for

---

[3]   This is a very important debate about the nature of syntax. See the exchange between Devitt and Rey and Collins in Fairweather and Montemayor (2023).

how to learn a language shares a similar kind of epistemic social background to that required for learning moral rules.

Both views, nativist and non-nativist, assume a process of convergent learning and coordination regarding the most basic rules, based on mental states or social agreements and structures. But there is an alternative to these types of theories that are based on *rules*, innate or consensual, which offers a different perspective on the linguistic analogy. This alternative proposal is suggested by Villoro, and it has been recently developed by Malcolm Bull (2019). The moral syntax view is universalist because it appeals to capacities that all humans share, regardless of their concrete situation of privilege, oppression, inclusion, or exclusion. As was just mentioned, the most influential alternative to the nativist perspective is conventionalism about norms, according to which both linguistic and moral norms are the result of consensual processes, dependent on agreements achieved by all subjects in conditions of equality. The universalist character of this proposal is that it assumes such circumstances of symmetry and equality as necessary for real consensus, ignoring concrete situations of asymmetry and inequality, such as the practices of exclusion that we encounter in polarized political exchanges.

In a social and political context, Malcolm Bull (2019, 82) argues for a notion of "radical sociability" that sharply contrasts with universal consensus views. Bull examines the ideas of David Hume about the role of conventions in the origin of justice, which Hume also justifies through an analogy with language. David Lewis (1969), inspired by Hume's account, proposed his own analysis of communicative conventions. For Lewis, the mechanisms underlying the reliability of our communicative exchanges are conventional. But, as Bull points out, Davidson (2001) offered counterexamples to Lewis's theory that can be extended, through the linguistic analogy, to the moral and social realm. In particular, Davidson says that there are cases in which the meaning of an expression cannot be determined by mutually understood conventions, given the presence of errors and malapropisms that we still manage to understand.

Davidson's solution to this difficulty is to propose a principle of charity or rational recognition, without which no genuine communication is possible. According to this principle, in cases where it is clear that the language being used is aberrant or in violation of established norms, speakers must assume that the person making the error has genuine communicative intentions that are coherent and rational, and that the speaker has the capacities needed to form true beliefs (Davidson, 1984). This implies that people cannot use a speaker's aberrant uses and errors as evidence against that person's communicative and epistemic status—people should not use this evidence as a *justification* for excluding non-standard speakers from membership in the linguistic community.

The principle of charity is not negotiable for Davidson because it is a presupposition of interpretative and communicative labor that must happen in *any* linguistic exchange. Violating this principle is a fundamental impediment to rational communication, which demands that members of a linguistic community are not excluded in arbitrary ways. In fact, Davidson argues that conventions do not precede, and are not presupposed, by our linguistic abilities. Since conventions are neither necessary nor sufficient conditions for linguistic communication, one can only converge towards a provisional theory of language, which will always depend on communicative charity, cooperation, and rational recognition. Hence, contra Lewis, language based on rational recognition comes prior to conventions, because *language*—linguistic meaning—is a necessary condition for agreements and conventions

Bull uses an equivalent principle to Davidson's charity principle in the political and moral domain by appealing to his notion of radical sociability, a reinterpretation of the term "radical interpretation." According to Bull's version of the linguistic analogy, the principle of charity can be understood as a principle of political mercy, which starts from concrete situations of injustice and cruelty (Bull 2019, 82–7). The linguistic analogy offered by Bull allows for a less asymmetric and patriarchal understanding of political mercy: mercy is, in this context, a way of attending first to injustices, the way Villoro requires, in order to then rationally accommodate the needs of those less favored. This is what is radically social about Bull's account of mercy. However, Bull somehow still requires the goodwill of those with privilege and power to accommodate those in need, which is the reason why I shall not adopt his view here. Crucially, for Davidson, the principle of charity does not depend at all on our inclination toward benevolence: charity is a necessary condition for linguistic exchanges of any kind. Therefore, in my interpretation of reasonable recognition, as opposed to Bull's and more in line with Davidson's, charity does not imply an act of generosity or "favor" from the privileged and powerful.

The work of Anne Phillips (2021) provides helpful guidance concerning how we should understand the principle of charity in the moral realm in an alternative way, which differs from the traditional notion of mercy. Phillips argues that equality is not, as has been assumed, a common characteristic of real political arrangements. To the contrary, real equality implies the *active rejection* of an individual to be treated as inferior, rather than the passive acceptance of an abstract conception of all the members of a community, independently of their differences in status, as equal. Communicative equality, for Davidson, has this communitarian and active character as well: if, as a speaker, I am always judged on the basis of my errors as if they were manifestations of a lack of rationality, or as evidence of cognitive incapacity and incompetence, I have the epistemic justification to reject silencing or unfair treatment from those who attempt to exclude me from the community on the basis of their uncharitable interpretations. This act of rejecting my exclusion from the community does not require, like the traditional conception of charity, an act of mercy from those in power.

For Villoro, this active refusal to be treated as inferior is reasonable and has both epistemic *and* moral consequences (here, Villoro's view differs from the perspectives of Bull, Phillips, and Davidson). The Central Normative Proposal integrates both principles of charity: the requirement that a person not be treated as inferior in an epistemic community of speakers, or any other kind of epistemic community;

and the demand that this person not be harmed by being judged as morally deficient or incompetent. It is this active character of our epistemic and moral agency—the rejection of inferior treatment for arbitrary reasons; the demand for constant rational recognition by people in situations of privilege that have created these asymmetries— that is at the core of Villoro's Central Normative Proposal.

Under conditions in which there are concrete impediments to becoming full-status participants, the cognitive capacities of people in inferior positions cannot be either developed adequately or exercised fairly. Various egalitarian and contractual theories address this problem, but without abandoning the assumption that equality and symmetry should be the starting point. In contrast, the principle of communicational charity starts from conversational asymmetries and, in the political realm, from injustice. Although eliminating injustice is a shared goal of all views, including contractual and deontic theories, the reasonable recognition approach emphasizes the contingencies of continuous action among asymmetrically positioned participants in any given community. This more concrete and realistic way of taking asymmetries as points of departure demands that we actively reject treating anyone as inferior. To be implemented, Villoro's proposal depends on our capacities to carefully attend to the social asymmetries and positionings of individuals and groups within a society. The proposal starts with asymmetries that exclude others and entail the worst kinds of epistemic silencing. This kind of epistemic injustice prevents the development of capacities for knowing and for being recognized as a member of groups that create knowledge and evidence. The Central Normative Proposal has, therefore, two postulates, both of them based on the principle of charity, actively implemented:

> *Epistemic non-exclusion: On the basis of communicative charity, members of epistemic communities must actively collaborate with disadvantaged members in order to guarantee the reasonable and justified transmission of knowledge, and attend to their concrete epistemic needs. Disadvantaged members should demand this reasonable recognition of their status.*

Ethical and political non-exclusion: On the basis of communicative charity, members of moral and political communities must actively collaborate with disadvantaged members in order to treat them with dignity, and attend to the concrete conditions that marginalize them. Disadvantaged members should demand the elimination of all conditions that keep them marginalized.

These are the duties that Villoro proposes for an epistemic and moral principle of non-exclusion: to allow all members of a community to access and achieve knowledge; to pursue the truth; and to be tolerant of those who differ radically from us, allowing them to actively refuse to be treated as inferior or deficient. It would be absurd to propose that these are not central preoccupations of all ethical theories, since one can certainly find similar norms in all alternative views. Few ideas are as fundamental to moral and political theory as the elimination of injustice and inequality. What distinguishes Villoro's account from others is his emphasis on always starting by attending to concrete injustices, as a methodological and empirical constraint; and by relating epistemology to ethics, meaning that we cannot assume the equality of participants without specific acts of rational recognition, what we have been calling epistemic and ethical "charity." Analogously to language, epistemic and moral agents must negotiate and rationally assert their status as participants. Their very status depends on the principle of linguistic charity and on the reasonable practice of being charitable. Their active rejection to be treated as inferior is fundamental for the possibility of conventions as sources of agreement rather than blind regularities or impositions. Ultimately, this type of active charity is our only hope to achieve equality, epistemic and moral, in contexts that are deeply warped by sociopolitical power.

It would also be absurd to suggest that any kind of exclusion is unjustified and unreasonable. Practical reason allows for various kinds of reasonable exclusion. For instance, the exclusion of children from entering into contracts or of fans from participating in games. The kind of exclusion that matters for Villoro is the one that is deeply unreasonable because it impedes the participation of disadvantaged members for unfair and arbitrary purposes, which lack any possible justification, including a practical one. Villoro's main insight is that we cannot assume equality, moral or epistemic, because the circumstances that make possible the development and interaction of our epistemic and ethical capacities are deeply asymmetric.[4]

This insight, at first, seems superficial, particularly because alternative approaches like the contractual or deontic perspectives share a substantial number of ideas about how to eliminate injustice and inequality, though their points of departure are different. But the difference is truly fundamental once one focuses on concrete processes of reasonable recognition and of exclusion-elimination. I will provide one such concrete illustration which very much preoccupied Villoro in the next section. However, this point can be made in a variety of ways. There are multiple concrete examples where practices of charity are essential in legislative and political exchanges. Peace and reconciliation processes, for example, take place precisely because conventions and laws were insufficient to guarantee peace and non-exclusion. Villoro's insight is that this practice should also be constantly exercised in our epistemic and moral communities. If we are drowning in injustice and exclusion, then the demands of charity become urgent. This urgency lies behind Villoro's plea to start with the asymmetries.

An alternative way to see the fundamental difference that results from Villoro's starting point involves Davidson's thesis concerning linguistic norms. As we saw, for Davidson, conventions cannot precede our linguistic abilities because conventions depend fundamentally on linguistic cooperation. Since conventions are neither necessary nor sufficient conditions for linguistic communication, our linguistic capacities cannot be assumed as given and equal in character. How we

---

[4]   According to a Marxist reading of Villoro's thesis, such asymmetries are the result of historical injustices that produce systematic and structural inequality. This reading is not necessary for understanding and appreciating the epistemic and ethical-political dimension of the Central Normative Proposal, although this proposal can certainly be compatible with a Marxist approach. But since the historical-structural interpretation is not necessary, the linguistic analogy suffices to appreciate Villoro's view.

arrive at our syntactic and semantic conventions is a matter of empirical research, and it remains a contested issue (Fairweather and Montemayor, 2023). Davidson's point is that our practices for communicating and cooperating with one another are the foundation for such conventions. We can only converge towards a provisional theory of language, always dependent on communicative charity, cooperation, and rational recognition—all *contingent* aspects of our communities. Likewise, our capacities to learn principles of equality that orient us in epistemology and ethics cannot be taken for granted because the process of learning also requires accommodation and mutual recognition. Unlike the presuppositions of equality and fairness of contractual and deontic theories, here we confront a process in motion, in which we must constantly improve ourselves, a process of constant amelioration that can be disrupted or even canceled by a variety of contingencies.

According to Villoro, the duty to search and promote the truth and the duty to be tolerant are present in any situation in which knowledge and beliefs are communicated. The epistemic value of reasonableness is to not be excluded from communities that generate and distribute knowledge. The moral value of reasonableness is to not exclude anyone from social benefits and from communities on which we all depend in order to live a dignified life. Villoro's account of epistemic and ethical inclusion can be interpreted as a capability approach, based on a theory of epistemic and moral needs as developed by Amartya Sen (1993, 1999), Martha Nussbaum (2011, 2020), and others (this interpretation will be developed in Chapters 4 and 7). If there are agents who are excluded from epistemic and ethical-political communities, their abilities will not develop as they should, and their needs will not be satisfied adequately. The application of principles and procedures can be considered "rational" because they achieve social goals, but these principles cannot be reasonable if, as a result of their application, we violate epistemic and moral charity and systematically exclude certain groups. Because of its emphasis on communication, the Central Normative Proposal is not equivalent to a criticism against ideal theories based on a capability approach. The principle of epistemic and moral charity that regulates reasonable communication is theoretically compatible with core theses from ideal theories (otherwise, it would be difficult to make sense of Villoro's firm commitment to universal human rights). However, we shall see that interpreting Villoro's account as a kind of pragmatically inspired capability view is quite illuminating.

To begin with concrete injustices as a departing point for a theory of knowledge and moral justification is an important and original methodological move by Villoro, and it informs not only the principle of non-exclusion but much of his philosophy. This section defends a specific interpretation of this principle through a linguistic analogy that reveals the vast scope of the Central Normative Proposal. Linguistic charity in communication, which is compared here with political, epistemic, and ethical charity, is not an act of benevolence or generosity; it is a necessary condition for the development of cognitive capacities that dignify the lives of people, with profound normative implications for epistemic and ethical communities. One must cooperate linguistically despite constant situations of asymmetry or disadvantage (malapropisms, accents, socioeconomic backgrounds). We do not cooperate in these situations out of a desire for benevolence, to benefit the linguistically oppressed. Rather, charity is essential to keep the entire linguistic community healthy and, in particular, to make reasonable communication possible. This kind of charitable effort implies the minimization and eventually, the elimination, of manipulative and oppressive linguistic practices. It might entail many other maxims of communication, such as the Gricean maxims, but without appealing to egalitarian or ideal principles of symmetry. In the next section, I expand on the proposal that our capacities to attend to the specific circumstances of members of our communities is crucial to understand how our communicative practices become *reasonable*, rather than merely rational. Attention is, therefore, intimately related to linguistic charity and the type of rational recognition required by the Central Normative Proposal.

Social epistemology: rationality, cooperation, and reasonableness

Bull (2019) argues that a political theory based on mercy (an asymmetric relation incompatible with principles of equality) is incompatible with any theory of *justice*, because justice assumes equality and symmetry. Unlike Bull, Villoro emphasizes the universality and validity of human rights, a commitment that is shared by ideal theories and theories of justice that articulate their justification of human rights through principles of justice and equality. The epistemic equivalent of this commitment to universality is Villoro's emphatic defense that truth can be pursued without falling prey to relativism or skepticism (Hurtado, 2008). The principle of epistemic and ethical charity, as we saw, clarifies and eliminates the apparent tension between Villoro's starting concern with injustice and asymmetry, and the goal of seeking truth and justice for as many people as possible under the best conditions available. I shall illustrate this principle of epistemic and ethical charity with a concrete political example that will justify the importance of cognitive processes of attention in achieving what Villoro calls "reasonable rationality."

Cooperation cannot be based on absolute certainties. Rationality and our general orientation towards truth are always mediated by situations and evaluations in which other orientations, for instance the well-being of others, must become a priority, with substantial consequences for action. Our orientation in navigating the world is central to the way in which Villoro distinguishes rationality from reasonableness.[5] He asserts that this distinction plays an important role in the theories of John Rawls and Jürgen Habermas, and emphasizes its significance for social epistemology and a theory of reasonable communication:

---

[5]　See Montemayor (2014) for a distinction between rationality and reasonableness in the context of a debate concerning legal methodology, a topic which also interested Villoro, particularly in its relation to human rights.

> All conceptions about rational communication and consensus in ethics must draw the distinction between what is purely rational and what is reasonable. This distinction is the basis, for instance, of John Rawls's "overlapping consensus" proposal, as a requirement for a democratic society. The same distinction is proposed—I believe—as a condition on the "community of dialogue", of Apel and Habermas.
>
> (Villoro, 2007, 218)

Communication must be based on epistemic values, like that of non-exclusion, which prevents forms of epistemic injustice. In contemporary epistemology, a central preoccupation is how practical and moral considerations can modify and modulate epistemic justification, influencing principles and norms concerning truth and evidence-gathering—effects that are studied as forms of *pragmatic and moral encroachment*.[6] This is a problem that Villoro addresses in his treatment of reasonableness at the collective level. A theme that Villoro examines with the notion of what we now call "encroachment" is the concept of ideology.

Villoro says explicitly in the appendix to *Los retos de la sociedad por venir* (The challenges of the society to come) that "What is reasonable is equally important in collective actions. It concerns, too, therefore, the use of reason in politics." (2007, 216) Although the notion of rationality based on norms and consensus plays a critical role in our epistemic and ethical practices, it is insufficient to explain what is reasonable, or how to be reasonable. Villoro's point of departure is to begin with injustice and oppression because it is *always reasonable* to challenge or eliminate them, independently of consensus that is either broadly accepted, or should be accepted. The political battle we must engage in, as a demand derived from the principle of non-exclusion and the Central Normative Proposal, is the energetic opposition to consensus and agreements that are oppressive or ideological, no matter how broad or robust they are. A pluralist theory of communication fosters human dignity by opposing prevailing ideologies that are erroneously accepted as legitimate

---

6   See for instance Basu (2019).

consensus based on allegedly valid norms. The gap between norms and practices and the way in which norms abstract from and ignore concrete circumstances both favor ideologies that result in exclusion. In *El concepto de ideología* (The concept of ideology), Villoro writes:

> A situation of domination requires that certain beliefs be destined to consolidate the prevailing order of things. A way of thinking that responds to the particular interests of a class or group, aims at justifying them. The concept of ideology corresponds to this type of thinking and to the beliefs that it generates. But in any situation of domination, a way of thinking that seeks to break or modify this order can present itself. Against ideological beliefs, this rational activity questions them, against a reiterative thought based on existent conventions, a disruptive thought emerges.
>
> (Villoro 1985|2007, 9)

What Villoro calls "disruptive thinking" is the active refusal to be treated as inferior mentioned in the previous section, both in the epistemic and ethical domains. Disruptive thinking, as mentioned earlier, is also a main goal of philosophy. It requires activity, and for it to succeed, genuine cooperation and charity are needed, because what disruptive thought challenges are the very presuppositions that are taken as rational because they are consensual. Ideological consensus is a constant source of oppression precisely because it can be considered as rational on the basis of consensual agreements. Recent work in epistemology seeks, in a variety of ways, to combat ideology as a system of beliefs that perpetuate oppression, either in the guise of unconscious bias or explicit norms, by appealing to the systematic influence of the practical and ethical on the epistemic.

Amia Srinivasan (2020) shows how internalism about epistemic justification may serve an ideological role that can only be eliminated on the basis of a radical and structural kind of externalism, which Villoro would call a reasonable externalism. One of the examples Srinivasan uses concerns the ideology of violence and oppression against women, a system of beliefs that is evaluated and evidentially "confirmed" within contexts of social oppression. Srinivasan argues that although these systems of beliefs are clearly oppressive, they also clearly satisfy internalist standards for coherence and rationality, according to the most canonical versions of the internalist view. The case against internalism can be extended along similar lines, as Srinivasan herself does, to other sources of exclusion and epistemic violence, justified by ideology. According to her, confronting ideologies requires a theory of *epistemic positionings*. Reasonableness is, in the work of Villoro, what allows for tolerance and, most important, for attention to the concrete positionings of others, which is a necessary requirement for disruptive thought and reason. Without our capacity to attend to the concrete realities of others and our immediate contexts or environments, we cannot appreciate epistemic positionings and we cannot, therefore, criticize established ideologies. Thus, one need not fully agree with Srinivasan's criticism against internalism to appreciate how her point relates to Villoro's principle of non-exclusion. I can make this adjustment because, as we will see further in Chapter 5, I take the central message concerning attention to the concrete circumstances of oppression to be neutral.

What does it mean to "attend" to the concrete circumstances of others less privileged? A key example for Villoro, discussed in the previous chapter, is how Mexicans have attended to the problems and needs of indigenous communities. We saw his three stages of "communication" with the indigenous world—first the collective forms of brutal oppression, ideologically justified in part on religious doctrine as ideological justification; then acceptance of indigenous people as members of a prevailing postcolonial community; and finally, their recognition as citizens and even "founders" of Mexican culture. Villoro finds in these stages structural forms of consensual rationality that never culminate in a reasonable approach. Certainly, the official recognition of indigenous people as citizens with equal rights is established by longstanding rational and democratic principles, and it is obviously better than slavery, forced conversion to Christianity, and persecution. But such recognition was deeply insufficient for establishing an epistemically and ethically robust Mexican community that could genuinely incorporate indigenous people as participants, one in which they have the same real access to possibilities and capabilities as their compatriots. This promise for genuine inclusion is, in fact, far from being achieved, after *five centuries* of rationally principled political action.

The rationality behind the Constitutional legal system of Mexico, which used the United States Constitution as a blueprint, grants indigenous people not only citizenship and equality before the law, but also communitarian autonomy. Nonetheless, despite all these nontrivial legal protections, the indigenous communities of Mexico remain abandoned and in poverty. Indigenous people remain *remote* and they are basically removed from the national conversation. Their languages, communities, even their geographical locations are perceived as remote and unfamiliar. They are not active members of the epistemic and ethical communities that shape national policies in Mexico, in sharp contrast to the perfect symmetry of the law. This dissonant reality excludes them almost as effectively as the practices of openly oppressive colonial regimes, although obviously, no one would consider those oppressive regimes as preferable to the current system from a moral or epistemic standpoint. Villoro invites us to seriously consider the fact that, despite this difference, the situation of indigenous people remains opprobrious.

To confront this puzzling and unacceptable situation, what Villoro recommends is to start with a brute fact: the profound and deeply immoral asymmetry that systematically excludes indigenous people from national conversations. We must begin not with equality, rights, and symmetry, but with this concrete injustice, and we must put *effort* into actively attending and incorporating these communities by accepting their challenge to not be treated as inferior, regardless of what the explicit text of the law says. Only by attending to the needs of all the members of diverse communities, with the charity that characterizes reasonable communication, will the Mexican community be capable of truly integrating an epistemic and ethical community—one that is acceptable and does not exclude indigenous and other groups both from the production and distribution of knowledge, and also from the goods and practices that allow people to improve their lives and live with dignity.

There will not be an ideal point in which everything will be homogenous and egalitarian, a kind of paradise where we can simply forget that all this ever happened. Villoro insists on this point, and we will return to its importance in subsequent chapters. This lack of ideal perspective is part of the justification for initially beginning from injustice. The concrete and actual *should demand our attention* in ways that the abstract and possible shouldn't. There will not be an ideal Mexican polity where all asymmetries are smoothed out, partly because one cannot change the past, and partly because past injustices inform the way we communicate, which communities we belong to, and how much effort we put in attending to the needs of other members of our communities. It is *rational* to claim that Mexicans have done "all they can" from a legal point of view; that the law recognizes the indigenous world to an extent that other jurisdictions, like the United States, do not; and that it would be rational for the indigenous world to appreciate this. But we know all too well that, in fact, and over a long period of time, all that indigenous communities have received from the dominant epistemic and ethical communities of Mexico is constant exclusion and rejection. What is rational, in this context, is not reasonable. The system of beliefs about equality among citizens, based on the Constitution, is not sufficient to change situations of exclusion and oppression. We must go beyond these beliefs, which confuse us into thinking that we have done all we can do. We must, in particular, put effort into attending to concrete situations of injustice, in their specific manifestations.

Notice that it is also insufficient to merely *know that, as a matter of fact*, there is injustice, the same way one knows that Jupiter has more than 70 moons. The existence of injustice is not a simple "fact among others" that one must abstractly assess and ponder (the next three chapters expand on this issue). It is, in itself, *an urgent demand* on reasonable communication, which asks from us to be more reasonable in our communicative efforts and in our relations to others. This demand requires us to change our perspective on the needs of oppressed communities. It is an urgent demand: if we do not actively attend to their needs, by ameliorating their situation and repairing the harms they have suffered, we are acting unjustly, epistemically and ethically. For this reason, Villoro insists that the Central Normative Proposal depends fundamentally on starting, methodologically, from injustice. To achieve this methodological goal of starting from injustice, one must *pay attention to what is unjust*. It is not enough to simply know, remotely, that there are injustices in the world and that, on the basis of such knowledge, we must develop systems of beliefs about the world that must cohere with one another.

Thus, we should not live merely rational lives that accord with norms and procedures. What is reasonable is eminently social and cooperative. As Villoro says: "What is reasonable refers to a dialogical rationality, as opposed to the soliloquy of a pure rationality." (2007, 218). We need to orient ourselves with the flexibility and openness of what is reasonable, considering the possibility that various options that might be rational might nonetheless become oppressive and unreasonable by blinding us from the concrete reality of other members of our communities. Attention is what allows us to pierce this shield of belief that can prevent us from engaging and seeing, as well as listening, to these members. It is because of this that reasonable rationality is diverse, uncertain, impure and not arrogant (2007, 221–2). Continuing with the linguistic analogy, in the words of Davidson, if linguistic ability is the ability to converge on a passing theory from time to time, then "we have erased the boundary between knowing a language and knowing our way around the world generally." (Davidson 2006, 265). There shouldn't be a gap between knowing our language and knowing our way around the world.

Reasonable rationality resolves the apparent tensions in the work of Villoro—tensions between pluralism and the universality of human rights and justice, and between tolerance and non-relativism. The rationality of abstract soliloquy leads to ideology or is at least favorable to it. As Srinivasan (2020) argues, one can perfectly comply with norms of belief, including those norms that concern experience and evidence and epistemically justify, from an internal perspective, what is both epistemically and morally unjustifiable. Epistemically unjustifiable, because our internally justified beliefs are not really producing knowledge of the relevant information about positionings, and morally unjustifiable because such beliefs can then justify ideological systems of oppression. This happens because beliefs are *non-factual* in the sense that believing a proposition, even with a good degree of justification, never guarantees its being true. Beliefs are not necessarily *anchored in reality*. Reasonable rationality is fundamental to a comprehensive theory of rationality precisely because it necessitates being anchored to concrete realities. For the same reason, contractual obligations cannot be the basis for reasonable rationality. Villoro writes:

> Both forms of association, a society based on a contract and a community based on a shared sense of goodness and common values, can break apart if in them exists a discrepancy that leads to the exclusion of part of their members [. . .] The solution of this antinomy in their form of association could only be possible through the construction of a new society in which there is no exclusion. It would be a plural society in which different cultures would have real possibilities to freely develop.
>
> (Villoro, 2007, 111)

The relation between freedom and knowledge depends on the cooperation and charitable communication of reasonable agents, which prevents epistemic and moral exclusion and promotes the integration of a plural society. This is, in essence, Villoro's Central Normative Proposal. For it to become possible, attending to concrete situations and positionings is crucial. The engagement of diverse groups or epistemic collectives in specific contexts is fundamental, and requires navigating overlapping social networks where asymmetries must be eliminated through reasonableness and epistemic charity. In this effort, equality should never be taken for granted, as a given. Rather, one must struggle, make attentive efforts, and fight oppression by actively rejecting being treated as inferior, while also preventing others from being treated as inferiors.[7]

---

[7] In this context, it is useful to consult the work of Ángeles Eraña (2021), which is particularly relevant for the interests of the late Villoro in Zapatismo and Zapatista social epistemology.

Toward an ethics of attention

Where should the Central Normative Proposal lead us, based on the comments made earlier about the importance of being attentive to properly understand the concept of reasonableness in Villoro? The short answer is that Villoro's proposal leads toward a unified theory of reason that integrates ethics with epistemology, the subject of the following chapters. What is important to appreciate now is that the kind of normative guidance that is not exclusively dependent on belief, provided by attention, can be more explanatory and comprehensive in its application to many cases, as demonstrated, for instance by Georgi Gardiner (2022). Assessing cases in which the problem is not the violation of evidential standards or norms of truth dependent on belief, but rather difficulties arising from our lack of attention to what is *relevant* in a specific context of evaluation, or the epistemic distortions that result from paying too much attention to something in a biased and inadequate way, is fundamental in determining whether our rational practices are reasonable or not.

In other words, attention is fundamental to the project of developing a comprehensive theory of rationality that clearly delineates not only the rational from the irrational, but also the rational but unreasonable from the rational and reasonable. Attention is required to expand the boundaries of our contemporary approaches in epistemology and ethics. This expansion includes practices of attention that play a critical role in the development of reasonable rationality. We can possess a vast compendium of knowledge, for instance, be experts in Constitutional law, and have very good evidence that several injustices are committed on a daily basis. From a strictly rational perspective, we are blameless since we are doing "all that can be done" to satisfy the demands of epistemic justification based on evidence. But we might still be epistemically incompetent if we comply with such requirements in a way that is unreasonable, by being irresponsive to the concrete needs of others. We become unreasonable because of our inattentiveness toward their suffering and their positionings. We are blameworthy if we do not put more attentive effort in engaging and communicating with them. This is a *norm of attention* that communicative charity demands.

Attention not only amplifies the norms of rationality, but it also serves a more basic epistemic and moral normative role than justified belief. This is a stronger thesis than the previous one concerning theoretical amplification, and it may not be crucial to interpreting the Central Normative Proposal (although it certainly helps clarifying how it operates—Chapter 4 expands on this issue). However, I shall argue that Villoro's unified theory of reason requires this stronger thesis. Although he expressed his epistemic views in terms of belief (and norms of belief), as most contemporary epistemologists also do, he used the term "orientation" in his definition of *reason*, which I take to be good, or at least initial, evidence, for the stronger thesis about the role of attention. Moreover, he defended a dispositional view of belief, which is compatible with interpreting doxastic orientations in terms of attention. Orientations based on reasonable rationality can be interpreted as acts of attention that are *anchored* in the needs and concrete characteristics of those who require our cognitive focus and communicative charity.[8]

If we don't interpret reasonableness as fundamentally involving norms of attention, then key claims in the work of Villoro become unclear and even paradoxical, given the non-factual nature of belief (even in a dispositional account of belief, justified belief is non-factual). One of these key claims concerns the very definition of "reason," as we saw earlier. For instance, the following definition of "reason" appears in the appendix to *Los retos de la sociedad por venir*, a late work of Villoro's, confirming the crucial role that attentive anchoring plays in reasonable rationality:

> By definition, reason is a human disposition that allows us to "tie" our beliefs and actions to reality. But this is not a reality "in itself", just as it

---

[8]   In the context of moral theory, the work of Iris Murdoch (1971) is highly relevant here. In the concluding chapters, views like Murdoch will be compared to Villoro's unified theory of reasoning.

would exist independently of all subjects. Reality is, in each case, that which opposes our will, which resists us, which confronts our attitudes and desires. The reality in which reason anchors itself is therefore a world that exists in relation to the activity that in each case humans deploy. Reason is a "tie" to our surrounding reality, the one that is given in a determinate situation and which can oppose human dispositions in that situation [...] We call "reasonable" the use of reason in a context, in accordance with the proposed goals of that context.

(2007, 221)

Belief, even if justified, cannot play this role of "tying" or anchoring reason to reality or to any determined and concrete situation.[9] As Villoro says, some mental ability must allow us to tie "our beliefs and actions to reality" and this is the key role of attention in human cognition.[10] Belief can *never* guarantee such anchoring capacities. It suffices to mention here classic cases such as the new evil demon in which justified belief leads to systemic falsehood (one of the key cases examined by Srinivasan, 2020). Notice, too, the more capacious realm of reason that is opened up by epistemically, socially, and morally tying beliefs and actions to reality. Attention, unlike belief, is the most essential capacity for anchoring ourselves in concrete situations: it orients us and "ties" us to objects, properties, and relevant aspects of the world that surrounds us. In the context of perception, the kind of anchoring that attention provides is essential to understanding demonstrative or de re reference, and also to explaining the most fundamental cases of perceptual epistemic justification (Dickie, 2020). Without attention and its selective functions, no type of anchoring to reality, concerning beliefs or actions in specific contexts, would be possible.

---

[9]   See Eraña and Montemayor (2025) for how this has substantial consequences for philosophy as a whole, including skepticism, as well as the binding problem in perception, and the other-minds problem.

[10] For a review of the evidence in support of this claim, including empirical findings on object based attention, see Montemayor and Haladjian (2015). This issue is further clarified in subsequent chapters.

Because what is reasonable depends on our cognitive capacity to fix the reference of our actions and beliefs in concrete reality, and because this function is exactly the role that attention plays in our cognition, it follows that the epistemic and moral value of attention is more fundamental, as well as more capacious, than that of belief. The beginning of Villoro's *El poder y el valor* (Power and value), in the section *Valor y actitud* (Value and attitude), says:

> On a first approximation, we can understand by "value" the characteristics for which an object or situation is the target of a favorable attitude. "Attitude" is an old term used initially by social psychology and then adopted in philosophy. It refers to an acquired disposition that distinguishes itself from other dispositions through its *"direction" favorable or unfavorable* towards an object, class of objects or objective situation. What characterizes it is therefore its *affective charge* towards something.
>
> (Villoro 1997, 13; the emphasis is mine)

This definition of value emphasizes the selective capacity of attention, and demonstrates its potential for being epistemically and morally charged (about the epistemic version of "charge" in contemporary epistemology see Siegel, 2017, examined in Chapter 6). Referring back to the previous example, one can have a distant or remote orientation, based on basic beliefs about facts concerning inequality among certain groups, and thus have some knowledge of the exclusion of a certain group, but at the same time, have an unfavorable charge in our orientation towards them. Reason demands that in this situation we should reorient our attention so that we can confront more directly what is at stake in this asymmetry, recharging more favorably the affective component of our orientation towards this group and its needs.

Therefore, on the principle of epistemic and communicative charity, epistemic non-exclusion is essential for reasonable communication. Political and moral non-exclusion is a necessary condition for pluralism and human rights.[11] What is reasonable can be interpreted as the positive and essential functions of attention, because attention anchors us in what is concrete, bypassing the soliloquy of private rationality. A stronger thesis can be defended here: what is reasonable *must be understood* in terms of attention, because only in this way will we be able to characterize the entirety and nature of epistemic and moral value, within a theory of reason that examines it in the widest possible sense. If the present analysis is correct, the functions of affective charges, epistemic or moral, and of our general orientation to navigate the world, are more clearly fulfilled by attention than by belief. The Central Normative Proposal and reasonable rationality depend on the broader normative guidance provided by the anchoring of attention. What we must do, then, paraphrasing the title of a book by Habermas, is to orient ourselves in order to become "an attentive society," rather than a merely rational one.[12]

Developing a more attentive society and reinvigorating our theory of reason so that the relation between ethics and epistemology is at its center, as Villoro does, has important consequences for ethics. Hurtado (2023, 22–3) reminds us that Villoro's negative approach to justice or *via negativa*, was a reaction against prevailing theories of the time, particularly Rawls's use of the "veil of ignorance" in order to guide the cognitive processes of evaluating our ethical intuitions. Hurtado argues that, unlike the ideal position Rawls wants to achieve, Villoro assumes a non-ideal standpoint, and begins his investigations through the concreteness of injustices in Mexico and Latin America. Hurtado is absolutely right about this, as I hope the discussion above demonstrates. But I would go further. Villoro's project is much larger than simply

---

[11] In the field of human rights theory, different senses of non-exclusion can be understood as formulations of a principle of "irradiation," which expands liberties progressively in the most encompassing way possible. The progressive character of this principle is also similar to Villoro's principle. See, for instance, Montemayor (2002).

[12] Habermas, J. (1971). *Toward A Rational Society: Student Protest, Science, and Politics.* Boston, MA: Beacon Press.

reacting to prevailing theories in the anglophone world in order to offer a more realistic perspective, as experienced in the situatedness of the global south. Indeed, in the next chapter I shall argue that, very much like Immanuel Kant, Villoro is interested in investigating reason in its most fundamental forms, in a way that can be updated with the psychology of attention, offering a more realistic and empirically valid account of the capacities involved in our encounters with others and in our practices of giving reasons to one another. The linguistic analogy defended here is only the first step toward a more thorough account of Villoro's unified theory of reasoning.

References

Basu, R. (2019), Radical Moral Encroachment: The Moral Stakes of Racist Beliefs, *Philosophical Issues*, vol. 29(1): 9–23.

Bull, M. (2019), *On Mercy*, Princeton: Princeton University Press.

Davidson, D. (1984), 'Radical Interpretation', In D. Davidson (ed.), *Inquiries into Truth and Interpretation*, Oxford: Clarendon Press (pp. 125–39).

Davidson, D. (2001), 'Communication and Convention', In Donald Davidson, *Inquiries into Truth and Interpretation*, Oxford: Oxford University Press (pp. 265–80).

Davidson, D. (2006), 'A Nice Derangement of Epitaphs', In Donald Davidson, *The Essential Davidson*, Oxford: Oxford University Press (pp. 251–65).

Dickie, I. (2020), 'Cognitive Focus', In R. Goodman, J. Genone and N. Kroll (eds.), *Singular Thought and Mental Files*, New York: Oxford University Press.

Eraña, Á. (2021), *De un mundo que hila personas (o de la inexistencia de la paradoja individuo/sociedad*, Mexico City: Instituto de Investigaciones Filosóficas-UNAM and UAM.

Eraña, Á. and Montemayor, C. (2025), *Anclándonos al mundo (la atención como umbral de la certeza)*, Mexico City: Bonilla and Instituto de Investigaciones Filosóficas-UNAM.

Fairweather, A. and Montemayor, C. (2023), *Linguistic Luck: Safeguards and Threats to Linguistic Communication*, Oxford: Oxford University Press.

Gardiner, G. (2022), 'Attunement: On the Cognitive Virtues of Attention', In M. Alfano, C. Klein and J. de Ridder (eds.), *Social Virtue Epistemology*, New York: Routledge.

Hurtado, G. (2008), Reseña bibliográfica de Luis Villoro, *Los retos de la sociedad por venir*, *Diánoia*, 53(60): 195–9.

Johnson King, Z. (2022), Radical Internalism, *Philosophical Studies*, 32(1): 46–64.

Lewis, D. K. (1969), *Convention: A Philosophical Study*, Cambridge, MA: Harvard University Press.

Mikhail, J. (2011), *Elements of Moral Cognition: Rawls's Linguistic Analogy and the Cognitive Science of Moral and Legal Judgment*, Cambridge: Cambridge University Press.

Mills, C. W. (2005), "Ideal theory" as ideology, *Hypatia*, 20(3): 165–83.

Montemayor, C. (2002), *La unificación conceptual de los derechos humanos*, Mexico: Porrúa.

Montemayor, C. (2008), Moral Innatism and Legal Theory, *Problema: Anuario de Filosofía y Teoría del Derecho*, 2: 407–30.

Montemayor, C. (2014), Rationality and Reasonableness in Legal Theory, *Problema: Anuario de Filosofía y Teoría del Derecho*, 8: 39–51.

Montemayor, C. (2023a), Luis Villoro y el Principio de No Exclusión, *Diánoia*, 68(90): 31–51.

Murdoch, I. (1971), *The Sovereignty of Good*, New York: Routledge and Kegan Paul.

Nussbaum, M. (2011), *Creating Capabilities: The Human Development Approach*, Cambridge, MA: Harvard University Press.

Nussbaum, M. (2020), 'The Capabilities Approach and the History of Philosophy', In E. Chiappero-Martinetti, S. Osmani and M. Qizilbash (eds.), *The Cambridge Handbook of the Capability Approach*, Cambridge: Cambridge University Press (pp. 13–39).

Phillips, A. (2021), *Unconditional Equals*, Princeton: Princeton University Press.

Sen, A. (1993), 'Capability and Well-being', In M. Nussbaum and A. Sen, *The Quality of Life*, Oxford: Clarendon Press (pp. 30–53).

Sen, A. (1999), *Development as Freedom*, New York: Knopf.

Siegel, S. (2017), *The Rationality of Perception*, Oxford: Oxford University Press.

Srinivasan, A. (2020), Radical Externalism, *The Philosophical Review*, 129(3): 395–431.

Villoro, L. (1985|2007), *El Concepto de Ideología y Otros Ensayos*, Mexico: Fondo de Cultura Económica.

Villoro, L. (1999|2022), 'Sobre el principio de la injusticia: la exclusión (Octavas Conferencias Aranguren)', In J. Villoro and G. Hurtado (eds.), *La identidad múltiple*, Mexico: El Colegio Nacional (pp. 65–128).

Villoro, L. (2007), *Los retos de la sociedad por venir*, Mexico: Fondo de Cultura Económica.

Villoro, L. (1982|2008), *Creer, saber, conocer*, México: Siglo XXI.

Villoro, L. (1997), *El poder y el valor; fundamentos de una ética política*, Mexico: Fondo de Cultura Económica.

3

Truth, Knowledge, and Freedom

The claim of reason

In the previous chapter, attention was characterized as the key cognitive capacity we depend upon to anchor ourselves to reality. It was defined as a normatively salient kind of cognitive action, in the sense that the agent orients with a particular charge and focus toward objects or situations.[1] This kind of mental action cannot be reduced to a single event or to merely causal relations. It is a fundamental source of cognitive freedom. Attention fosters creativity and cooperation. Beliefs, by contrast, are fixed, so that there is certitude about their content and a discrete "totality" about them. Even if they are about uncertainties or degrees of credence, beliefs are *items* that can be mapped, added, subtracted, mutually supported, and quantified. A calculation of doxastic evidential updates that depends on this abstract formulation of belief-structure is at the very foundation of contemporary formal epistemology.

As we saw earlier, beliefs are non-factual because they represent the world without ever guaranteeing accuracy. This is why justification plays such an important role in Western, belief-based, epistemology. Without evidence or some way of successfully anchoring them, beliefs cannot play the role of "maps by which we steer" (an expression introduced by Frank Ramsey, who plays an important role in the discussion that follows). The anchoring of the map is independent from that map; something else needs to guarantee its accuracy by verifying or measuring it. Attention is essential for anchoring cognition, including

---

[1]   For definitions of attention see Mole, et al. (2011); Montemayor (2023a).

beliefs. As Villoro remarks, reason itself is a kind of anchoring and, as such, is an activity that is never complete—it cannot be a fixed item. Reason, based on the anchoring provided by attention, can improve or deteriorate; it can be positively or negatively charged; but it is never "done" or packaged into a unit. Attention, in particular, can never be itemized in such a way because it is the manifestation of epistemic agency (Fairweather and Montemayor, 2017). Attention is, therefore, largely responsible for our cognitive autonomy, our mental freedom, and the spontaneity of reason (Montemayor, 2023a).

The proper function and core purpose of attention is to select relevant content for the execution of the right kind of mental activity, so as to anchor our reasoning capacities. This deserves emphasis. The proper function of belief is to represent or depict a situation, without guaranteeing that the depiction is true. By contrast, the proper function of attention is to anchor our minds to concrete objects and situations. This seemingly simple point is critical to the project of developing a comprehensive theory of rationality. In particular, Villoro's characterization of reason as an anchor to the world is crucial to delineate the rationality of arrogant soliloquy from reasonable rationality. The anchoring function of attention, on which reason depends, is well understood in the philosophy and psychology of perception.[2] For instance, attention solves the "binding problem" of assigning the right properties to the correct and properly integrated perceptual objects. Attention also provides the orientation to focus on what is relevant, gaining a causal rapport with objects in the world that opens them to inspection. As Dickie (2020) has argued, this kind of epistemic grounding also plays a fundamental role in semantics and is the foundation of singular thoughts. It is no surprise that attention plays a key justificatory role in non-Western philosophical traditions, where it is understood as the main source of knowledge and the fundamental cognitive connection with the world and our conspecifics (Ganeri, 2017).

---

[2] In philosophy, see Ganeri (2017). In psychology, see for instance the literature on object based attention: Pylyshyn (2000, 2001), Kahneman, et al. (1992).

The orientation of attention shapes the epistemic profile of beliefs. The most basic influence of attention on beliefs is that the grounding of attention provides some perceptual beliefs with true contents, but not others—specifically not those based on phenomenally identical experiences that are not anchored by perceptual attention and which are, therefore, non-veridical. But the orientation of attention shapes beliefs in other, more subtle ways. I explain below how some pragmatists examined and categorized these more nuanced influences, and how they illuminate Villoro's own dispositional account of belief. The basic idea here is that attention can be oriented toward the world, towards other agents, and toward joint actions, plans, or schemes for the coordination of joint attention. The orientation of attention makes the world cohere, presenting it as a familiar and welcoming place for our actions through the integration of various motoric and sub-personal routines. Attention shapes our agency by making it cohesive and well-integrated for action (Wu, 2014, Chapter 2).

The orientation of attention specifies various options for anchoring the maps by which we steer. This is fundamental to understanding the limits of reason, since reason depends on being properly anchored. Villoro saw a connection between the topic of anchoring cognition in reality and the work of Wittgenstein, particularly the *Tractatus*, which will be a central theme in this chapter. Given the essential role that attention plays in being reasonable, it is no surprise that Villoro became interested in a book devoted to the foundations of mathematics and language that centers on mapping relations to the world and ends with a few cryptic passages about the unity of ethics, logic, and aesthetics. Attention is a remedy for skepticism (Eraña and Montemayor, 2025), and Villoro was keen on showing how reasonable rationality prevents us from falling into skepticism and relativism, both about truth and about moral goodness.

Delineating the bounds of reason, as we discussed in Chapter 1, is a key task of philosophy. For Villoro, this project had practical and political consequences. Villoro was deeply interested in the disruptive nature of justified reasoning in the fight against oppression and ideology. The limits of reason also concern the foundations of science and morality. To explore these limits, a methodological starting point should delineate how to relate the entirety of our available knowledge about the world and about ourselves. As Kant wrote about the purpose of the *Critique of Pure Reason*:

> This attempt to alter the procedure which has hitherto prevailed in metaphysics, by completely revolutionising it in accordance with the example set by the geometers and physicists, forms indeed the main purpose of this critique of pure speculative reason. It is a treatise on the method, not a system of science itself. But at the same time it marks out the whole plan of the science, both as regards its limits and as regards its entire internal structure.
>
> (Kant, 1929, 25)

Villoro decided to explore this foundational issue with the initial methodological point of attending to injustice, following the programmatic ideal of relating knowledge and freedom to concrete actions. Knowledge should lead to increases in our freedom, while also making us accountable to one another. Good reasoning should lead to the disruption of various forms of oppression and epistemic injustice. Reason-guidance must make possible the integration of knowledge, participatory democracy, and liberation. This methodological strategy is, as Kant envisioned, the demarcation of a critical program against bad reasoning and superficial or purely speculative rationality.

As pragmatism is also a programmatic and critical project, it provides a perspective that is very congenial to Villoro's philosophy. A central theme in some pragmatist views is that education is essential for liberation as political action.[3] To cultivate reasonable attentional practices we must engage in attentional resistance against forces of homogenization and oppression. Education is about building cognitive tools, and we need such tools to fight injustices. Education is a collective

---

[3]   See Pappas (2017), who examines the role of Zapatismo and Villoro's engagement with it, highlighting the pragmatic commitments of Villoro's philosophy. This commitment to education as a core value of pragmatism is particularly salient in the work of John Dewey and Richard Rorty.

activity and, when we cooperate, we are better able to identify patterns of mistreatment. In the Latin American context, Paulo Freire conceived of the education of the oppressed as a struggle for hope: a *cultivation* of hope.

In the United States, bell hooks continued this tradition, highlighting that education occurs everywhere, particularly in the dominant centers of culture production delivered as mass media, where ideological and oppressive education is imposed on the excluded. hooks thought that encasing education in classrooms that replicate oppressive dynamics is a disservice to liberational education. She writes that in contexts of domination, the "will to learn," which Villoro would categorize as a basic need that we must satisfy for everyone if we don't want to create exclusion, requires that education be a powerful source of insurrection. The will to learn is a plea to learn what one needs to know, and to liberate subjugated knowledges—the awareness of the "need to create justice in education" (hooks, 2003, 7). In Chapter 7, I shall argue that this pragmatist liberational project entails what I will call "a bureaucracy of intimacy."

Joint attention is fundamental to understand how both virtuous or vicious attention practices scale up to social, and even global, patterns of behavior and social interaction, now more than ever through social media. Generally speaking, joint attention is necessary for communication and joint action (Clark, 1996). A more political and structural kind of joint attention is also important here, one that shapes affiliations and modes of attentional fairness regarding the distribution of knowledge, in ways that either enhance or inhibit reliable communication—for instance, through trust or polarization. Joint attention also needs to be grounded in concrete contexts. In this sense, it needs to be anchored in reality in a way that goes beyond mere ideology or opinion, as Villoro's notion of reasonable rationality demands.

Collective attention in public education is essentially political, because it can be interpreted as a form of resistance against social inequality, as hooks said. The relation between attentional practices and education can in fact be understood as a requirement for any democracy to work properly. Pragmatists have emphasized the role of education in preventing injustice and inequality. For instance, for John Dewey (1916), the purpose of education is to become partners in knowledge production and distribution, rather than simply staying in the asymmetric situation of trainer and trainee. Dewey explicitly says that, unlike the relation between trainer and trainee, the learner is a "copartner" in a shared activity (Dewey, 1916, 13). The asymmetry between trainer and trainee is compatible with the kind of social hierarchy that leads to various forms of attentional invisibility (Harris, 2017). Education is, therefore, a natural place to look for powerful and scalable kinds of attentional coordination and resistance.

An understanding of how disruptive and reasonable rationality has developed through history is also important for Villoro. As we saw in Chapter 1, the Renaissance, according to Villoro, emancipated our intelligence. This disruption transformed philosophy itself, creating a dynamic force in our understanding of reality that still fuels our scientific investigations. This is the kind of transformation that emancipatory education strives for—not to satisfy metrics in classrooms, but to benefit humanity as a whole. Knowledge in unison with liberation is the core claim of reason.

Knowledge is a socially produced, collective achievement. The Renaissance doesn't belong exclusively to Leonardo or Galileo, yet their personal commitments, and the commitments of others who joined them, made the Renaissance possible. Now heroes of humanity, scientific inquiry, and the arts, Leonardo and Galileo were the outcasts and rebels of their time. Galileo, like many other free thinkers of his time, suffered from oppressive practices, and even overt condemnation based on ideological thinking. But the hope for liberating education prevailed over these practices of oppression. The Renaissance reoriented and expanded the limits or "figure" of the world. In aesthetics, it reoriented attention to new forms and styles of beauty; in politics, it reoriented political agendas towards new liberal ideals. In science, knowledge was reoriented toward new scales and formal approaches. It was a reform of our intelligence and learning.

Villoro's notion of the "figure" of the world is at least partly inspired by his engagement with Wittgenstein's work on the limits of reason and language, as I argue below and in subsequent chapters. For Villoro, genuine knowledge liberates, and it is always courageous in its search for truth. Responsible reasoning applies not only to beliefs, but also to actions and behaviors oriented towards specific social goals on a foundation of attentional grounding. Collective attention reoriented us, in the case of the Renaissance, toward a new understanding of humanity, turning us into a different kind of community—a more knowledgeable and just collective. Reasonable rationality is transformative and disruptive exactly in this way. It has a *basing* character, and it is also profoundly political.

However, Villoro is not a radical communitarian, since personal commitment can never be replaced by social conditioning or design. But it is fair to say that reasonable rationality produces *collective* transformative experiences.[4] Individual transformative experiences count for very little in this context. They become relevant only when reasonable rationality is firmly in place. Similarly, isolated, coherent, and evidentially based belief counts for little if knowledge is not distributed properly and is kept in the hands of a few privileged individuals in an enclosed silo, without helping the goals of education and liberation. The *house of reason*, for Villoro, is not a monolithic temple. Various epistemic cultures, the dominant and the oppressed, struggle to shape a dynamic and politically infused space of reasons and actions. A theory of rationality is incomplete without a clear distinction between reasonable and unreasonable reason-giving in such a dynamic context. The highest forms of rationality, our greatest epistemic achievements, require the highest degree of *integration* between epistemic inquiry and moral, as well as aesthetic, reasoning. This normative requirement makes Villoro, in my opinion, one of the most original and encompassing social epistemologists and theorists of rationality.

---

[4] Some of this material on the Renaissance and the norms of belief is based on in my review of Guillermo Hurtado's compilation of Villoro's work at *Notre Dame Philosophical Reviews*, Montemayor (2024).

Villoro, like many contemporary epistemologists, offered an account of the norms of belief and rationality, which will be examined in detail in Chapter 5. These norms are guides for concrete action by a socially embedded agent with a personal grip on reason. Villoro is emphatic about this. He begins his analysis of the ethics of belief by clarifying that belief and knowledge have an essential practical function that is best understood as a guide for action, uniting epistemology with ethics. This kind of pragmatic guidance, as I argue in the next section, also plays a *foundational* role. Viewed properly, these are norms of *integration* between the epistemic and the ethical domain. Villoro distinguishes between two forms of the Spanish verb "to know." *Saber* requires *intersubjectively achieved*, objectively sufficient justification, while *conocer* requires *successful action*, *trust* and reliability. Interestingly, wisdom is one of the highest forms of "conocer," while science is a form of "saber."[5]

A unique feature of Villoro's norms of belief is that they are postulated as *social* rights and duties. This is why intersubjectivity, more than "truth," plays an essential role in his epistemology. In fact, Villoro does not require truth as a necessary condition for knowledge, although, as I mentioned earlier, he never denies that pursing the truth is a central goal of epistemology. To see why Villoro does this, it is important to emphasize the social and pragmatic commitments of his view. His norms of belief concern: (1) the duty to pursue the highest degree of justification, in accordance with the practices of specific epistemic communities, and the right to communicate one's reasons for adopting beliefs and acting in a certain way (a right that counters testimonial injustice and epistemic silencing); (2) the duty to achieve and maintain epistemic autonomy while respecting the autonomy of others, and the right not to be manipulated or oppressed; and (3) the duty that one's actions must be consistent with one's beliefs, and the right to be considered as coherent by others (the equivalent of Davidson's charity principle).

---

[5]   In their translation of Villoro's *Creer, Saber, Conocer*, David Sosa and Douglas McDermid (1998) translate "saber" as personal knowledge, and "conocer" as propositional knowledge. I prefer not to use their translation because it misses (1) the social dimension of "saber," (2) the relation between wisdom and "conocer," and (3) the orientation towards action of all forms of "conocer."

The aim of these norms is the integration of ethically robust epistemic communities. They concern not just individual belief, but collective belief and crucially, action. For Villoro, solipsistic rules for the guidance of subjective belief contradict the essence of the ethics of belief. He says that the ethical validity of these norms depends on the prevalence of the general interests of the epistemic community above individual ones, and that these norms do not guide belief in isolation, but only in the context of situations for actions that lead to their formation. Villoro argues that these norms help us avoid dogmatism and skepticism, which are forms of *epistemic intolerance.* Ultimately, the goal of following these norms is to use our reasoning and knowledge for the purpose of liberation (Montemayor, 2024).

The conditions for disruptive rationality and reasonableness require much more than subjective belief. Reasonableness requires personal and constant alertness and attention to the needs of others, and a constant commitment to intersubjectively achieved truth and justice. This is the importance of the scope of the norms of reasoning, which necessarily include actions and dispositions to change our world, in which injustice, epistemic and moral, prevails. Villoro takes injustice, ethical and epistemic, as the starting point for a non-ideal social epistemology. This justifies exploring in more detail how Villoro's non-ideal theory of justice and communication relates to similar or supporting views, particularly pragmatically oriented ones—we need to look beyond Villoro's (1982) *Creer, Saber, Conocer.* We will come back to Villoro's account of knowledge in Chapter 5. We shall now focus on Villoro's account of the scope of reason.

The origins of reason and meaning: Villoro on Wittgenstein

Kant's *Critique of Pure Reason* "marks out the whole plan of the science, both as regards its limits and as regards its entire internal structure" (Kant, 1929, 25). As Villoro (1975) shows in his essay "The unsayable in the *Tractatus*," Wittgenstein was interested in a similar project concerning the delineation of the bounds of language and reasonable communication. Wittgenstein's project, as Villoro interprets it, is similar in spirit to Kant's because it demarcates the limits of what is reasonable to communicate, showing that there is a transcendental relation between ethics, aesthetics, and logic. This relation determines the limits of language and its meaning. Villoro writes the following about Kant and Wittgenstein, regarding the project of establishing the grounding conditions of reason, in the context of explaining why, for Wittgenstein, ethics and logic are transcendental:

> Using a distinction of Kantian origin, we can say that what is mystical does not *transcend* the world, but that it is *transcendental*. "Transcendental" is what goes beyond any possible experience and which is assumed to exist beyond its limits. It refers to the existence of certain things or facts that cannot be captured either by experience or by expressions in a scientific language, but that subsist in some ontological region that differs from experience. This kind of transcendence does not fit the conception of the *Tractatus*. What is properly "transcendental," on the other hand, according to Kant, is not "far away" all possible experience, but rather "closely near" it. It is a set of conditions that make it possible; these conditions cannot be experienced, because they are not constitutive parts of experience, but I must admit them to account for the totality of experience.
>
> (Villoro, 1975, 18)

Villoro insists that what is transcendental must be understood in terms of the totality of the world, a *vision*, or *figure* of the world. He continues explaining that, similarly to Kant, "for Wittgenstein, logic is 'transcendental' because it is the condition for any language to be capable of providing a figure of the world." (Villoro, 1975, 18) Villoro then explains why ethics and aesthetics have the same transcendental status. But how is it possible to see the unity and totality of the world by experiencing what is transcendental, making all our experiences a coherent "figure of the world," without ever being able to experience what is transcendental as a specific fact or object *in* the world? To address this foundational question, Villoro appeals to attention (he explicitly uses the Spanish word "atención"), as a cognitive attitude and orientation that *shows us how* what is transcendental delineates the figure of the world as a totality:

> The sentences about the totality of the world in the *Tractatus* "refer" me (in the pragmatic sense in which they "indicate" or "direct") to *another thing*, however this is no longer something *in* the world, but rather something that can only manifest itself in the vision of the world as a limited totality [. . .] Just like an allegory, they allow us to fix our attention on something that only we can see for ourselves, in our world. But they can only do this to the extent that we understand that they do not represent anything (they lack meaning).
>
> (1975, 31–3)

Wittgenstein thus takes a *negative route* (*via negativa*), appealing to nonsense in order to reveal the foundations of all that is meaningful. This reorientation of attention leads to achieving the "correct vision of the world" (1975, 33). Villoro says that there is a three-stage operation facilitating the proper understanding of the sentences in the *Tractatus* concerning the totality of the world: (1) the cancellation of standard reference to facts in ordinary language; (2) the transference of this "reference" to the limits of the world and of language; and (3) *an orientation of our attention* to what can show itself in our language and our world, not as a representation of facts and objects, but as a vision of the totality of the world as such—the totality of its meaning and value. Margarita Valdés rightly characterizes this reorientation toward a comprehensive vision of the world as one that demarcates the limits of scientific explanation, making possible an ethical perspective on the world (Valdés, 2024, 159–64).

We can help each other orient our attitudes and attention towards the value of the world, by practicing a "negative" approach that anchors our reasoning without representing anything specific. Of course, we can also be anchored to objects and situations, but for us to appreciate their value, a more "charged" kind of attentional orientation is required. Describing the nonsensical statements of the *Tractatus*, Villoro says that although they lack meaning, they play a fundamental *pragmatic* role. They "redirect" our attention to alert us about something we *must* see (Villoro, 1975, 29). This is part of our education and our good practices of attention. We cannot deduce through an argument the right vision of the world. Habits of attention must shape our attitudes and beliefs, charging our orientation toward the world positively or negatively. They allow us, for example, to attend to the context and nuance of a conversation, rather than to the mechanically reproduced sequences of words. We will see how this issue about attentiveness was part of a conversation between Wittgenstein and Alan Turing on the mechanical or computational aspects of intelligence.

Meaning in mathematics is a key concern in Wittgenstein's entire work. Many of his observations about mathematics are in his later work, particularly *Philosophical Investigations*. The examples he presented concern difficulties regarding following rules, which leads to various puzzles. They also concern "forms of life" that provide meaning and value to our interactions through what we can call "patterns" of contextualized attention. The pragmatist Charles Sanders Peirce thought of beliefs as guides to action based on habit. Habits of the mind can be characterized as attention protocols, or attentional biases. Peirce thought that norms of thought were habits that need to be put *to use in action*—in a way similar to a protocol of attention that is designed to achieve a purpose. In his essay "What Pragmatism Is" he says:

> But for one who had learned philosophy out of Kant, as the writer, along with nineteen out of twenty experimentalists who have turned to philosophy, had done, and who still thought in Kantian terms most readily, *praktisch* and *pragmatisch* were as far apart as the two poles, the former belonging in a region of thought where no mind of the experimentalist type can ever make sure of solid ground under his feet, the latter expressing relation to some definite human purpose. Now quite the most striking feature of the new theory was its recognition of an inseparable connection between rational cognition and rational purpose, and that consideration it was which determined the preference for the name *pragmatism*.
>
> (Peirce, 1905|1998, 333)

The Kantian project still inspires the pragmatist project in a foundational and methodological way, but the grounding is now, for the pragmatist, in action and purpose *as a unity*. This change is crucial for understanding Villoro's philosophy, as Pappas (2017) has argued. In fact, it is what makes Villoro's epistemology and ethics compatible with non-ideal theories. The reorientation and charging of attention are versatile and, even in mathematical abstraction, provide grounding, purpose, and an orientation that make action more efficient. Peirce was a skilled mathematician who was particularly interested in the way we attend to abstractions. His notion of *hypostatization*, or counting abstractions as real, resembles the way in which many of the objects of attention are "postulated" in order to do things with them. Ian Hacking quotes the following passage from Peirce in the context of a discussion on Platonism in mathematics:

> It may be said that mathematical reasoning (which is the only deductive reasoning, if not absolutely, at least eminently) almost entirely turns on the consideration of abstractions as if they were objects. The protest of nominalism against such hypostatization . . . as it was and is formulated, is simply a protest against the only kind of thinking that has ever advanced human culture.
>
> (Hacking, 2014, 255)

There are clear cognitive risks in reifying abstractions without justification and paying attention to abstract entities like possible visitors from other galaxies, which is why Peirce says that hypostatization must be done intelligently and with *action and purpose* in mind. Villoro would say that it must be done *reasonably*—a reasonable, rather than a merely rational, use of abstraction. Properly understood, hypostatic attention is a kind of "delineation" that makes our thinking and our acting more flexible and open to diversity by properly grounding, in this case, the most powerful kind of collective reasoning, the kind we use to launch rockets and predict the behavior of elementary particles. Attention can segment, diversify, and make not only objects, but also their elements or properties, salient or more vivid, turning them into new objects of attention. In his essay "On a New List of Categories," Peirce defines the *act of attention* as "the pure denotative power of the mind, that is to say, the power which directs the mind to an object." He then writes:

> The terms "precision" and "abstraction," which were formerly applied to every kind of separation, are now limited, not merely to mental separation, but to that which arises from *attention to* one element and *neglect of* the other. Exclusive attention consists in a definite conception or *supposition* of one part of an object, without any supposition of the other.
>
> (Peirce, 1868|1992, 2)

Charge, orientation, and mental focus unite thought and action. Any number contains, inherently, a combination of many numbers. For example, 2 is 1+1 (3–1, 10–8, etc.) and it is also the number that yields an irrational number when its square root is taken. How we pay attention to the number 2, or to which aspects of it, makes a big difference. If we want to give an example of an irrational number, we select the square root of 2. If we are buying oranges at the local market, we "act upon" 2 and select the best two oranges for a salad. *What* and *how* we pay attention to can energize or enfeeble our minds, making us do or not do things, increasing or decreasing our curiosity. Hypostatic attention is the only kind of thinking that has advanced human culture in all directions. We pay attention to abstractions, and this makes our joint attention remarkably robust and independent from our immediate surroundings. We attend to contracts, deadlines, plans, expectations, authorities, numbers, scientific theories, the calendar, our bank accounts. It is not an exaggeration to say that most objects of our attention in contemporary culture are hypostatic. But this does not mean that we are looking at the world from an eternal and ethereal perspective. We are still very much acting *in* the world, and the meaning and value of our interactions still derive from it.

Going back to an example from the last chapter, we can attend to the misery of others as a "fact among many," the same way as we might orient our minds toward the rings of Saturn. Such a distant approach to the pain of others is ungrounded partly because it prevents action. The dignity of others is not a fact among many other facts. Properly seeing the world requires that our attention be reoriented, from the itemization of belief contents and their truth-conditions to the meaning and value of the world in its totality. This cannot be done through belief or representation alone: it requires the proper and reasonable practice of our attention. We can have as many maps through which we steer as we want. But unless they are grounded by the proper vision provided by attention, they will remain unanchored. We can have a representation of the world in which some people are classified as suffering more than others. However, if we don't dignify these people with our attention, our representations of them remain ungrounded. This is important if we want to understand any kind of reasoning, including abstract mathematical reasoning.

Joint attention and common ground: the case of mathematics

All objects of attention are a kaleidoscope: attention can always hypostasize, segment, or abstract one aspect as the most salient object of attention and ignore others to focus mental energy on the new object derived from the original one. The vitality of our cognitive energies depends on this diversity of objects of attention. But as Villoro says in his interpretation of Wittgenstein, attention is fundamental to reorient our minds from the specificity of truth-conditions, such as objects and their properties, to the integrity and totality of the world as such. This is not optional, and no other kind of mental action can substitute this foundational reorientation of attention. It is the source of whatever charge, positive or negative, our beliefs might have since beliefs are incapable of reorienting our minds in this fundamental way. We will return to the topic of charge in subsequent chapters, particularly in Chapter 7.

We can view the world as a collection of facts—objects, their properties, their behavior and regularities. In this scientific view of the world, we are among those objects, seen "from outside." Our lives are facts among other facts. When attention reorients our view toward the world as a whole, we appear not merely as a mechanism moving around according to the laws of physics, but rather as part of the conditions for the world to *appear at all* with any meaning to anyone. But this is not because we convey meaning to the world: it is because the world in its totality, with us inside it, is not merely a set of facts. The world has a figure and a value that escapes any factual description and yet, it is its figure and value that grounds meaning. This is true of mathematical knowledge as well.

On the topic of mechanical versus spontaneous perspectives on our thinking, Hacking worries about proofs that can only be reached through computer power, which he calls "Leibnizian proofs," versus proofs that are done through our understanding of them, all at once, which he calls "Cartesian proofs." Hacking's preoccupation is that if mathematics becomes fully computerized, it will be arid and alien to human interests. Even if everything goes well with the results, a mechanical intelligence cannot be held accountable. Mathematicians would have to trust the humanly unverifiable results of such computations: "An author submits a paper with a proof or proof sketch, together with a programme for checking the proof, and a confirmation that, when run, the computer says, 'OK'. Who checks that the programme is sound?" (2014, 25–6). This is a situation of blind trust in computational oracles. Mathematics might become a matter of luck—we would be lucky if everything goes well because our trust cannot be *grounded on reciprocal attention*.

Agency is what is critical here, rather than, as Hacking and many epistemologists think, the role of phenomenal consciousness. Leibnizian proofs are based on automatic and reliable procedures. This notion of proof cannot account for the experience of mathematical discovery and the accepted standard of normative strength typically associated with mathematical reasoning, such as deductive inference. One experiences a kind of revelation when a proof is clearly grasped. To a large extent, one accepts a proof on epistemic grounds when we can see that it follows rational norms. But neither mechanical reliability nor the phenomenology of experiencing the clarity of a proof can explain why the proof is attributable to an agent on the basis of the agent's capacities. Revelations, even if profound, can be wrong and unanchored from interests and truth. One needs the proof to be the result of a *mental action* on the part of the agent. This is something that Wittgenstein appreciated much better than other philosophers of mathematics, and it is a deeply pragmatist insight.

One can think of this distinction in terms of Daniel Kahneman's systems 1 and 2. System 1 delivers results quickly and unconsciously through heuristic reasoning, while system 2 requires slower, conscious understanding. This distinction addresses the problems raised by Hacking, because both systems are part of a complex integration of inferential and attentional routines that constitute mental agency (Montemayor, 2019). More important, the kind of guidance needed as one "goes through" the proof is *attentive*, not merely experiential. Mathematical reasoning is an activity attributable to us because of how we attend to proofs and mathematical objects. This mental action is irreducible to consciousness (what is it for each of us to feel the way we feel) or to the authority of reason, abstractly conceived: going through a proof is something we must *do*. We need to update and revitalize our understanding of mathematics and its underlying psychology the way Peirce and the pragmatists suggested. What gives a charge and orientation to mathematical proofs as mental actions is how they are integrated to our goals and purposes. This is why attention is essential in an account of the foundations of logic and mathematics.

Hacking quotes Wittgenstein's remark that mathematics is a *buntes Gemisch*, a colorful "MOTLEY of techniques of proof. And upon this is based its manifold applicability and its importance." (cited in Hacking, 2014, 57).[6] Mathematical reasoning involves a colorful mixture of

---

[6]   Some of this material on mathematics, in this and the following paragraph, is based on Montemayor (2016).

inferential capacities, including analogy, induction, deduction, and creative, abductive leaps of faith, which lead to new discoveries. Why would such a colorful mixture of inferential reasoning account for the manifold applicability and importance of mathematics? Because these are *attention routines* that are integrated for multiple kinds of mental action in accordance with various goals and purposes. Their importance lies, therefore, in making possible new kinds of mental routines, problem-solving techniques, and social interactions. Mathematics certainly is a colorful mixture of cognitive capacities. The motley of mathematical techniques is a motley of mental activities. What unifies and gives epistemic status to all this cognitive multiplicity is the agential nature of attention, and this is what neither mere reliability nor phenomenology can sufficiently account for. The reliability of computers is not sufficient because what is needed to create common ground in mathematics is joint attention. Similarly, what it is like to be you from the inside is not sufficient to create common ground. Joint attention is fundamental for mathematics as a joint activity, as well as for *any* kind of reasonable communication. We focus on mathematics here because it is important to show that many pragmatically inclined thinkers, like Villoro, thought that an emphasis on action is critical to explain the foundations of even our most abstract forms of reasoning.

The experience of discovery that comes with Cartesian proofs is also infused with aesthetic value and analogical reasoning. If one takes the aesthetic value of mathematics seriously—and the centrality of symmetry in aesthetics seems to demonstrate that one should take it seriously—then the normative aspects of mathematics become intricate. Aesthetic experiences are clearly important to mathematicians, physicists, and scientists who seek to find simple and beautiful equations. Their interest here is also transcendental, for the sake of mathematics itself. Mathematics is not reducible to a collection of facts, and it also has an aesthetic transcendental value. Central to this transcendental experience is "seeing" a self-evident truth in an obvious way that *anyone else should* be able to see. It is a seeing that we should all be capable of sharing through *joint attention*. Otherwise, what would be the point of mathematics if all it brought were incommunicable aesthetic revelations?

Philosophical views about the nature of mathematics capture the diversity of cognitive skills involved in mathematical reasoning, and they are all best understood as kinds of joint attention. For instance, one can characterize certain approaches to the foundations of mathematics as normatively inductive. The work of John Stuart Mill (endorsed by Philip Kitcher) falls in this category because, for Mill, "The truths even of arithmetic are merely the most general inductions of all, confirmed in all our experience." (Hacking, 2014, 114) Other authors, by contrast, emphasize analogical reasoning and abduction, or inference to the best explanation (e.g., Polya, 1954; Putnam, 1975; Steiner, 1973). Wittgenstein's remark concerning the "motley of techniques" favors the view that all forms of inference are at play in mathematical reasoning. Deductive reasoning and attention to a priori contents that involve certainty is only *one* of the techniques we use in doing mathematics. It is the diversity of inferential patterns of reasoning, integrated through attention, that explain the colorful motley of techniques involved in mathematical reasoning.

Wittgenstein emphasized in his later work that what makes mathematical reasoning not a matter of luck or a mere accident of random associations is the guidance that joint action provides, which we follow as a community. He was strongly opposed to the idea that mathematics is grounded in some mysterious realm of abstract objects or set of rules that we must explicitly follow. It is our mental capacities and actions that explain the usefulness of mathematics, but also reveal its foundations. In line with what Ramsey thought about propositional content and truth, determined by successful action, the foundations of mathematics and rationality must be anchored to the concrete ways in which we engage the world and each other.

Mathematics does not descend from heaven and does not depend on how it feels to be conscious, in our own private minds. Its role in our reasoning must remain anchored to our actions, goals, and interests. Villoro was interested in unifying various types of rationality into a balanced and reasonable view of the world. He became increasingly worried about the prevalence of instrumental and scientific rationality in realms where deliberative reasoning is essential. His examination of the *Tractatus* already reveals this preoccupation. In contemporary epistemology, this topic includes the role of technology in shaping our collective attention, imposing a scientistic and technocratic approach to human-decision making that becomes unanchored, opening the door to ideological thinking.

Wittgenstein was also very concerned about this issue, and he talked about it, and related topics, with none other than Alan Turing, at Cambridge. Turing and Wittgenstein largely agree on their approach to intelligence and the foundations of mathematics, although they had some disagreements concerning the nature of inferences and rules. The key to understand their agreement is their appreciation of *contextualized action* and the variety of concrete situations in which intelligence operates. It is precisely because of this that an attention-based approach is crucial to appreciate how their views overlapped. Juliet Floyd writes:

> Wittgenstein and Turing are often regarded, in a misleading caricature, as philosophical opponents. Wittgenstein is taken to be a humanistic philosopher of meaning and "forms of life", hostile to mathematical logic and the very idea of a Turing machine; Turing is taken to be a mechanistic or behaviouristic theorist of the mind, intent on reducing the concept of meaning to that of information. Neither picture is correct.
>
> (Floyd, 2013, 250)

We are agents who succeed at achieving collective goals on the basis of mathematical calculations because of how mathematics helps us coordinate action and attention. We are mathematical thinkers because of the repertoire of diverse actions we can produce with the help of mathematics, mental and physical. Floyd argues that this purposeful and action-oriented perspective is crucial for both Wittgenstein and Turing: "On their view, it is the everyday, purposeful use we humans make of language that crucially animate and frame the notions of meaning and information." (Floyd, 2013, 250) Wittgenstein and Turing object to the view that subjective awareness is the foundation of meaning. Meaning is fundamentally related to use and action.

This discussion about the foundations of mathematics and intelligence is relevant for Villoro's expansive kind of social epistemology, beyond his interest in Wittgenstein. Villoro would be very concerned about the current fascination and obsession with artificial intelligence. The distribution of knowledge depends now on technologies produced by a handful of companies that serve capital interests, located in powerful militarized states. Social media and the instrumental technification of society have profoundly changed knowledge distribution and education. The battle for non-exclusion must be fought now at a much larger scale (see Montemayor, 2023b). In later texts, inspired by his analysis of the *Tractatus*, Villoro warns that we have leaned too heavily on instrumental rationality, with great costs to our dignity, education, and the planet. In the concluding pages of his book on the Renaissance, where he discusses the Renaissance as a reshaping of the figure of the world, Villoro writes about the dangerous role that instrumental rationality can play in the justification of epistemic oppression:

> The use of rational means that should lead not to the domination of humans, but rather to their integration with the totality of which they are part. Matter would not be manipulated as an instrument for the use of humans alone, it would be used for the binomial humans-nature. *This would entail a radical change in the exercise of instrumental rationality, which has prevailed until now in modern times*; not the suppression of this kind of rationality, but rather, its subordination to a higher kind of rationality: that which establishes the ultimate goals and values that are worth living by.
>
> (Villoro, 1992, 146, my emphasis)

Radical changes to the purposes underlying our rational practices, including mathematics, require changes in what Villoro, following Wittgenstein, calls the *figure of the world*. Reasonable rationality becomes disruptive because it must confront oppression that is imposed through instrumental rationality. Philosophy is defined by Villoro as the disruptive *activity of reason*, which delineates the proper scope of rationality, including science. Radical change that benefits most humans depends on reasonable and clear communication. Risky communication favors exclusion and the accumulation of power in the hands of those who can impose an instrumental approach to social interactions.

Villoro's engagement with Wittgenstein's early work is relevant for these themes in social epistemology and politics. Villoro would agree with Wittgenstein and Turing about the importance of everyday purposes as foundational for reasoning. But given the extent to which we have algorithmicized society, it is fundamental to analyze what we mean by "everyday purposes." An example discussed by Wittgenstein and Turing will help illustrate the problem of reducing rationality to its norm-following component, thereby elucidating how we should understand the types of purposes underlying reasonable and meaningful communication—a central goal in identifying the limits of reason.

Wittgenstein and Turing on the instruments of reason

Wittgenstein and Turing met in Cambridge on multiple occasions. Although the precise period during which they interacted is uncertain, Wittgenstein's influence on Turing seems to have been significant early on, perhaps even during Turing's undergraduate years, particularly at the meetings of the Moral Sciences Club (see Floyd, 2017, 123). We know for certain that Turing was a key participant, in fact Wittgenstein's main interlocutor, in Wittgenstein's 1939 lectures on the foundations of mathematics. In his acclaimed biography of Wittgenstein, Ray Monk characterizes this remarkable exchange in more confrontational terms than Floyd. But I hope to show that even in Monk's rendition of their exchanges, the disagreement is not as deep as many think, therefore leaning in favor of Floyd's interpretation.

My goal in exploring this exchange is to show not only that Wittgenstein and Turing agree on the centrality of action for determining conversational background and common sense, but also on the importance of providing a *non-idealized or non-metaphysical* foundation for mathematics and linguistic meaning. Monk focuses on a disagreement between Wittgenstein and Turing concerning the role of contradictions in mathematics. According to Monk, for Wittgenstein, a contradiction cannot be a fatal flaw in a system of mathematics; by contrast, for Turing, this was a decisive flaw in the system. Monk describes this difference in opinion as follows:

> 'You seem to be saying', suggested Turing, 'that if one uses a little common sense, one will not get into trouble.' 'No', thundered Wittgenstein, 'that is NOT what I mean at all.' His point was rather that a contradiction cannot lead one astray because it leads nowhere at all. One cannot calculate wrongly with a contradiction, because one simply cannot use it to calculate. One can do nothing with contradictions, except waste time puzzling over them.
>
> (Monk, 1990, 421)

According to Monk, Wittgenstein sees contradictions as pointless, as irrelevant to action guidance, and therefore, as irrelevant to assessments concerning epistemic risk—an issue related to Wittgenstein's two notions of "nonsense" in the *Tractatus*. By contrast, Turing conceives of contradictions as a grave form of epistemic mistake. At the core of this debate is the issue of *rule-following* and the success-conditions for action. I reproduce the exchange Monk comments on at length for the reader to appreciate the importance of successful action, in the light of the notions of epistemic risk, rule-following, and reliable attention routines:

> *Turing*: You cannot be *confident* about your applying your calculus until you *know* that there is no hidden contradiction in it.

> *Wittgenstein*: There seems to me to be an enormous mistake there. For your calculus gives certain *results*, and you want the bridge not to break down. I'd say things *can go wrong in only two ways*: either the

bridge breaks down or you have made a mistake in your calculation—
for example you multiplied wrongly. But you seem to think there may
be a *third thing wrong*: the calculus is wrong.

Turing: No. What I object to is the bridge falling down.

Wittgenstein: But how do you *know* that it will fall down? Isn't that a
question of physics? It may be that *if one throws dice in order to calculate*
the bridge it will never fall down.

Turing: If one takes Frege's symbolism and gives someone the
technique of multiplying in it, then by using a Russell paradox he could
get a wrong multiplication.

Wittgenstein: This would come *to doing something which we would
not call multiplying*. You give him a *rule* for multiplying and when he
gets to a certain point he can go in either of two ways, one of which
leads him all wrong. (cited from Monk, 1990, 421; my emphasis)

The disagreement here seems to be serious, but an epistemic gloss on it
may put the issue under a different light entirely. Instead of interpreting
this disagreement in terms of the nature and consequences of
contradictions, as Monk does, I believe this issue should be understood
as one concerning the *sources* of epistemic trust and epistemic risk.
Wittgenstein argues that there is no *extra* epistemic risk that an analysis
of contradictions could uncover—the risks are either in our understanding
of *how to do* mathematics or in the *outcomes of our actions*, in our efforts
to pursue goals. Turing rejoins that the risk of having a system with
contradictions is that *rules* cannot be followed *consistently*, and therefore,
that there is a quite significant third source of epistemic risk.

But if one interprets Wittgenstein as saying that there can only be
two types of epistemic risk concerning bad outcomes, one based on
lack of understanding or proper mental action, and one based on lack
of reliable skills or execution, then he is at least concerned with the type
of failures that Turing is also trying to avoid. They both want to prevent
the bridge from falling apart, and the consistency of mathematics to be
related to everyday events. The difference, then, is one of emphasis,

rather than substance. Turing believes that a system with contradictions cannot guide action at all, and Wittgenstein believes that this issue is moot, since action and goal-oriented guidance within a context are all there is—there is no such thing as the *system itself*, beyond our practices.

Their disagreement does concern rule-following. Epistemic risk and luck are to be avoided, either by following rules or by the capacities of agents that satisfy their goals in accordance with rational guidelines. We trust agents who have these capacities, and trust that certain nomological necessities or regularities also hold, e.g., that other speakers are competent, and that they are identifying the syntactic structure of a sentence, without the need to consciously rehearse the syntactic rule explicitly or engage in the arduous task of identifying irregularities and contradictions in formal systems of rules that may affect grammaticalness. Wittgenstein argues that having the explicit knowledge that a system lacks any contradiction is too high a standard for *reasonable* mathematical reasoning. But this is also because there is no such thing as a complete system of rules that determine what we say. If one considers syntactic structure and meaning, Wittgenstein's point extends to all kinds of communication. We rarely stop mid-sentence to verify consciously and explicitly that we are following the right syntactic rule, testing for violations of linguistic norms and principles—an exercise that even professional linguists may find difficult. On the contrary, if we did this regularly our conversational exchanges would be very difficult and risky—a lot of information would be lost in such awkward and untimely interruptions, which would not invite much trust from other speakers. Expecting that speakers should engage in such unreasonable interruptions is indeed a mistake, and it violates the principle of charity examined in the previous chapter.

Turing would agree with Wittgenstein that conscious reflection concerning abstract systems of rules would impede reasonable communication. In his famous paper from 1950, Turing explicitly objects to conscious introspection of rules or meanings as the basis of intelligence, considering it an obstacle for an account of machine learning. Wittgenstein asserts, like Turing, that reliability and guidance are crucial. Reliability and guidance are the main feature of attention routines, so if this is correct, Wittgenstein and Turing characterize the foundations of mathematics in terms of epistemic agency, understood as mental *actions* that are reliable because they are based on the communicative capacities of speakers. The foundations of meaning are the concrete actions of communication and cooperation of linguistic communities, rather than the abstract systems or ontologies proposed by philosophers of mathematics. Monk, who emphasizes their disagreement, says the following about Turing's very active participation in Wittgenstein's lectures:

> It must indeed have taken a certain amount of courage to attend the classes as the single representative of all that Wittgenstein was attacking, surrounded by Wittgenstein's acolytes and having to discuss the issues in a way that was unfamiliar to him. Andrew Hodges, in his excellent biography of Turing, expresses surprise at what he sees as Turing's diffidence in these discussions, and gives as an example the fact that, despite long discussions about the nature of a 'rule' in mathematics, Turing never offered a definition in terms of Turing machines. But, surely, Turing realized that Wittgenstein would have dismissed such a definition as irrelevant; the discussion was conducted at a more fundamental level. Wittgenstein was attacking, not this or that definition, but the very motivation for providing such definitions.
>
> (Monk, 1990, 422)

It is surprising that Turing did not invoke Turing machines as a clear example of guidance through the mechanical instantiation of algorithms—a literal "instrument of reason." Turing might have felt that Wittgenstein was focusing primarily on agency-dependent guidance, rather than mere mechanical instantiations that could "do the job." Here it is useful to consider two types of epistemic risk that could hinder cooperation. One of them is based on the unreliability of an agent—it is risky to be guided by an agent who is unreliable and rarely succeeds in fulfilling goals. The other type of risk is based on poor cognitive integration. An agent that is very successful in fulfilling goals but cannot integrate how those goals compete with or prevent the satisfaction of other important goals or preferences is risky because such a configuration would result in the satisfaction of some very reliably achieved goals at the high cost of ignoring more central needs, both of the agent and of others. Ultimately this agent will be rational but unreasonable by not taking the right approach to which purposes should be subordinated to which others, the way Villoro says that instrumental rationality should be subordinated to a higher kind of reason. Both kinds of risk are involved in the exchange between Turing and Wittgenstein.

"It may be that *if one throws dice in order to calculate* the bridge it will never fall down," asserts Wittgenstein. But not if we use artificial intelligence and computer machinery. Using a Turing machine or a computer would be a lot less risky than throwing dice. In fact, computers are a paradigm of reliability. They are *actually* what we now use to build bridges, fly planes, and perform difficult calculations. But perhaps Turing hesitated mentioning Turing machines as an example of rule-following because they clearly are not good at cognitive integration or, for that matter, any kind of cognitive agency that involves reasons and purpose. Monk is right in saying that computer intelligence is irrelevant to Wittgenstein's inquiry. Epistemic agency is not something we can prove mechanically or through consistency tests and benchmarks. It always manifests itself in concrete actions and in the success these actions have in meeting goals because of the capacities of the agent. Action cannot be substituted by algorithms, and agential guidance cannot be examined and dissected as rules and propositions. This basic point is crucial to properly see the limits of reason and the foundations of knowledge.

Turing would be surprised by our current reliance on computers. He would be intrigued by the kind of architectures that dominate contemporary artificial intelligence and by our fascination with it, especially, our willingness to leave to machine intelligence what used to be the exclusive task of human reasoning: the guidance of our knowledge production. Turing pioneered instrumentalized and computerized intelligence. But I don't think he would have expected that many of our daily interactions and behaviors are dependent upon computer code and interfaces with automatized technologies. The bridge not only stayed firm—we have built our societies around computer power. But if Floyd is right, Turing would be concerned with the extent to which we rely on automation. Turing, like Wittgenstein and Villoro, would not equate the instruments of reason with reason itself. For Villoro, the massive scale of our new collective "instruments of reason" would signal the collapse of *reasonable communication*, since we have placed instrumental rationality above reasonable rationality, making automation the main source of social coordination. We risk weakening our moral and epistemic capacities. If we don't regain control of instrumental rationality by subordinating it to reason, we will lose the battle against unreasonable rationality. We will not be able to develop the humanistic technology that Villoro envisioned as the new figure of the world.

Automatism, spontaneity, and purpose in action

Precision in thinking is fundamental for communication and inquiry, and yet there is no "system of rules" that guarantees with certainty that precision will always be achieved. The pragmatist takes this basic truth as fundamental. We can only achieve precision through our actions. This requires cooperation and attention in communication, not a soliloquy about rules and regulations. This insight is at the core of Villoro's Central Normative Proposal. Peirce, as the quote above indicates, thought that attention plays a key role in achieving precision. Both Peirce and Frank Ramsey cared deeply about the foundations of mathematics, and they were committed to provide a theory of meaning with a firm pragmatic footing.[7]

---

[7]   For an overview of Ramsey's pragmatism and his influence on Wittgenstein see Misak (2016). This influence is documented in more detail in the next chapter.

Ramsey's "success semantics," originally proposed as a pragmatic theory of meaning, can be also interpreted as a key component of a reliabilist virtue theory in epistemology grounded on attention (for details see Fairweather and Montemayor, 2017). The full details of these views are not necessary here. The main idea is that, according to Ramsey's success semantics, meanings become precise through what is called a "utility condition": the condition that must obtain for an action to satisfy a specific purpose, desire, or need. If such a condition is satisfied, then the content of the intention to act qualifies as true. Content is, therefore, intimately related to action and purpose. An important contribution from Peirce here is that attention is crucial in specifying how purposes become relevant in executing actions by providing intentional guidance from purpose to execution.

The way Villoro articulated this action principle in his theory of knowledge is that "truth," abstractly conceived, is not necessary for knowledge. What is needed is successful action through *intersubjectively achieved guidance*, which provides what Villoro called "objectively sufficient" justification. We approximate the truth through coordination and cooperation. Just as there is no "absolute set of rules" sitting in some abstract realm to guarantee precision, there is also no "absolute truth" out there, waiting to be "grasped." To fully appreciate why the previous discussion on Wittgenstein matters for understanding Villoro's proposals about knowledge and communication, it is useful to consider an interpretation of Davidson's view of meaning. In the previous chapter, Villoro's principle of non-exclusion was interpreted through Davidson's charity principle. However, Davidson also defended a truth-functional account of meaning that seems in tension with the cooperative character of interpretation. Paul Horwich says that Davidson's account combines the following:

1. the Wittgensteinian idea that we should interpret a foreign-language speaker by pairing each of that speaker's words with a word of our own that is used, fundamentally, in the same way; and

2. a reformulation of this idea in *truth*-theoretic terms. Specifically, Wittgenstein's requirement that the pairing preserve basic dispositions of word-use (so that they yield agreement in basic beliefs-forming dispositions) becomes the requirement that our interpretation of the words of the foreign language has the result that the preponderance of the sentences the foreign speaker accepts express beliefs that are true. (2017, 29)

The second principle is the charity principle. Horwich argues that charity is the key to Davidson's view, and that the truth-requirement is unnecessary and problematic. A key problem he raises is that no manual for interpretation of a specific conversation can be deduced from truth-theoretic values. Even if this could be possible, it is doubtful that the meaning of sentences is equivalent to their best logical expressions. Meaning depends on a kind of *know-how*, which consists of our propensities to deploy certain terms in specific contexts (2017, 38), rather than our understanding of compositional truth-value assignments to propositions. Truth, according to Horwich's criticism of Davidson, is a generalization device governed by the principle that each attribution of truth to a proposition is equivalent to the proposition itself (Horwich's own deflationist view of truth). He then concludes:

> Davidson's two-pronged account of meaning combines the good, the bad, and the ugly. The good is the 'meaning as use' picture of what makes for a plausible interpretation—a picture that's visible (but with some difficulty) in his principle of charity. The bad is his truth conditional account of the compositionality of meaning. And the ugly is the ungainly result of sticking them together.
>
> (Horwich, 2017, 45)

This is a fair criticism because Wittgenstein would indeed find a truth-functional analysis inadequate. But it misses Wittgenstein's main concern of providing an anti-skeptical approach to *language use*, which opposes automatism and rule-following as the basis for our understanding of meaning. Wittgenstein's proposal for linguistic interpretation is not at all based on the kind of "matching" that a computer or other mechanical automatisms could perform, even in the idealized version of Turing's machine infinite tape. No amount of matching, patterns of behavior, sequences of responses, or artificially intelligent output can bring you to understand an expression. Meaning is not merely pattern recognition. Philosophy should not be in search of a foundation that sits outside (above or below) our communication practices in specific contexts. There is no super-procedure that could explain human understanding as implementing a matching automatism at its foundation.

Meaning depends on how we use it in accordance with our practices, based on our agency and the familiarity that gestures and tone bring to a conversation. For Wittgenstein, matching words (something that contemporary large language models do much better than us) operates from "outside" meaning, treating the meaning of expressions as a *mere fact or phenomenon* (see Stroud, 2012, 23). Following a rule is not an interpretation—following a simple *matching rule* is not conducive to understanding. Understanding is a *practice*, as Wittgenstein says in response to the paradox of rule-following in *Philosophical Investigations*. Fundamentally, it is our practices, grounded in attentive communication, that allow us to *use* language, rather than merely *describe it as a phenomenon*. As Katherine Glüer says about the Davidsonian approach to the problems of rule-following and objectivity, a radical-interpretation account of meaning determination requires "a background of shared sensitivity, of commonly detectable similarity." (Glüer, 2017, 93)

What is eligible for meaning? What is expressible, which practices are relevant for communication in a social context, which gestures are meaningful? Our varying abilities to respond to these questions in specific contexts of communication are all there is to understanding meaning, and they all require attention to salient contents in a meaningful background. These abilities provide the grounding or anchoring of what is meaningful and *reasonable* to say in a concrete situation, rather than a description of facts or norms based on a grand soliloquy about rules and interpretations that, in fact, leads to a paradox or infinite regress: we are told about syntactic, semantic, and pragmatic rules, but do not know which rules apply in a concrete situation. There has to be another norm that indicates what is meaningful and permissible to say in a given situation, and then, yet another norm for applying that norm.

In his *Remarks on the Foundations of Mathematics* (VI-31), Wittgenstein addresses the problem of rule-following and the correlative descriptions of mental states with the phrase *"our disease is one of wanting to explain."* The sequence of numbers produced by the student who does not follow the rule of adding two each time shows that no *list* of outcomes or performances, no matter how long it might be, can *prove* that the student understood the instruction (*Philosophical Investigations*, 185). But instead of falling into skepticism and despair, we must see that there is a problem with our expectation that something above and beyond our practices guarantees that we are all following the same rules: some kind of meta-mechanism, or super-rule system. The meaning of communication occurs *within* our practices. From the outside, our practices are a mere fact among others, something to be described like the number of rings around Saturn, something we can predict and manipulate. There is an essential lesson here for the way in which we implement our instruments of reason, particularly artificial intelligence. The key philosophical point is that, from the outside, everything we do is mere automatism, as if the life that fuels the world has been taken away from it. Based on the points made above, it is attention that allows us to *use* language from inside its meaning, in a spontaneous, sensitive, and responsive manner. This helps us solve the puzzle about how to explain meaning because, as Barry Stroud puts it: just as Kant thought that thinking must be addressed within thought itself, Wittgenstein thought that meaning must be approached within meaning itself.

In a similar vein, for Villoro, we can describe poverty without attending to it: we can create rules, explanations, constitutions and plans, all in order to help the poor, and yet, still fail to see what poverty means to the poor, and how it really affects those who suffer it. The same holds for other kinds of oppression. If all we have is the soliloquy of personal belief, then we have blinded ourselves to these injustices. The world *should matter* as foundational for our reasoning, rather than merely our beliefs about the world. This is the idea behind the anchoring of reason on attention. The limits of the world also delineate the limits of what I can do. I am not the center of the universe, nor is the world a set of rules, beliefs, dispositions, or pixelated impressions that I can manipulate willingly. The world has its own value and is the foundation for everything that has value. If slavery were legal, I should attend to the injustices it would create in a way that few other things would demand of my attention. Reasonable rationality demands that I break through my opinions and doxastic attitudes and attend to the people who suffer as such, in their suffering. It forces me to communicate with others and with the world *as such*.

If we are unreasonable in our communication, if we only follow unreasonable kinds of rational rules or optimal solutions to problems, we cannot really engage the world, even if we generate the appearance of rationality and justification through the representation of rules. We become unanchored, and we lose sight of the world. This is a substantial danger that we are creating with automation, by putting instrumental rationality and algorithmic thinking above more fundamental kinds of reasoning. Wittgenstein's remark that "our disease is one of *wanting to explain*" has a moral equivalent in Benjamin Constant's condemnation: "I hate that fatuousness of a mind that excuses what it explains . . . and that analyses itself instead of repenting" (cited in Shattuck, 1996, 137). No amount of moral "calculation" or "rule-examination" can substitute for genuine and attentive engagement with others. The needs of other people and the value of the world are not mere maps by which we steer—the value of the world transcends its instrumental or navigational value. Similarly, the world is not a simulation based on a clever program. There is no set of rules that explains how meaning emerges from the world. Even if there is a grand theory of information from which the events in the world could be derived with mechanistic precision, that would still be a description of the world *from outside* meaning and value. Eliminating the illusion that an explanation from outside is an adequate account of meaning, value, and reason is key to understand the influence of Wittgenstein's work on Villoro's social epistemology. As Villoro would put it, we should never take the instruments of reason to be reason itself—instrumental reasoning depends fundamentally on reasonable rationality for its proper grounding and justification.

In 1990, four years before the Zapatista uprising, Villoro wrote an article on technological knowledge. Technological knowledge, Villoro says, is a kind of second nature (Villoro, 1990, 131). It is an essential part of our efforts to enhance knowledge and freedom because, unlike scientific knowledge which aims toward neutrality, technological knowledge is a collective kind of instrumental rationality that depends on interests and goals. There is potential here, then, of bridging the neutrality of the scientific knowledge we achieve collectively for the sake of finding truth with the knowledge we must achieve for the purpose of improving our society. The instruments of reason can bridge the relation between science and public reason. The collective "knowledge that" of science, can become the assistant of the collective "knowledge how" of technology and social transformation (Villoro, 1990, 133–4).

For Villoro, however, to prevent this bridge between science and human interests from collapsing, the instruments of reason must never be prioritized above reasonable communication and engagement. The project of reforming intelligence can be supported and accelerated by the social impact and transformative action of technology. But for this transformation to be valuable and positive rather than enfeebling and oppressive, our practices for cooperation must be considered from "inside" our meanings and communication. Instrumentalizing our reasoning capacities through automation is perhaps the worst kind of epistemic and moral exclusion because it *dehumanizes* our practices of communication by eradicating the sensitivities that are required for the identification of meaning and value. It excludes reason from instrumental problem-solving. Our "background of shared sensitivity, of commonly detectable similarity" fades away. There is no option here for Villoro: instrumental rationality and science must depend for their grounding and justification on reason.

As a good pragmatist, Villoro asserts that the fundamentality of reasonable communication and human interests for technological knowledge is essential to properly *project our future* (Villoro, 1990, 139). Reason is what provides sense and meaning to scientific and technological knowledge—it is what allows us to see our external descriptions and predictions from inside our practices and interests. If reason is eliminated from scientific and instrumental rationality, they can easily become powerful sources of collective domination over nature and humanity. Reason provides intimacy to the otherwise distant knowledge produced by science and technology. Bureaucracy is typically a negative word, but bureaucracies are essential for controlling large societies, for good and ill. In the final chapter of this book, I argue that Villoro envisioned a kind of "bureaucracy of intimacy" that must exist if we want to maintain the bridge between instrumental rationality and reason safe. That chapter further examines Davidson's notion of charity as essential to an account of meaning as use, which illuminates Villoro's negative route as well as his pragmatism in his own analysis of Wittgenstein's work. The next two chapters focus on how Villoro's negative route needs to be interpreted as the active and disruptive transformation of intelligence, and on how this shapes Villoro's account of knowledge.

References

Clark, H. H. (1996), *Using language*, Cambridge: Cambridge University Press.

Dewey, J. (1916), *Democracy and education*, New York, NY: Columbia University Press.

Fairweather, A. and Montemayor, C. (2017), *Knowledge, Dexterity, and Attention: A Theory of Epistemic Agency*, New York, NY: Cambridge University Press.

Floyd, J. (2013), "Turing, Wittgenstein and Types: Philosophical Aspects of Turing's 'The Reform of Mathematical Notation' (1944-5)," In S. B. Cooper and J. van Leeuwen (eds.), *Alan Turing—His Work and Impact*, Amsterdam/Burlington, MA: Elsevier, (pp. 250–3).

Floyd J. (2017), 'Turing on "Common Sense": Cambridge Resonances', In Floyd, J. and Bokulich, A. (eds.), *Philosophical Explorations of the Legacy of Alan Turing*, Cham, Switzerland: Springer (pp. 103–52).

Ganeri, J. (2017), *Attention, Not Self*, New York: Oxford University Press.

Glüer, K. (2017), 'Rule-Following and Charity: Wittgenstein and Davidson on Meaning Determination', In C. Verheggen (ed.), *Wittgenstein and Davidson on Language, Thought, and Action*, Cambridge, UK: Cambridge University Press (pp. 69–96)

Hacking, I. (2014), *Why is There Philosophy of Mathematics at all?*, Cambridge, UK: Cambridge University Press.

Harris, L. T. (2017), *Invisible mind: Flexible social cognition and dehumanization*, Cambridge, MA: The MIT Press.

hooks, b. (2003), *Teaching Community: A Pedagogy of Hope*, New York: Routledge.

Horwich, P. (2017), 'Davidson's Wittgensteinian View of Meaning', In C. Verheggen (ed.), *Wittgenstein and Davidson on Language, Thought, and Action*, Cambridge, UK: Cambridge University Press (pp. 28–45).

Kahneman, D., Triesman, A. and Gibbs, B. J. (1992), The reviewing of object files: Object-specific integration of information, *Cognitive psychology*, 24(2): 175–219.

Kant, I. (1929), *Critique of Pure Reason, translated by N. K. Smith*, Hong Kong: Macmillan.

Misak, C. (2016), *Cambridge Pragmatism: From Peirce and James to Ramsey and Wittgenstein*, Oxford: Oxford University Press.

Mole, C., Smithies, D. and Wu, W. (eds.). (2011), *Attention: Philosophical and Psychological Essays*, Oxford: Oxford University Press.

Monk, R. (1990), *Ludwig Wittgenstein: The Duty of Genius*, New York: Penguin Books.

Montemayor, C. (2016), Review of *Why Is There Philosophy of Mathematics At All?* By Ian Hacking, *The Mathematical Intelligencer*, 38(3): (85–90).

Montemayor, C. (2019), Inferential Integrity and Attention, *Frontiers in Psychology: Consciousness Research*, 10: 2580.

Montemayor, C. (2023a), 'Attention: Mechanism and Virtue', In D. G. Burnett and Justin E. H. Smith (eds.), *Scenes of Attention: Essays on Mind, Time, and the Senses*, NY: Columbia University Press (pp.103–23).

Montemayor, C. (2023b), *The Prospect of a Humanitarian Artificial Intelligence: Agency and Value Alignment*, London, UK: Bloomsbury.

Montemayor, C. (2024), Review of 'La Razón Disruptiva, Antología compilada por Guillermo Hurtado', *Notre Dame Philosophical Reviews* (online).

Pappas, G. F. (2017), Zapatismo, Luis Villoro, and American Pragmatism on Democracy, Power, and Injustice, *The Pluralist*, 12(1): 85–100.

Peirce, C. S. (1868|1992), 'On a New List of Categories', In N. Hauser and C. Kloesel (eds.), *The Essential Peirce, Vol. 1 (1867-1893)*, Bloomington, IN: Indiana University Press.

Peirce, C. S. (1905|1998), 'What Pragmatism Is', In the Peirce Edition Project (eds.), *The Essential Peirce, Vol. 2 (1893-1913)*, Bloomington, IN: Indiana University Press.

Polya, G. (1954), *Mathematics and Plausible Reasoning, vol. I: Induction and Analogy in Mathematics*, Princeton University Press.

Putnam, H. (1975), "What is mathematical truth?" In: Putnam, H. *Philosophical Papers, vol. I: Mathematics, Matter and Method, second ed.* Cambridge University Press, 60–78.

Pylyshyn, Z. W. (2000), Situating Vision in the World, *Trends in Cognitive Science*, 4(5): 197–207.

Pylyshyn, Z. W. (2001), Visual indexes, preconceptual objects, and situated vision, *Cognition*, 80(1–2): 127–58.

Shattuck, R. (1996), *Forbidden Knowledge: From Prometheus to Pornography*, New York: Harvest, Harcourt Brace & Company.

Steiner, M. (1973), *Mathematical Knowledge*, New York: Cornell University Press.

Stroud, B. (2012), 'Meaning and Understanding', In J. Ellis and D. Guevara (eds.), *Wittgenstein and the Philosophy of Mind*, Oxford: Oxford University Press (pp. 19–36).

Turing, A. M. (1950), Computing machinery and intelligence, *Mind*, 59(236): 443–60.

Valdés, M. M. (2024), Incursiones en el *Tractatus* de Ludwig Wittgenstein, Mexico: Fondo de Cultura Económica and UNAM.

Villoro, L. (1990), Sobre el Conocimiento Tecnológico, *Revista Latinoamericana de Filosofía*, 16(2): 131–48.

Villoro, L. (1975), Lo indecible en el *Tractatus*, *Crítica: Revista Hispanoamericana de Filosofía*, 7(19): 5–39.

Villoro, L. (1998), *Belief, Personal, and Propositional Knowledge, translated by D. Sosa and D. McDermid*, Amsterdam: Rodopi Philosophical Studies.

Wittgenstein, L. (1953), *Philosophical Investigations*, In G. E. M. Anscombe and
    R. Rhees (eds.), G.E.M. Anscombe (trans.), Oxford: Blackwell.
Wittgenstein, L. (1956), *Remarks on the Foundations of Mathematics*, In
    G. H. von Wright, R. Rhees and G. E. M. Anscombe (eds.), G. E. M.
    Anscombe (trans.), Oxford: Blackwell.
Wu, W. (2014), *Attention*, Oxford: Routledge.

4

Reforming Intelligence

The concreteness and familiarity of the world

Reasonable communication expands the limits of meaning. Attention to what matters expands the world, our horizons, into what Villoro calls new *figures* of the world. Reforming intelligence, as it was done in the Renaissance, depends on this enhancement of meaning. It requires eliminating exclusion and increasing the integration of epistemic and moral communities. Villoro starts his essay on the *Tractatus* by emphasizing the importance of Wittgenstein's statement that the main point of the *Tractatus* is an ethical one. He refers to the following passage, from a letter to Ludwig Fricker, cited by Janik and Toulmin:

> *The book's point is an ethical one* [...] My work consists of two parts: the one presented here plus all that I have *not* written. And *it is precisely this second part that is the important one.* My book draws limits to the sphere of the ethical from the inside as it were, and I am convinced that this is the ONLY rigorous way of drawing those limits.
>
> (Janik and Toulmin, 1973, 192)

This explicit recommendation to interpret the book in a fundamentally ethical way was, as Villoro says, largely ignored. We saw how meaning and sense require practices and an understanding of those practices "from inside" meaning and reason. Reversing the orientation of this passage, Wittgenstein says in the *Tractatus* 6.41: "The sense of the world must lie outside the world" (Wittgenstein, 1922|1974). Seen from within, sense and value are never reducible to facts, propositions, or phenomena. But if one decides to see the world as a set of facts and phenomena that require classification and manipulation, then the view we adopt is from "outside" meaning and ethics. Wittgenstein's key insight is that no explanation of meaning or value can derive from facts and phenomena. This limit demarcates and specifies the anchoring of reason. We must attend to the world as a totality in order to see its value and meaning.

Reorienting ourselves to the world as a totality is not daunting, exhausting, or dependent on lengthy training and a sophisticated education. Our *familiar stance* in the world is already immersed in value and meaning. Consistent with Wilfrid Sellars' characterization of "the manifest image," we find ourselves in the world "inside" its meaning and value. It is looking at the world as a set of facts and phenomena that takes effort and training. Thus, anchoring ourselves to the world requires paying attention to it within our *natural attitudes* towards value and meaning. It is critical to see that the anchoring of reason from inside meaning is to the *concreteness of the world as such*. We cannot anchor ourselves in the world through theories, descriptions of facts, predictions or any such depictions of phenomena. All of these reductive strategies to match meanings with words, theories with facts, and so on, depend on the meaning and value of our communicative practices, which are naturally anchored to the world.

Villoro frequently mentions in his essay on the *Tractatus* that attending to the concreteness of the world produces a mystical or religious experience. The world is there, as a totality I cannot change, but I find myself *in it*, understanding it from *inside* its totality. It is not an alien entity or a set of phenomena that I must interpret and study—at which school or university? This grounding or anchoring of our understanding is foundational; it immediately reveals the world to us as the source of all meaning and value. If the world were a simulation, a set of phenomena, or a set of pixelated impressions, it would not produce such a profound experience—or as Villoro wrote, it would not be experienced as a miracle but would rather be perceived as a complex artifact. We would not be able to anchor ourselves in the world if we approached it through an artificial perspective in which the world is itself an artifact. We are *immersed* in the meaning and value of the world. This *is* the anchoring of all meaning and value. No external explanation is needed. The world is concrete to us not because it is a bunch of facts that we can describe or theorize about, or a set of pixels and bits of information that we can manipulate and calculate. The world is concrete because *we naturally and familiarly find ourselves in it*—it constitutes who we are, as well as what we find meaningful and valuable.

A few intriguing paragraphs in the *Tractatus* tie these ideas to ethics. Villoro refers in particular to 6.43, where Wittgenstein writes:

> If the good or bad exercise of the will does alter the world, it can alter only the limits of the world, not the facts—not what can be expressed by means of language. In short the effect must be that it becomes an altogether different world. It must, so to speak, wax and wane as a whole. The world of the happy man is a different one from that of the unhappy man.
>
> (Wittgenstein, 1922|1974)

War and genocide shape the world in its totality, but not because they are additions to the "facts about the world" that make some propositions true. Rather, they change the *contours* of what is valuable and meaningful in the world. They matter not because they change the cardinality and truth conditions of propositions about facts or phenomena, *this or that* data set, but rather because they transform the *way we live and orient ourselves in the world*. Major confusions emerge from not fully understanding this point about our anchoring in the world. Villoro writes that "this vision does not correspond to thought nor does it fall under the sphere of representation" (Villoro, 1975, 14). It is a vision of the totality of the world that comes naturally to us, which is why it doesn't require theoretical evidence and justification. If it needed further evidential support or theoretical analysis the world could not be the ultimate anchoring of meaning and reason. Villoro continues his interpretation of 6.43 as follows: "To have this vision, we must go beyond that sphere and let the world offer *itself* to our sentiment. It thus depends on the attitude we adopt *before the world*." (1975, 14, my emphasis)

We let the world offer *itself* to us from "inside" meaning, through our attentive attitude. This is the world in all its concreteness: it is neither a representation nor a simulation of it. How can the world reveal or "offer" itself to us, as a whole? The answer is that the world exists independently of our will, and we are in it surrounded by its meaning and value. We don't need to take courses or acquire information, let alone run computations on massive amounts of data. What is hard to understand about the anchoring of reason in the concreteness of the world is that once we are immersed in its meaning, which happens automatically for us, there is nothing else left to explain. What we need to do in order to let the world offer itself to us is simple: we need an attentive attitude to the totality of the world that speaks to our sentiment.

When belief and rationality are not grounded in the world, but in the soliloquy of an arrogant and opinionated rational agent, then belief *distances* us from the world. Beliefs that are not grounded on attentive anchoring foster skepticism, solipsism, and relativism about truth—epistemic issues that Villoro associates with epistemic arrogance and injustice. We need to be attentive to the world by being receptive and spontaneous, rather than merely *doxastic (opinionated) and rationalistic.* This attentive perspective on the totality of the world critically involves other people and their needs. Sometimes, to properly let the world reveal itself, we need to pay attention to it by not believing anything in particular about it—by not forcing our opinions into it, turning it into our own biased representation. In fact, this is true of some of our most transformative experiences: falling in love or being amazed by something beautiful.

The world has a way of getting our attention independently of what we do, and despite the multiplicity of erroneous beliefs. Even justified, yet still erroneous beliefs, can powerfully create distance between us and the world through a thick wall of doxastic fog—the world becomes a set of facts expressed by *my opinions*, which are relative and easily falsifiable. This is how Cartesian skepticism operates, by targeting entire sources of belief, challenging their anchoring with three scenarios in which the world progressively disappears *in its entirety*. We are left with sensorial impressions, pixelated bits of information, and overall falsehood. We cannot trust our experiences of the world, which become simulations and mimicry. Only one belief, the *most solipsistic of convictions*, remains fully justified for Descartes: I think, therefore I must exist.

What happened to the world? The Cartesian skeptical response is that the world needs to be *restored* through evidence and epistemic tricks that we must learn from science—an unnatural and absurd situation. This is a modern and astonishing feat of cognitive distancing that removes our anchoring from the world, which was helpful in promoting and justifying the scientific method. It is certainly not our standard way of coping with the world (Wittgenstein addresses many of these issues in *On Certainty*). Contrary to what Descartes proposed in the *Meditations*, we never experience animals and other humans as automata, or ourselves as the *only mental thing* in a mechanistic universe. Alice Crary (2016), for instance, argues that Wittgenstein's work helps us see how the expressive and imaginative capacities that allow us to be "inside" ethics clearly involve nonhuman animals. Our moral powers depend on being anchored in the world, rather than being epistemically distant from it.

The world can compel our attention in powerful and immediate ways, in a great variety of circumstances, positively and negatively charged. The pain of someone we love, our own pain, the beauty of a landscape, falling in love, mourning death, are all instances of the world revealing itself to us. We might have become accustomed to distancing ourselves from the world, through skepticism, or rationalistic and empiricist strategic reasoning—approaches that conceive of the world as reducible to a bunch of beliefs that require evidence to be justified, or a bunch of pixelated sensations that need repeated organization and statistical analysis for them to gain meaning and coherence. We may rationally prefer to sacrifice current people and our planet to save future generations, escaping current reality as a justification to help abstract people. Global warming and poverty come to mind here—*actual* suffering is epistemically inhibited in order to create rational plans that will help *future, simulated, or possible people and their potential suffering*. Even in actuality, profit is prioritized over real meaning and value. But the world in its totality, including the natural world, is there, in front of us, and it is the foundation for all our plans and escapist tendencies. Whatever rational force there is in these kinds of epistemic escapism, it must, paradoxically, be grounded in the world as a totality. The world is there, as it were, watching. We need to attend to it. If we don't, we become *unreasonable*, despite being rational about our small plans—small and insignificant in comparison to the might and dignity of the world as a whole. We embrace the paradoxical distancing of our reasoning from the world at our own peril. In the *Philosophical Investigations*, Wittgenstein writes:

> "I believe that he is suffering."—Do I also *believe* that he isn't an automaton? It would go against the grain to use the word in both connexions. (Or it is like this: I believe that he is suffering, but am certain he is not an automaton? Nonsense!)

> Suppose I say of a friend: "He isn't an automaton."—What information is conveyed by this, and to whom would it be information? To a *human being* who meets him in ordinary circumstances? What information *could* it give him? (At the very most that this man always behaves like a human being, and not occasionally like a machine.)

> "I believe that he is not an automaton", just like that, so far makes no sense.

> My attitude towards him is an attitude towards a soul. I am not of the *opinion* that he has a soul.

> (178e-Part II, section iv)

The normal expression "I believe that he is suffering" demands our moral and epistemic attention; it is anchored and reasonable. The artificial expression "he is not an automaton" is unanchored and absurd. Yet, the latter expresses a *rational* belief, which is even logically entailed by the veridical proposition that automata don't have experiences. However, *saying* this absurd expression in the presence of someone who is suffering is a piece of *nonsensical indifference*, a kind of meta-cruelty, based on unreasonable rationality. The anchoring of the reasonable expression that "someone is suffering" depends on our attentive attitude toward the person who is suffering, *in the normal circumstances*. The interpretable and rational, yet unreasonable and offensive expression that the suffering person is not an automaton depends on unanchored rationality (based on belief-generated skepticism or relativism). These passages from Wittgenstein are very relevant for understanding Villoro's notions of *anchoring reason in reality* and of the *figure of the world*.

On genuine philosophy

In the interview, "On the philosophical tasks of the present," Mario Teodoro Ramírez asks Villoro if he could elaborate on the idea that philosophy must be anchored in what is concrete, which is essential to Villoro's concept of *reasonable rationality*. Ramírez specifies that he would like to know the reasons for and conditions of this kind of anchoring. Villoro responds that: "good philosophy has never been unfamiliar to criticizing the beliefs accepted in society; therefore, philosophy is a very important element of social reform." The anchoring of good, one could say *genuine*, philosophy, thus depends on its critical role in criticizing bodies of beliefs that are largely taken for granted for the sake of maintaining the status quo. Villoro clarifies:

> It is not an element that resembles that of a revolutionary or a politician, no, its remedy is the mending of opinions, a remedy of intelligence: a "reform of intelligence", as Spinoza said. In this sense, philosophy has a concrete mission: it cannot be based on simple speculation concerning certain problems that might be very interesting, but which cannot fulfill this function of criticizing beliefs and reforming received opinions. When it is good, philosophy necessarily has an immediate relation with society.
>
> (Villoro, 2022, 22)

Villoro defined this immediate relation between philosophy and a historically concrete society in terms of principles for communication that demand epistemic and ethical non-exclusion. According to his proposal, the reform of intelligence has two aspects. One of them requires direct contact with the concrete rational and communicational needs of societies, and with humanity in general. The other aspect implies a critical revision of properly philosophical assumptions. If such assumptions are abstract, conservative, sterile, or fragmented, philosophy becomes a form of escapism or skepticism, a kind of intellectual entertainment that impedes the anchoring of our cognitive capacities in what is reasonable, turning philosophy into *ideology*.

These two facets of the anchoring that philosophy should provide can be understood, as Villoro argues, as an activity of criticism in two directions. A first orientation is philosophy's critical labor against external bodies of entrenched beliefs. It is directed toward ideologies or sets of manipulative beliefs that oppress social groups by maintaining the status quo. The oppressive effect of such ideologies may affect vast groups, even most people, depending on how we measure the negative impact of ideologies. These groups are kept in a situation of exclusion at various levels. Chapter 7 examines Villoro's views on ideology and how it is central to his political philosophy. A second orientation of criticism is internal, directed toward the kinds of "philosophy" that are ideological, and impede the reasonable labor of criticism that constitutes philosophy's main purpose. This second orientation challenges philosophy's unreasonable assumptions, and has expressed itself throughout the history of philosophy, for instance, in Kant's critical philosophy. Ideological philosophies prevent the anchoring of philosophy in concrete societies, such as recent forms of vacuous scientism and, as Villoro repeatedly says, escapist forms of skepticism and relativism, which are, unfortunately, quite popular today.

When philosophy is good, it reforms our communicational practices in order to prevent and eliminate exclusion. Part of this effort consists in dismantling and criticizing byzantine systems of philosophy that pretend to provide the ultimate truth, when in fact they prevent us from eliminating exclusion by distracting us from society, becoming ideological. Philosophy should not be an empty exercise in rationality that is disconnected from society—a kind of arrogant soliloquy that fuels exclusion by ignoring the needs of society. For these reasons, philosophy is an activity that criticizes and rejects forms of communicational exclusion, and that requires an anchoring in concrete social circumstances. Philosophy is an activity that reforms and reorients our *attention toward concrete circumstances*, fostering a reevaluation of epistemic and ethical values in favor of non-exclusion.

Philosophy must unify our search for truth with our search for freedom. The relation between truth and freedom is the nucleus toward which all good philosophy gravitates, and it is at the core of Villoro's Central Normative Proposal: our duty to search the truth must be accompanied by our duty to prevent exclusion, thereby amplifying the freedom of those who are oppressed or disadvantaged (Montemayor, 2023a). Any act of communication presents an opportunity to eliminate exclusion from epistemic and ethical communities. These are opportunities to engage philosophy as a criticism of ideology. Our communication has become too commodified and governed by the crudest kinds of strategic rationality (see Chapter 7). This is partly because most philosophy today is either compatible with ideology or deeply ideological itself. Philosophy, according to Villoro, is not the property of a few specialists at elite universities, and it is not "contained" in the almost unreadable articles published in largely inaccessible journals that catalogue the highest forms of academic prestige. When it is good, philosophy leads to social transformation. Genuine philosophy is the best hope we have to fight ideology and oppression. Philosophy is for everyone, not just for experts. It is *achieved* through our daily and very concrete practices of reasonable and non-exclusive communication. Philosophy is incompatible with intellectual domination of any kind. From its very beginning, philosophy aims at liberation and at fostering a multiplicity of approaches, rather than ideology and the homogenization of thought.

Belief and reasonable communication

As mentioned earlier, beliefs can be false and still be epistemically justified. The distance between truth and justification fuels most of contemporary epistemology. This approach clearly favors skeptical views, which is a source of concern for Villoro. Skepticism is compatible with exclusion and lack of cooperation, and some formulations of skepticism may even directly lead to injustice (see Srinivasan, 2020). Attention is crucial for anchoring reason precisely because belief is incapable of such anchoring, even when it is justified. Beliefs, according to Villoro, are dispositions but our epistemology is incomplete if *attitudes* are not included. Attitudes orient dispositions, including doxastic ones, toward concrete objects and socially relevant situations, determining the ways in which subjects respond. (Villoro, 1985|2007, 100). Crucially, Villoro argues that while attitudes and beliefs are related because they dispose individuals to act, attitudes are defined by the *affective and evaluative* aspects of our dispositions to act, unlike beliefs, which are defined by their *cognoscitive* aspect (ibid., 101). This distinction plays an important role in Villoro's conception of ideology, examined in Chapter 7.

Notice the pragmatic elements of these definitions. Attitudes, which I shall interpret as attentive attitudes, have a kind of energy and charge. They can powerfully orient us through our evaluations of objects and situations. We can ignore what should be salient if they are negatively charged or unjustified, or they can energize our epistemic capacities in a way that we are not only successful in achieving multiple epistemic goals, but also cooperative and creative. Villoro defines this rich affective orientation as being essentially geared toward *action*. In a similarly pragmatic spirit, Villoro conceives of beliefs as doxastic attitudes that dispose us to act, but with a more cognoscitive or semantic component rather than an affective one. This cognoscitive orientation is also best understood as a kind of attention because attention, unlike belief, is necessary for de re reference (reference to particular objects as such, rather than descriptions) and for a relation between justification and aboutness (Dickie, 2020). Belief cannot guarantee this kind of factual relation to concrete objects or situations—de re beliefs, which ground other types of descriptive reference, depend on the attentive focus of an agent on a singular object or situation for them to be veridical.

The relation between ethics and epistemology requires an evaluative orientation towards concrete objects and situations and a proper comprehension of their attributes. Both capacities necessitate attention, and both are fundamental for the anchoring of reason and philosophy in concrete reality. Our evaluative and cognoscitive orientations should seek to comply with the principle of non-exclusion in communication. Here too, attentional orientation is of the essence. Villoro's account is thus best understood as requiring attention in order to anchor reason to reality, and as requiring cooperative joint attention in order to articulate practices of non-exclusion in communication. Attention also helps explain crucial aspects of epistemic agency that cannot be accounted for exclusively with belief, such as epistemically and morally justified curiosity as well as creativity (see Fairweather and Montemayor, 2017). Since curiosity and creativity are also components of epistemic and moral cooperation, they are essential aspects of Villoro's political and social philosophy, as subsequent chapters demonstrate.

This attention-based interpretation of Villoro's theory of rationality can be synthesized by the following slogan: *reason is rooted in reality through our attentive orientations.* This is a key commitment of Villoro's philosophy. To properly understand it, we must unfold the meaning of "being rooted" in reality. Rationality (instrumental, strategic, moral) needs to be reasonable for it to be part of the pursuit of knowledge and freedom. Unreasonable rationality is a form of ideology that conduces to oppression. The metaphor of the tree of knowledge needs to be taken literally and biologically. Rooted trees suffer when their branches are cut off. To maintain its vitality, the tree of knowledge must maintain its integrity and be rooted in the concrete needs of its society.

Because beliefs don't have to be true to be either justified or strongly endorsed, they can serve as the basis for collections of falsehoods or partial compartmentalized opinions that unify a group, serving as common ground while systematically excluding beliefs that are different. Thus, collections of beliefs, as Villoro warns us, can ground ideologies for political and moral oppression. Villoro's epistemology is designed to prevent ideological thinking. This is why attention should play the role that he assigned to reasonable attitudes, because when attention works properly, it anchors us to concrete situations. In fact, attention is the most important cognitive skill that guarantees that we are acquainted with concrete, rather than possible, objects and situations. Moreover, Villoro explicitly appeals to our capacity for attention in his interpretation of Wittgenstein in order to ground reason in reality, distinguishing meaning and value from collections of facts and abstract theorizations.

Because of these characteristics, Villoro's epistemology offers a unique advantage: it can explain a phenomenon that escapes contemporary accounts of ideology in contemporary epistemology. This phenomenon is the *invariance of structures of oppression across opposing ideologies*. Governments that claim to be far right as well as far left, parties that seem to present completely different visions of the world, and various regimes throughout history with radically different forms of government, turn out to be consistent with very similar degrees of oppression and exclusion. This is the importance of concreteness in an account of knowledge and freedom. Villoro has the conviction that what makes our actions reasonable is that they cannot be merely ideological—they have to be anchored in the concreteness of the world. Since they are unanchored by their very nature, we follow ideologies at our own peril. Reforming these practices depends on the elimination of ideologies by paying attention to concrete individuals and situations. The reform of intelligence is an attentive one.

Villoro, in other words, allows us to avoid what seems to be a dilemma for all *exclusively doxastic views* of rationality. The *dilemma of ideology for doxastic views* can be expressed as follows:

1. Confronting an ideology is an act of opposition, a conflict between groups.
2. The moment the confronting or critical discourse opposes "the other," it stops being reasonable because it promotes the exclusion of the other group's perspective as irrational.

3. Thus, as the action of opposing an ideology implies the risk of becoming ideological itself (because of 2), the only way to be reasonable is to avoid any conflict that could lead to the exclusion of a group (prohibiting the situation described in 1, which seems essential for the project of making liberation from ideologies possible).

How to solve this problem that seems to trap us into an option between arrogance and indifference, similar to Agrippa's skeptic trilemma? The options, under an exclusively doxastic understanding of rationality, seem to be either skeptical inaction or overt confrontation. Inaction could be interpreted in two ways. One is to not oppose the exclusionary effects of ideology by finding ways of peaceful resistance to epistemic arrogance and exclusion. This first interpretation is the equivalent of Pyrrhonian withheld judgment, where no belief or opinion crosses the bar for full assertion. The other version of inaction is to not oppose the ideological group directly, by offering it a persuasion strategy. This is the equivalent of dialogical accommodation without open resistance, a kind of "reframing" of the issues that could, in the end, resemble an infinite regress of accommodations. Both strategies can be complementary, but they differ fundamentally in that one of them leads to inaction while the other leads to perpetual accommodation. A third route is to go for the other fork of the dilemma: direct confrontation, asserting the exclusion of the other group as irrational. This is the fork of arrogant rationality, or as the ancient skeptics call it, dogmatism.

One must not interpret this problem as an entirely theoretical difficulty, the kind of problem that can be dissolved purely in thought. This kind of speculative rationality is criticized by Villoro. There is a *historical dimension* to this problem as well, which is essential to understand Villoro's philosophical views on knowledge and freedom. These *rational paths* have been taken time and again with very mixed results, and the structures of oppression seem to be, to this day, rather intact in terms of their pervasiveness and resistance to real or concrete change. Some political advances are clear, and no one denies that we live in much less cruel societies than we used to. But we would fool ourselves into thinking of our current situation as one in which there is no pervasive oppression and inequality. To the contrary, some may think of our current situation as being much worse than it has ever been given the amounts of concentrated wealth in the hands of few individuals and the very urgent threat of the automatization of intelligence and knowledge.

Thus, our doxastic strategies to address this skeptical difficulty sustain the invariance of structures of oppression. The reason for this is that the conflict it presents is one of *opinions*, rather than a tension in more deeply entrenched attention patterns that sustain inequality. The effect is one of excessive attention to some issues at the cost of others on the basis of our opinions, preventing joint attention to what really matters: concrete forms of exclusion and oppression. In reality, these opposing discourses are not changing anything; they don't really help anyone in disadvantage to improve their status. As a result, there is a certain *theatricality* to the situation described in the dilemma of ideology. The opposing parties are immersed in their arguments, without looking at reality. This has been the biggest difficulty, according to Villoro, of contemporary epistemology and ethics, defined as the unified search for knowledge and freedom, as illustrated by the three moments of "dialogue" between mainstream Mexicans and the indigenous world, explained in *Grandes Momentos*. The theatricality of ideology will be further explained in the next chapters, particularly Chapter 7.

Communication and concreteness

According to Villoro's principle of non-exclusion, and following Phillips' understanding of equality, the active character of our moral and epistemic agency consists in refusing to be treated as inferior. The concreteness of the world includes the communicative needs of other members of society, particularly those who are unjustifiably deprived of knowledge and the freedom to communicate. Attention is at the heart of the reliability of communication.[1] To make something common, to create common ground, we need to be anchored in similar ways to concrete contents. This is a necessary condition for any kind of cooperation. If there were no possibility for common ground, based on concrete reality rather than opinions, we would have only ideologies. We achieve our *social existence* through communication. If we are excluded, we become irrelevant and immaterial for the production of knowledge, which entails that we are not free to think or speak in ways that matter to others because we are invisible to them. The other becomes concrete when we jointly attend *with* that person and when we pay attention *to* that person's communicative needs. Joint attention substantiates our agency.

Depriving someone from becoming a solid and visible member of society can occur at many levels. From early education in a family to the hierarchical clustering of power by groups, networks of knowledge distribution and moral support profoundly shape who will have decision-making power and to what degree. Epistemically, various stages of bureaucratized education segregate people into profiles that range from very significant ones that give privileged access to the best education to successively more inconsequential ones whose members are never given access to knowledge. Even in systems where there is considerable social mobility, the epistemic profile of most individuals who try to become visible and active members of communities without real access to resources, gradually waters down so that in the end only a few have consequential decision-making in knowledge production, or solid epistemic standing. This, of course, does not mean that the communicative and epistemic needs of those who are degraded are any less concrete than those with power. We all have the same epistemic needs to be recognized as a member of knowledge-producing communities. Their needs are real, but they become permanently unfulfilled.

---

[1] For a general discussion of linguistic luck, including the importance of attention as a way to eliminate it, see the essays in Fairweather and Montemayor (2023).

Something similar happens with moral standing: exclusion implies invisibility, which in this case means that the moral dignity of the excluded erodes. The question is also about trust: can we trust this person or this group of people? The emphasis here, however, is not on their epistemic competence, but their basic qualification as good human beings that we can trust, however that state of goodness is defined. Villoro's insight is that denying one type of status to someone reinforces the denial of the other; he sees this happening both historically and at various stages of individual development. By not recognizing the epistemic needs of entire groups of people we reinforce the process of dehumanizing them as morally irrelevant as well. This is how entire groups lose the epistemic and moral entitlements they deserve. How is it that we manage to ignore the concrete needs of other people, their concrete *humanity*? Ideological thinking blinds us to their reality, forcing us to use only very specific kinds of unreasonable rationality, mostly strategic reasoning. The way out of this problem is to reorient our attention to the concrete needs of others.

What makes people socially significant is their *capacity to participate in society*. This capacity that should be taken for granted in any free community is systematically denied to a vast number of people, entire groups of them, who are certainly the majority. An abhorrent aspect of slavery is that it entirely precludes the possibility of social significance. We abolished slavery, but we have developed new forms of exclusion that resemble the crude forms of slavery humans practiced before. Instead of physical chains and punishment, we have socially implemented systems of exclusion that depend fundamentally on ideologies and vicious patterns of attention surveillance. We prevent people from participating fully in society by excluding them from a good education, and by ignoring the basic needs any human must satisfy to live a decent life. As part of their exclusion, we stop cooperating with them. We don't trust their opinions and their actions, shaping the meta-semantic level in which meanings are contextualized as systematic exclusion. The worst part of this systemic miscommunication (or anti-communication) is that because the dominant groups operate under ideological thinking, they believe that the opposing groups, who are actually oppressed, are effectively excluding them by not trusting them in return. Everyone becomes frustrated, angry, and uncooperative.

Anthropological and sociological approaches to language show that cultural significance and the semiotic character of expressions—the use and interpretation of symbolic expressions at a context—are determined by specific actions in concrete situations that are hierarchically organized. Meaning is assigned once a situation is *concretized* by the actions and the context. Political bias easily shapes epistemic and ethical guidance, orienting our attention to status. Cultures of attention based on such biases frame patterns of collective attention that can deeply divide us, instead of helping us become more grounded in cooperation— what Villoro would call unreasonable, as opposed as reasonable, attentional patterns. This happens because attention is no longer grounded on the concrete needs of others, but is rather directed through the biased and powerful convictions of ideological group-thinking. As a consequence, our epistemic and moral capacities have become *opinionated*, rather than *attentive*.

Legal systems, religious traditions, and any hierarchy of power provide classic examples of meta-pragmatic guidance for the concretization of meaningful contexts of communication, which shape linguistic communities at large. Michael Silverstein (2023, 6–9) offers the following example of context-setting in which the intentions and actions of speakers determine how expressions will be interpreted. If "A" (a researcher that is looking at her computer and doesn't turn around to see who has entered her office) says: "there is more trash under the table," this expression is not merely the description of a fact, it is also, and prominently, a command, justified by a structure of power in which the researcher has superior status than the cleaning staff. "B" (the person who enters the room, who is actually the head of the lab) silently stares at A, who then turns around, looks at her and realizes her mistake. What A should do is to apologize, not because it is false that there is more trash under the table, but because she issued a command to the wrong person by stating that fact.

The presence or absence of a person changes what we mean when we say something and it also changes how we attend to situations, including the garbage under the table. Silverstein calls this a *meta-pragmatic indexicality* that accompanies our acts of communication. There are two kinds of assertability conditions at work here, which speakers must identify in a non-lucky manner. The statement "there is more trash under the table" is assertable if it satisfies the basic norm of being true or justified—there is indeed some trash under the table. However, the intended meaning of the expression as a *command* to the cleaner requires the indexical pointing to the correct individual entering the room. This latter condition is not satisfied in the example above. Getting either assertability condition wrong would get the speaker in trouble. But the second kind of trouble is conducive to potential insult and confrontation. The intended meaning is to issue a command that assumes the truth of the simple fact that there is more trash under the table. Thus, the assertability of "there is more trash under the table" as a basic fact is too trivial for it to specify the relevant context. A hierarchical structure is presupposed as common ground between A and B, and it is this structure that serves as the fundamental condition for the assertability of the sentence as a command. The indexicality contained in the expression concerning the target of the command, the cleaning person, depends on the joint attention of the speakers to this hierarchical structure.

This kind of meta-pragmatic and meta-semantic specification of concrete contexts seeps through language. The invisible hierarchy of power and status distribution that we jointly attend to as we speak is crucial for specifying which concrete situations will count as meaningfully relevant. This tapestry of joint attention does not depend on our beliefs or our conscious states alone—it is *common ground*. I cannot see the conscious beliefs inside your head, but I can tell if our cooperation leads to success or not, and I can also tell in which hierarchical structures of power we are allowed to cooperate. I can also assess whether your assertions are reliable or not—how much you get things right, how much you joke when you shouldn't, etc. Language is flexible and we can distort the use of meta-pragmatic effects to mold our attention ideologically. If I start asserting facts to "school you" and humiliate you (as if I were in a position to issue commands and instructions to you), it won't matter if I am satisfying the standard norm of assertion, that what I am saying is true. It won't even matter if the beliefs accompanying those assertions are always justified. You will resent my assertions, and with justification, because I am demeaning you, excluding you from the group of people I cooperate with. Ultimately, I am diminishing your status and putting your competence into question.

There are various degrees to which I can stop cooperating with you. I could assert sentences as if you were in principle incompetent to grasp them, without any other communicative intention than showing other people that I will not cooperate with you. I could also start doubting everything you say and ignoring what you intend to communicate, clearly violating Davidson's charity principle. I can turn my attention away from everything you care about, focusing exclusively on things I find relevant and blinding myself to what you cherish. Again, I could be rational in treating you this way—after all, I consider you to be a poor source of information and it is a *norm of belief* to acquire good evidence. Ignoring you is exactly what this norm requires me to do. One can go further: a meta-pragmatic version of this norm is that I should prevent you from communicating or cooperating with others—I should go "after you" in order to police what you say. The problem here is that, according to Villoro, I am using my attention and communication capacities unreasonably, in an opinionated fashion. I am following a rational norm of belief, but only in order to demean you and demote your epistemic and moral standing.

Attention and reasonableness

Not joking at a funeral, and avoiding saying something offensive, even if true, about the departed, is as important for linguistic cooperation as satisfying basic assertability conditions regarding the truth. In fact, insulting you "with the facts" will lead much faster to confrontation than the mere lack of linguistic cooperation. If you suspect that I am manipulating you or demeaning you, that will justify not only your decision not to cooperate, but also your decision to actively *resent* my participation in a conversation. We have moved from potential lack of cooperation to direct confrontation. These emotional components of communication become the main drivers of how we pay attention to our interlocutors. Most of our conversations are shaped by them. We don't want to be treated as conversational inferiors even in situations where we are open to learn from someone, and we resent being treated as inferiors in any conversational context. Unfortunately, while anger and resentment are legitimate reactions to being treated as inferior, instead of fostering cooperation, they exacerbate exclusion.

Attention patterns like the ones illustrated in Silverstein's example determine concrete situations of asymmetry or cooperation, thereby defining which conversational exchanges are adequate or even possible. The semantic and pragmatic aspects of language thus acquire political and ethical dimensions. Villoro's social epistemology and political philosophy centers on how this happens: namely, how is it that our search for freedom and knowledge becomes concrete through specific capacities for communication. This constitutive character of joint attention that concretizes situations for communication and power dynamics makes attention essential for the normative requirement of reasonableness in our rational practices. It should be clear by now that Villoro's epistemology requires attention, rather than belief, to play this role. The question is what *kind* of role attention should play in shaping the norms of rationality and communication. There are three possibilities here, which I shall label *compatibility*, *necessity*, and *superiority*:

> **Compatibility:** *A unified theory of epistemic and ethical orientations that prevents exclusion does not need to be based fundamentally on beliefs or doxastic orientations. Attention is sufficient to account for the*

normative relation between epistemology and ethics—although attention
may not be necessary to account for it.

This is a weak version of the attention requirement for reasonableness
if we take into account the importance of rooting reason in reality for
Villoro. But even Compatibility would require a revision of
contemporary epistemology, moving it more substantially toward social
epistemology and political philosophy. Demarcating which
combinations, replacements, or expansions of doxastic norms with
attention norms would require insights from political philosophy and
philosophy of language. However, Villoro's Central Normative Proposal
and the associated reform of our intelligence seem to entail a much
stronger principle, one in which attention is not merely sufficient to
explain reasonableness, but is actually necessary and not replaceable by
any doxastic norm—attention is not an optional requirement in a
theory of reason:

> **Necessity:** *A unified theory of epistemic and ethical orientations that*
> *prevent exclusion, or the theory of reasonable rationality, fundamentally*
> *depends on attention capacities to anchor doxastic attitudes on concrete*
> *situations.*

Unlike the previous version, this account of reasonable rationality
asserts the fundamentality of attention for epistemic and ethical norms
over doxastic norms. Following Silverstein, and in accordance with
what Villoro says about attitudes and value, attention norms may play a
meta-normative role, determining which doxastic norms are relevant
in a specific context. They also play a basing role, giving doxastic norms
the anchoring they need to be reasonable. In order to capture the
context-determining and basing aspects of reasonable attention, a
principle of reasonableness could be stated as follows:

> **Superiority:** *A theory of reasonable rationality not only depends on*
> *attention; it is also wider in scope, more fundamental, and centered on*
> *the unifying relation between knowledge and freedom than theories of*
> *rationality based on belief.*

For Villoro, the anchoring role of reason is what justifies all the epistemic and ethical norms concerning how we should cooperate and communicate with each other. Since attention is the cognitive capacity that anchors our beliefs and attitudes, attention is essential to explain reason. Some philosophers have already pointed out that a full theory of epistemic norms needs to include attention (Gardiner, 2022). According to the updated version of Villoro's reasonable rationality theory, which assumes attention as fundamental, one must go beyond most contemporary philosophers by asserting that without attention, a theory of rationality is radically incomplete. According to Villoro, there cannot be reasonable rationality or a reform of intelligence without attention. To be reasonable, we must worry fundamentally about being attentive, rather than opinionated.

Philosophy is defined by Villoro as *disruptive reason*. It is not mere confrontation. Philosophy should provide us with better ways of cooperating, rather than with new forms of opposing and hating each other. Therefore, solving the problems of philosophy clearly goes beyond any distributive justice approach. The issue is not to distribute wealth and knowledge, but to equip everyone with the capacity to participate in society to the extent that is possible by becoming as visible to others as possible. The real possibility of not being treated as inferior in concrete situations of communication is part of the project of reforming intelligence through philosophy, which is not necessarily dependent on wealth or means of production—this is why Villoro also opposed Marxist ideological thinking. The final chapter explains why these commitments make Villoro's view a robust version of the capability approach to epistemic and ethical justice. The role that attention plays in Villoro's capability approach provides his social epistemology with the notions of *charge* and *force*, which allow us to explain what he calls the gnoseological and sociological roles of ideology (see Chapter 7).

The Villoro archive at the Institute for Philosophical Research of UNAM includes documents that confirm Villoro's deep interest in Wittgenstein—not only his notion of *figure of the world* and the unification of knowledge and freedom, but also his early work on existential philosophy, including the research he conducted with collaborators at the Grupo Hiperión. Villoro was planning on writing a book on the *Tractatus*, and had even drafted a table of contents based on a series of seminars he taught in 1967, 1972, and 1979 (see figures 4.1 and 4.2). He kept papers from his students, one of them on the notion of "figure" in Wittgenstein. The draft of the table of contents included sections on figures, elements, forms, truth, and the transcendental (figures 4.2 and 4.3). It also included a section on the "theory of the figure."

A remarkable document in the archive is a text that Villoro wrote in 1982, the same year he published his major work on analytic epistemology, about Jean-Paul Sartre (see fig. 4.4). In it, Villoro first makes a connection between Sartre's philosophical views and Mexican existentialism. He asks: what made Sartre's thought so attractive to generations of Latin American philosophers? What did they discover in it? Villoro answers by saying: certainly, neither rational rigor nor the intimation of a more critical philosophy (Villoro, 1982, 23). My generation, continues Villoro, believed it had found rigor and a critical

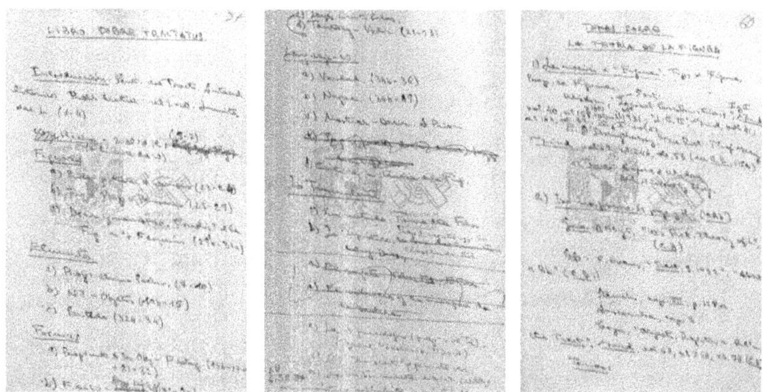

Figure 4.1 FLV-C6-E32-F57 (Anverso)

Figure 4.2 FLV-C6-E32-F57 (Reverso)

Figure 4.3 FLV-C6-E32-F60

philosophy first in phenomenology and then in some forms of analytic philosophy (ibid.) Villoro writes:

> What fascinated us about Sartre's writings was his deep comprehension of the sense of human life, linked to an enlightening proposal for a new morality. It was this passionate, liberating conception of humanity what gave an answer to the basic concerns of various generations. In Sartre we saw a more vigorous expression of a morality of authenticity and freedom [. . .] a conception of humanity as freedom.
>
> (ibid.)

Villoro then says that the problem with Sartre's liberating conception of humanity is that value and the sense of life cannot be found in the world because they are not reducible to facts. How should we conceive of them then? Freedom is to deny what is factually given by projecting what is valuable. If humanity cannot be merely factual, then what is it? Sartre, who understood how difficult it is to articulate this notion, found only one word, according to Villoro, to describe the situation: transcendence. Freedom is transcending what is factual. This negative route to freedom, which inspired Villoro's own *via negativa*, is characterized by Sartre as nothingness or pure negation. *Nothing* or *nothingness* are vague terms, but they are indispensable for Sartre's characterization of freedom.

Then, surprisingly, Villoro compares Sartre to Wittgenstein (Villoro was fluent in French and German, and translated various texts from these languages—some of the references in the archive are to French and German texts). Villoro writes that Wittgenstein's *Tractatus* makes the same point that Sartre is making but in clearer terms because nothingness is inaction while being silent implies an active engagement with the world, which is the right attitude towards what is not merely factual (1982, 25). Villoro points out, however, that in Sartre's engagement with Marxist ideology one can identify this active dimension of freedom that, when we speak in metaphysical terms, gets systematically lost. Humanity is transcendent of materiality, including historical determinants that make its materiality culturally concrete (see figures 4.5 and 4.6).

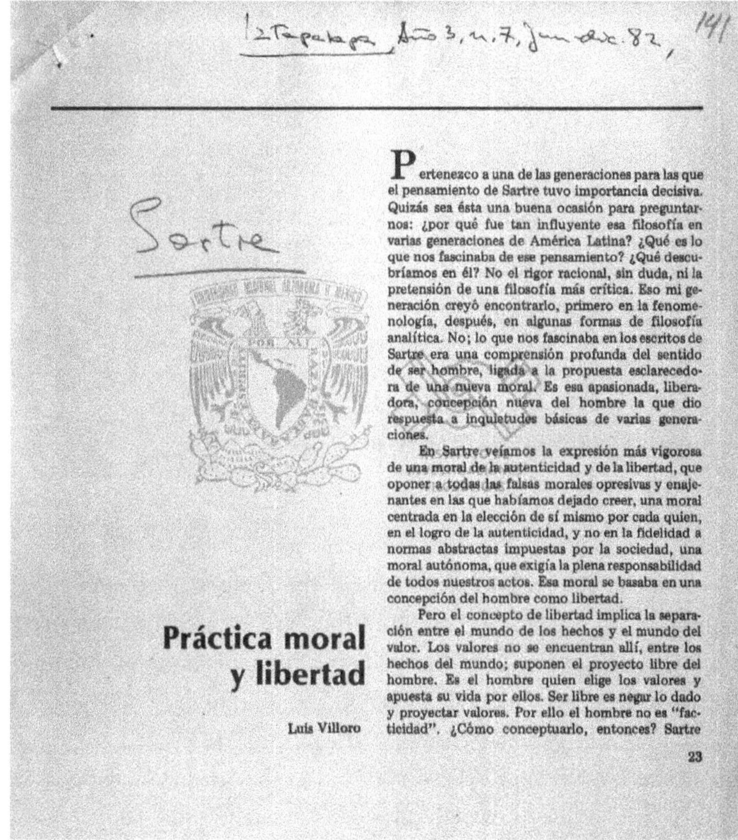

Sartre

Práctica moral y libertad

Luis Villoro

Pertenezco a una de las generaciones para las que el pensamiento de Sartre tuvo importancia decisiva. Quizás sea ésta una buena ocasión para preguntarnos: ¿por qué fue tan influyente esa filosofía en varias generaciones de América Latina? ¿Qué es lo que nos fascinaba de ese pensamiento? ¿Qué descubríamos en él? No el rigor racional, sin duda, ni la pretensión de una filosofía más crítica. Eso mi generación creyó encontrarlo, primero en la fenomenología, después, en algunas formas de filosofía analítica. No; lo que nos fascinaba en los escritos de Sartre era una comprensión profunda del sentido de ser hombre, ligada a la propuesta esclarecedora de una nueva moral. Es esa apasionada, liberadora, concepción nueva del hombre la que dio respuesta a inquietudes básicas de varias generaciones.

En Sartre veíamos la expresión más vigorosa de una moral de la autenticidad y de la libertad, que oponer a todas las falsas morales opresivas y enajenantes en las que habíamos dejado creer, una moral centrada en la elección de sí mismo por cada quien, en el logro de la autenticidad, y no en la fidelidad a normas abstractas impuestas por la sociedad, una moral autónoma, que exigía la plena responsabilidad de todos nuestros actos. Esa moral se basaba en una concepción del hombre como libertad.

Pero el concepto de libertad implica la separación entre el mundo de los hechos y el mundo del valor. Los valores no se encuentran allí, entre los hechos del mundo; suponen el proyecto libre del hombre. Es el hombre quien elige los valores y apuesta su vida por ellos. Ser libre es negar lo dado y proyectar valores. Por ello el hombre no es "facticidad". ¿Cómo conceptuarlo, entonces? Sartre

23

Figure 4.4 FLV-C7-E39-F141 (Anverso)

There are many things to say about these passages written by Villoro right around the time he finished *Creer, Saber, Conocer*, which anticipate his views on power and value. I will focus on one of them. Villoro thought of Wittgenstein, and some analytic philosophers (like Rawls), as pinnacles of rigor. This comparison between Sartre and Wittgenstein suggests that Villoro's mature thought was a revision of his earlier encounter with a liberating perspective on morality through existentialism, including Mexican existentialism, now filtered through the epistemic and ethical analyses of analytic philosophers, primarily

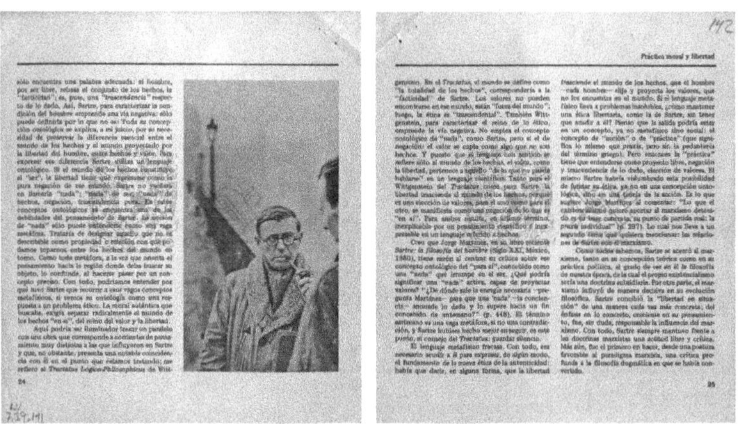

Figure 4.5 FLV-C7-E39-F141 (Reverso)

Figure 4.6 FLV-C7-E39-F142 (Anverso)

Wittgenstein. The anchoring of reason in the world was something that impressed Villoro deeply about the ethical and transcendental aspects of Wittgenstein's work. This is why the anchoring of reason on attention discussed thus far is so essential for Villoro's philosophy as a whole.

The norms of rationality are radically incomplete without attention. The norms "justify your beliefs" and "follow the beliefs you endorse as correct" are, at best, partial rules for rationality and cooperation. However, without attention, these norms can become sources of ideology and confrontation. Moreover, without attention, the transcendental nature of freedom and the anchoring of reason become problematic. The norm: "focus on what is most relevant" is essential to make our capacities for rationality reasonable. *Am I focusing on the right things?* is a more fundamental question in our lives, in their entirety, than the question *Are my beliefs correct?* This is not to disdain the importance of belief, but rather, to emphasize the centrality of attention in a philosophical account of knowledge and freedom rooted in what is concrete, like Villoro's. *Attention makes possible the rootedness of reason*. To be free we must transcend facticity, and this requires the activity of attention.

References

Crary, A. (2016), *Inside Ethics: On the Demands of Moral Thought*, Cambridge, MA: Harvard University Press.

Janik, A. and Toulmin, S. (1973), *Wittgenstein's Vienna*, New York: Simon and Schuster.

Silverstein, M. (2023), *Language in Culture: Lectures on the Social Semiotics of Language*, Cambridge, UK: Cambridge University Press.

Villoro, L. (2022), 'Sobre las tareas filosóficas del presente', In J. Villoro and G. Hurtado (eds.), *La identidad múltiple*, Mexico: El Colegio Nacional.

Wittgenstein, L. (1922|1974), *Tractatus Logico-Philosophicus*, D. F. Pears and B. F. McGuinness (trans.), New York: Routledge.

Pragmatism, Attentive Engagement, and Contemporary Epistemology

A pragmatic account of belief

Saber, creer, conocer (SCC) is considered Villoro's most rigorous work in analytic philosophy. Previous chapters have addressed issues in Villoro's epistemology, which he deeply cared about from early on in his career. These themes, on political philosophy, social epistemology and the foundations of reasoning are briefly examined in section three of SCC, particularly concerning the ethics of belief and the relation between knowledge and wisdom. Section three of SCC plays a bridging and transitional role from the themes of the first two sections (on the theory of knowledge) toward a wider theory of reasonable rationality, which as I have argued, is the ultimate goal of Villoro's social epistemology. In the first two sections, on belief and knowledge, respectively, Villoro engages with what is known as the *justified true belief* account of knowledge (or JTB), with all the literature beginning with Edmund Gettier's (1963) challenge to JTB, up to the time Villoro was working on these issues. Because of their emphasis on JTB and traditional analytic epistemology (of an individualistic and abstract or idealized kind), one may think that these two sections are irrelevant to Villoro's non-ideal theory of reason and freedom. In this chapter, I argue that, although they are not clearly related to Villoro's social epistemology, and they are not obviously continuous even with the third part of SCC, they certainly are *consistent* with Villoro's overall project.

SCC was supposed to be part of a two-volume treaty on epistemology and political domination (Hurtado, 2024). Villoro didn't write the second volume, but the relation to ethics and politics is present in the third part of SCC and in his book on the concept of ideology. Villoro wrote a book on ethics and domination *El Poder y el Valor* (Power and value), his major book on political philosophy. As Hurtado (2024, 235) says, on a first approximation, the project of SCC and this book on political philosophy seem to be unrelated, independent philosophical accounts of epistemic and moral/political value. Previous chapters have shown that this cannot be true of Villoro's entire work. But it is interesting to see how exactly the traditional and analytic approach of SCC relates to Villoro's social epistemology and political theory by examining the first two sections of SCC in more detail.

Analyzing the first two parts of SCC is also important because of the rigor and originality with which Villoro engages analytic epistemology. He articulates the JTB view and Gettier's challenge in a way that matters in Spanish, which has two terms for "knowledge" (*saber* and *conocer*). His positive account of knowledge is insightful and oriented towards issues in social epistemology. Villoro's account of the necessary and sufficient conditions for knowledge, unlike the standard approach that seeks to identify a fourth condition (safety, sensitivity, anti-luck, etc.) *removes* one of the three necessary conditions: truth. Initially, this seems preposterous. One of the reasons why no one in analytic epistemology thought of removing one of the three necessary conditions of JTB is because they all agreed that knowledge *entailed* them. Knowledge necessitates belief, justification, and truth.

According to JTB, S knows that p, if and only if: a) p is true; b) S believes that p; and c) S is justified in believing that p. Gettier presented famous counterexamples to JTB, showing that although these three conditions are necessary, they are not sufficient. Naturally, the post-Gettier literature focused largely on providing a fourth condition that would be sufficient. Thus, before explaining how the first two parts of SCC relate to Villoro's social epistemology, as articulated in other writings, one must show that his proposed analysis of knowledge within the analytic context is plausible and coherent. The previous chapters help explain why removing truth, abstractly conceived, from the necessary conditions for the achievement of knowledge is something that one would expect from a non-idealized, politically engaged, and historically oriented social epistemology. But here, I aim to show that even within the resources and discussion of the first two chapters of SCC, one can still defend Villoro's account, not only as plausible and coherent, but also as original and important.

First, as was previously noted, Villoro doesn't deny the vital role that truth must play in epistemology and, in fact, his account of knowledge is intended to oppose dogmatism and relativism about truth, which is a form of skepticism that Villoro battles throughout his work, both in epistemology and in ethics. His main concern is with the conditions for knowledge from the perspective of an agent embedded in a particular and contingent epistemic culture. It is well known that the quest for the necessary and sufficient conditions for knowledge did not lead to final and fruitful resolutions. Some authors question the very assumption that the JTB view reflects genuinely universal conditions on knowledge (Weinberg et al., 2001), while others opted for the irreducibility of knowledge to any component conditions (Williamson, 2000). Villoro's removal of the truth condition should be taken in this spirit. Seeking to reduce knowledge and other concepts to necessary and sufficient conditions that are highly idealized has not been productive, and Villoro's emphasis on knowledge as a social accomplishment shows that he would have agreed with these recent criticisms. He would have sided with experimental epistemologists in their challenge against an idealized and intuitive way to arrive at universal conditions for knowledge, and would have supported proponents of the knowledge-first view in their claim that knowledge cannot be simply deconstructed into idealized component conditions.

Villoro conceives of knowledge as an achievement, a view that resonates with contemporary views on knowledge, particularly in virtue epistemology (Sosa, 2007, 2009; Greco, 2010; Fairweather and Montemayor, 2017). There is a potential to develop his dispositional and social perspective on belief into a virtue epistemology, just from the resources provided in the first two sections of SCC. This would be an interesting project in traditional analytic philosophy, and it might be worth pursuing. But Villoro was not interested in just doing this. He was concerned with the unfortunate prevalence of domination in ethics and epistemology and, therefore, he was also trying to provide conditions for a theory of knowledge that would prevent dogmatism and ideology, unlike contemporary efforts in analytic epistemology that challenge JTB approaches, such as those just described. Unlike most standard views about epistemic virtue, Villoro's account is deeply concerned with politics.

On the question of knowledge and ideology, Villoro's approach caused mixed reactions. The Marxists at UNAM, who sympathized with Villoro's anti-domination epistemology, were not interested in the two first sections of the book, devoted to analytic epistemology, and they were frustrated with the third part because it didn't appeal to concrete social categories and stratifications, such as class. The analytic philosophers in Mexico had the opposite reaction, they were uninterested in the third part but they were very approving of the first two (see Hurtado, 2024, 235). Villoro could not be simply classified as a Marxist or analytic philosopher, and this made him an uncomfortable fellow traveler, even though his ideas were valuable for both sides. I agree with Hurtado's assessment that what made Villoro's view uncomfortable back then is what makes it unique and important today.

A central question for this chapter is how to incorporate the insights from the three sections of SCC into Villoro's broader project, given that none of them focus explicitly on attention, although section three focuses on analogous notions, as we just saw. Villoro's proposals in section three stand on their own as original contributions to social epistemology. However, his analysis of JTB in the first two sections is quite original as well, and consistent with section three. Here are the key definitions of belief and knowledge that Villoro offers in the first two sections. His dispositional view of belief is inspired by R. B. Braithwaite's (1932–1933) pragmatist account. Braithwaite defines the necessary and sufficient conditions for belief as follows: *S* believes that p, if and only if: a) S represents that p; and b) S has a disposition to act as if p were true.[1]

After addressing a variety of criticisms against Braithwaite's definition of belief, which includes a review of relevant work in the psychology of motivation and intentional attitudes, Villoro proposes improving Braithwaite's definition as follows: S believes that p, if and only if: a) S is in an acquired dispositional state x of responding in a specific way in various circumstances; b) p has been grasped by S; and p determines x. This definition can be examined from various angles, but the most salient is that, in contrast to Braithwaite, Villoro's definition dispenses with truth. In his definition, the subject need not act as if the propositional content of her belief were true. Villoro argues that if the subject had to act as if p were true, then she would already need to believe that p is true, with some standard of certainty, which would initiate a regress into other beliefs that would need to be considered as true in order for her to have a good degree of certainty about p.

Success in action based on reliable dispositions, essential to the pragmatic understanding of belief, does not depend on ultimate guarantees for truth. Even if one assumes that belief necessitates a representation of the content of p, p need not be represented as satisfying standards of certainty. The reliable disposition and motivation to act according to p suffices—no further explanation is needed. This is completely consistent with Ramsey's account of success semantics explained in Chapter 3. Given the importance of grounding reason in reality, attention is, as I argued before, a more powerful way to interpret both Ramsey's and Villoro's proposals. However, even if one focuses exclusively on belief, Villoro's definition already appeals more directly to action than to truth. Following this pragmatic interpretation, the requirement that the disposition be acquired through psychological processes is best understood in terms of the socially driven aspects of such a disposition, conducive to assertion, action, and joint attention.

---

[1]   For recent formulations of a dispositional account of belief see Schwitzgebel (2002).

Villoro dispenses with truth in his definition of knowledge for similar reasons. Before examining his definition of knowledge, and other topics in section two of SCC, the relevance of using Braithwaite's definition to motivate his own definition of belief is salient and deserves further scrutiny. It confirms Villoro's pragmatist leanings. Given Villoro's decades-long interest in Wittgenstein, it is intriguing to ponder how much Villoro knew about Braithwaite's relationship with Frank Ramsey and Bertrand Russell. These thinkers launched the beginning of analytic philosophy, an event which, as Cheryl Misak (2016) has forcefully argued, has been deeply misunderstood. In particular, the interaction between the "two Cambridges," as Misak says, set the course of what was to become the analytic philosophical tradition. In Cambridge, Massachusetts, William James, Charles Peirce, Chauncey Wright and Oliver Wendell Holmes created pragmatism. In Cambridge, England, Russell, Ramsey, G. E. Moore and Wittgenstein opened the path (or at least a central path) for analytic philosophy. These Cambridges, according to the standard historical accounts, were in opposition to each other. Misak writes:

> The standard story has it that Russell, Moore, and, to a lesser extent, Wittgenstein savaged pragmatism, leaving it never to fully recover. The standard story also has Ramsey and especially Wittgenstein putting forward novel positions, drawing upon few influences outside their tight local circle.
>
> (Misak, 2016, 1)

Misak shows that both parts of this story are wrong. Ramsey and Wittgenstein were "strongly influenced" by pragmatism and "even Russell took cues from it" (Misak, 2016, 2). She also argues that Ramsey's early pragmatist objections to Wittgenstein were decisive in his abandonment of the *Tractatus*, towards his "second" phase. It is remarkable that even Russell owes key insights to pragmatism. Peirce's influence on Ramsey is well documented, and Ramsey prefaces "Truth and Probability" with a quote from Peirce, explicitly acknowledging his influence on his thinking. Surprisingly, Ramsey also said that he learned his strand of pragmatism from Russell. How can this be, given Russell's famous and repeated indictments of pragmatism, and Ramsey's own indictment of Russell's logical-atomist theory of truth? Misak explains that:

> The key to unlocking this mystery lies in the fact that by 1926 Russell had in fact adopted some pragmatist claims about the link between belief and behaviour. He could not, however, enrol fully in the pragmatist project, since he took this to require endorsement of the pragmatist theory of truth that James was inclined to articulate. Russell understood that pragmatist theory of truth as the claim that truth is what 'works', and he found the idea an abomination. Nevertheless, Russell's new account of *belief* was pragmatist in spirit, and it provided a pragmatist steer for Ramsey. But as Braithwaite indicated, Ramsey was on the path also to a pragmatist account of *truth*, a path Braithwaite thought would result in a slide to relativism. Russell was not the inspiration for that.
>
> (Misak, 2016, 2)

There is much to say about this fascinating, as well as historically critical, nexus of ideas that crisscrossed both Cambridges, and I highly recommend that the reader consult Misak's book for details. This historical information is relevant to understanding the context in which Braithwaite was working. It was a remarkable time in which the field of analytic philosophy was just taking shape. The philosophers at Cambridge, England, including Russell, were clearly interested in the pragmatist conception of belief as a disposition towards concrete actions in various circumstances. Ramsey was the one who took this insight concerning action as a *standard of objectivity* to its ultimate consequences, applying it to truth, knowledge, and scientific understanding. Belief, as a cause of behavior, demands this standard because the action must be grounded in reality for it to succeed. Since beliefs are non-factive (one can easily believe what is false) their role as causes of behavior demands an explanation. In addition, a full understanding of how actions reflect our knowledge and convictions also requires motivations to feature more centrally in an analysis of knowledge.

In the section that precedes his proposed definition of belief, Villoro addresses this question concerning the objective standard for epistemic achievement. The section is titled "The distinction between belief, attitude and intention." In it, Villoro explains that we have various dispositions toward objects, positive and negative, as we have seen in previous chapters. Here, however, he says that the important thing about these dispositions, including belief, is that they satisfy *cognitive needs*—they are useful to the agent in satisfying goals (Villoro, 1982, 68). Like Ramsey with his utility condition, Villoro proposes that it is the combination of goals, desires, and representations that fix the content of beliefs. After addressing Elizabeth Anscombe's and Donald Davidson's views on *intention*, Villoro says that beliefs are implicit in all our attitudes as a kind of conviction, but he then refers to a distinction introduced by Edmund Husserl, between objectifying and non-objectifying acts. He defines the objectifying nature of perception and memory in terms of what we can collectively share—or as I have suggested, collectively *attend to*. Villoro says that this is what distinguishes the objects of belief from those of desire and intention; namely, that although they all require an objective standard to succeed in satisfying the needs of an agent, only the contents of belief are shared by an epistemic community. They can all have collective beliefs in a way that differs from their desires and intentions. The key point is that Villoro emphasizes the importance of action and shared contents within a community in order to motivate his definition of belief. This is why attention is needed here too, because attention can anchor the contents of belief and action in a way that belief by itself cannot.

A pragmatic reading of Villoro's definition of belief and of his philosophical views in general is particularly enlightening (Pappas, 2017). We can further develop this interpretation through the historical references Villoro uses. Even if Villoro was unaware of the deeply consequential debate about pragmatism in Cambridge, England, the connections are there in the historical record, and they are also present in Villoro's adoption of the dispositional view. For Villoro and the pragmatists, belief is a *habit of action*, under certain circumstances.

Cognitively, attention is more fundamental as a habit of action that then guides belief, so this is my proposed update to Villoro's view of belief and knowledge. However, this is not a major update: Villoro's view makes perfect sense as a pragmatist account of doxastic attitudes once the *contents* of non-factive states like belief are grounded. Another way of making this point is through Ramsey's requirements for a success semantics, which relate action and assertion, and on how this relation depends on attention (Fairweather and Montemayor, 2017).

This essential relation between cognition and action is crucial for Villoro's definition of belief and knowledge, as well as truth, conceived as a kind of joint standard for success tied to motivation. According to this understanding, belief habituates in order to succeed in various tasks, in many contexts, so that belief "does not disappoint," as Peirce would say. Belief does not disappoint because there is not only something objectifying about the contents of beliefs, but also something *objective* about how they are grounded in attention and also geared toward action. Perception presents the clearest case of this relation, but it is a relation that must hold in general in a theory of knowledge.

A pragmatic account of truth and knowledge

Given the commitments of Villoro's definition of belief, it is not surprising that his account of knowledge is also deeply pragmatist. An apparent discrepancy is that, like most analytic epistemologists, Peirce and Ramsey thought that belief is essentially related to truth. This is the main reason why belief is the propositional attitude of choice in epistemology: belief is oriented toward the truth, or it aims toward the truth. Villoro substitutes the truth condition for knowledge with conditions about the *intersubjective* determination of a disposition, as a habit for action under specific conditions. The previous discussion shows that, if the intersubjective conditions for knowledge are understood as a pragmatic commitment according to which truth is essentially related to action, then Villoro agrees with Peirce and

Ramsey's action-based account. He does not use the word "truth," because he disagrees with the idealization of truth as absolute for all speakers and times, but he means the same thing as Peirce and Ramsey: beliefs are habits of action that lead to the satisfaction of our cognitive needs. Those conditions of satisfaction determine how the content of the belief is fixed, and the success of our actions determine its truth.

The situation is similar with respect to knowledge. Villoro's elimination of the truth condition is meant to satisfy a pragmatic constraint: do not appeal to absolutes or abstractions that play no role in our social interactions and the manner in which we actively cope with the future. Villoro briefly discusses Gilbert Ryle's distinction between *knowledge that* and *knowledge how* in this context, clarifying that in the first case there is an object that is apprehended while in the second case the content is determined by possibilities for action, showing that both are compatible with his pragmatic definition of belief. Then, in contradistinction to the JTB view, and against the prevailing tendency to identify a fourth condition for knowledge, Villoro defines knowledge as follows: S knows that p, if and only if: a) S believes that p, and b) S has objectively sufficient reasons for believing that p.

Villoro justifies the second condition through the distinction between believing and knowing. He says that knowing implies not only the certitude of the strong sense of "believe" from the first-person point of view (more about this below), but also the satisfaction of a rational standard determined by a concrete and historically situated epistemic community, from the third-person point of view. The reasons we provide when we claim to know that p can never be based solely on our conviction that we strongly believe that p—knowledge requires a publicly available standard of evidence. This standard of evidence, for well-known reasons, cannot be very high—most people know a very substantial number of things, all required for successful action on a daily basis. If the standards for knowledge were very high, then we would quickly fall into skepticism and epistemic despair.

More important, the standards for knowledge depend on a *concrete epistemic community*, and they should apply to all its members. Thus, although our beliefs are intersubjectively determined because they are habits of thought that we acquire through our epistemic community, the reasons we provide when we claim to know something must directly appeal to the publicly accessible standards of our community, regardless of how we acquired our beliefs. Certainty and even degrees of credence can suffice for belief, but such *subjective reasons* are never sufficient for knowledge. This is essentially what condition b) requires. One way to understand this difference, suggested by Ramsey, is in terms of standards for credence versus standards for assertion (see Fairweather and Montemayor, 2017, Chapter 5). Our practice of assertion may vary geographically and temporally, but it determines a public standard that cannot be reduced to mere subjective confidence—it would be inadequate to respond to the question: "why did you tell me the car was safely parked when it was in the middle of the street" by saying "I strongly believed it was safely parked." Our interlocutor deserves a better reason than this.

Moreover, because of the pragmatic approach that Villoro embraces in his epistemology, the standard for knowledge cannot be "the truth," absolutely and abstractly defined. There is no absolute standard that the contents of our beliefs must "correspond to." Rather, it is our concrete practices that determine such standards. This is why, according to Villoro, it is so important to eliminate inequalities concerning the access and production of knowledge. Depriving individuals from participating in epistemic communities prevents them from satisfying the most basic epistemic needs, since they cannot have access to the standards concerning the truth without actively participating in concrete epistemic practices: there is no "truth out there" that they could access without participating in such collective epistemic practices.

When we believe we take a first step toward action, but the standards for belief are never epistemically sufficient if all we have are the subjective standards of personal conviction. Assertions, on the other hand, must comply with a variety of verifiable or publicly available standards. Knowledge, from ordinary perceptual truths to science, allows us to attend to what is relevant in order to act and regulate our expectations—it organizes our habits of thought and action, preparing us for what comes next. Accordingly, Ramsey thought of scientific theories as systems with which we *meet the future*. They are public systems that are always revisable. Even if some parts of the system look as rigid as an eternal axiom, new practices may question their axiomatic status by enhancing the possibilities for new actions and thoughts—for instance, the paradigmatic shift from Euclidean to non-Euclidean accounts of space in physics. In this pragmatist sense, belief and assertion do a lot of work in our explanation of the concept of *truth* because how we succeed in these communicative practices is exactly what determines what is true. Assertions have *objectively sufficient* satisfaction conditions. As Villoro would put it, they have "third person" standards. On Ramsey's account of truth, the equivalence of "p" and "it is true that p" is based on the fact that the satisfaction conditions for epistemic practices like assertion are all there is to know about how contents are true—succeeding at these practices is what we *mean* when we say that something is true. There is no further "truth" hiding in a higher dimension.

The revisability of all our epistemic practices is also consistent with Villoro's definition of knowledge. According to pragmatism, laws and inferences are habits and generalizations through which we meet the future. The fact that they are revisable explains why there are scientific revolutions and major systematic revisions, even in mathematics. Truth is getting things right for the here and now in order to face the future, and we depend on our epistemic communities to get things right. We never get to meet the absolute truth from a perspective of omniscience. The safe ground of truth is where *our practices* are tested, confirmed, and proven right.

C. I. Lewis was emphatic about how truth, understood in this way, also includes ethical, political, and legal truths. There is no mystery associated with how they could possibly be true when there is no difference in our practices that allow us to face the future—epistemic practices are on a par with ethical ones if they are helpful, and they include scientific theories and legal codes. He called the view that values are mere expressions of emotion "one of the strangest aberrations ever to visit the mind of man." (Lewis, 1946, 366) An example of a clearly assertable truth today is that slavery is deeply immoral. However, this was not the case until very recently. Frederick Douglass's condemnation of the United States' legal system was that this truth was contradicted by the legal practice of slavery. Ramsey proposed that since belief is partly a disposition to behave, we could measure the strength with which someone believes through her actions, evaluating these actions in terms of their consistency and success rate. The legal practice of slavery showed Douglass and others like him that very few people with power truly believed in the immorality of slavery—quite the contrary. Thus, this pragmatic "measure" of conviction extends to ethics and politics as much as it does to science and mathematics, and Villoro incorporates this insight into his philosophy.

Villoro was criticized for being a relativist about truth because of the elimination of truth from his definition of knowledge (Hurtado, 2003; Ornelas, 2017). Although Villoro rejects relativism about truth because it is a form of skepticism, eliminating the truth condition from the concept of knowledge is indeed a radical departure from the traditional view, one that seems to lead toward relativism. I hope to have shown that once we interpret Villoro's epistemology through his overall pragmatic commitments, the threat of relativism is eliminated. But given that there are various kinds of pragmatism, some more sympathetic to relativism than others, more elucidation on Villoro's strand of pragmatism might be illuminating.

I have argued that Villoro's kind of pragmatism is in line with Ramsey's given Villoro's definition of knowledge. This is also supported by Villoro's adoption of the dispositional theory of belief and by his overall interest in Wittgenstein (including Wittgenstein's later work). But let us concentrate on Ramsey's work here, given that Wittgenstein was never as explicitly pragmatist as Ramsey. Misak explains how Peirce and Ramsey articulate a view of knowledge according to which we believe with certainty when oriented toward action, and in which knowledge must lead to success reliably. This is a kind of epistemic reliabilism, but keep in mind that for Ramsey the equivalence between "*p*" and "*p* is true" depends on the assertability conditions for *p*. So our *normative commitments* and communicative practices also matter, besides reliability. Unlike the functionalist or behaviorist versions of reliabilism, Ramsey's pragmatism (and Villoro's) is, as Misak puts it, as thick with norms as are our practices of assertion and inquiry (Misak, 2016, 230). Misak writes about this issue:

> Some contemporary pragmatists, such as Robert Brandom and Michael Williams, refuse to take this normative step from the equivalence thought to the standards embedded in assertion and inquiry. They fail to see, as Price puts it, that disquotational truth is too thin to play a proper role in an adequate theory of assertion, commitment, and judgment [...] They would do well, I suggest, to return to Ramsey. For one thing, they would then retain a notion of constraint by 'objective factors', without which they appear to be as cut adrift from the world as Rorty.
>
> (2016, 230)

We can say, following Misak, that Villoro belongs to the "objective factor" strand of pragmatism, one that is compatible with virtue reliabilism (Fairweather and Montemayor, 2017). There are many details about the history of pragmatism within analytic philosophy that are relevant to how Ramsey influenced, among others, Wittgenstein. It is unfortunate that this history has been documented and established only recently by the valuable work of Misak. I have argued that key elements of Ramsey's kind of pragmatism can be identified in Villoro's epistemology, although Villoro does not articulate his view by following Ramsey explicitly. Yet, the connections are there, all over the first two parts of SCC. Pappas (2017) is right in affirming that Villoro belongs to the pragmatist tradition, which is also compatible with philosophical traditions in Latin America where action and liberation are central to inquiry. We can now give a few more details about this important claim by Pappas. Villoro presents other views about the role of belief in epistemology, beyond SCC, which we are about to address. The main conclusion of this section is that Villoro, like Ramsey, is not a relativist about truth, and this is why he commits to the "objectively sufficient" condition on knowledge—his account of knowledge is not just norms and commitments towards non-exclusion. Non-exclusion is a necessary condition for the existence of healthy epistemic communities, but it is not sufficient to guarantee knowledge.

Strong belief and the figure of the world: Ortega y Gasset and Wittgenstein

If attention fulfills the anchoring role that pragmatists assigned to action in relation to belief and knowledge, which is particularly true of Villoro given what he says about attitudes and motivation, what is the proper role of belief in a pragmatist account of knowledge once attention is in place? Beliefs we consider safe can be false in a variety of close contexts, and the degree to which one is confident about them varies from just above doubt to absolute certainty. The standards for believing are actually very weak. For instance, one can always deny the content of a belief if we also qualify the degree of certainty with which we believe it, as in "I believe it is raining, but I am not sure." The standard is so weak, that it questions the assumption that full belief is either the norm of assertion or the standard commonsense non-factive attitude (Hawthorne et al., 2016). Since this weak standard applies to full beliefs, it does not help to switch to degrees of credence—although degrees of credence capture much better the way in which belief is weak. Moreover, according to skepticism, particularly of the "Academic" kind, common ordinary beliefs may be systematically false and we would believe them with a great degree of certainty anyway. So it is abundantly clear that, by themselves, beliefs cannot anchor cognition on facts—at least not without the aid of attention or another fact-involving capacity.

However, beliefs can certainly *provide an orientation* toward the world. It is just that it is not a fundamental or grounding one. Villoro adopts the dispositional, or what I am calling the *pragmatic* view of belief, because of its essential orientation toward action. Villoro was aware of the key debate among the Cambridge pragmatists in England concerning the relation between belief and action. He says in a footnote that Ramsey and Braithwaite effectively respond to Russell's criticism that not all beliefs are conducive to action (Villoro, 1982, 33). We will see that, as Villoro says, it is not *immediate* action that determines the content of belief, but the assumption that if some condition is satisfied, given some goals and motivations, then the belief would lead to action. The previous chapters also make clear that Villoro is committed to the kind of assertion-based normativity of communicative practices concerning standards for justification and non-exclusion. It is this conditional and normative orientation toward action that makes attention a more suitable candidate for grounding in reality the kind of reliable epistemic capacity associated with communicative norms that Villoro has in mind—otherwise one cannot meet the "objectively sufficient reasons" condition for knowledge. But the framework provided by our beliefs is also part of our cognitive orientation and collective mental habituation. In fact, belief, even if ungrounded, can provide a powerful orientation toward the world that convinces us of the veracity of the belief's content. This is why Villoro is so interested in defending an epistemology that combats dogmatism, skepticism, and ideology. If belief didn't exert a powerful impact on our psychology, there would be no need for such combat.

Beliefs can play important, if less fundamental, roles in a pragmatist epistemology that is based on attention. Attention explains the reliability and action-oriented nature of Ramsey's strand of pragmatism, based on success conditions and reliable motivations. But the overall orientation that beliefs can provide constitutes a "figure of the world," a term we already encountered in Villoro's interpretation of the *Tractatus*. The metaphor mentioned before of "a map by which we steer" captures this idea of cognitive orientation. In the words of Peirce, inquiry "is not standing upon the bedrock of fact. It is walking upon a bog, and can only say, this ground seems to hold for the present. Here I will stay till it begins to give way." (Peirce, 1931, 589). This applies to *any* kind of inquiry, in science, morality, or jurisprudence. There is no absolute, indefeasible, or sacred path to the truth. Therein lies the enormous power of conviction, based on belief—even if false or unjustified, it provides a path that orients.

The bog can give way in a variety of ways. Because of the importance of assertability conditions for truth as success in action, given some motivation, our practices for assertion and the varying degrees of justification we use in asserting propositions can change with time. Some areas of doxastic certainty may become probabilistic, and we could start holding only partial beliefs concerning those areas (e.g., the position of particles after the quantum revolution). In other cases, full belief of the most fundamental kind may become conditional on a choice, given a larger and renewed doxastic landscape (e.g., the inviolability of the axiom of the parallels being true only in a geometry with no curvature). While not immediately conducive to action, as perceptual beliefs are, these general beliefs, like universal generalizations, laws, and mathematical statements, put us in a situation to make choices, open inquiry, and confront the future, in order to take action. This is all dependent on choice, inquiry, and reliable success at a context within a specific epistemic community and its contingent standards of evaluation. At the same time, some beliefs must "stay put" for inquiry to proceed at all. Not *everything* can give way. Something needs to be firmly there, ready for us to act in a multiplicity of ways. The territory might be provisional, but some of its sections are much firmer than others.

In this vein, Villoro distinguishes between a weaker and a stronger sense of "belief" in SCC. Interestingly, he characterizes the weaker sense with an example like the one used above, which denies the degree of certainty required for an assertion. This distinction is part of a larger discussion on subjective certainty and objective sufficiency. Villoro's example of the weak sense of belief is "I believe Juan is there, but I might be wrong." (Villoro, 1982, 130). As in contemporary analyses of epistemic modals, Villoro explains that the fact that there is no contradiction here reveals the higher standards we have for knowledge. For instance, "I am sure about this, although I might not know it" is paradoxical and nonsensical. Villoro then describes the strong sense of belief as incompatible with any lack of certainty. He says that Wittgenstein could only have had in mind the strong sense of "belief" when he wrote, in *Philosophical Investigations*, that we could distrust our feelings but not our beliefs, and that if there were a verb that meant "to believe falsely" such a verb would lack meaning in the first-person indicative (Villoro, 1982, 133).

Wittgenstein indeed devoted his attention to what Peirce called the "fixation" of belief, using epistemic and psychological perspectives. Wittgenstein's epistemology, in line with the pragmatist tradition, seeks to eliminate unreasonable forms of skepticism, such as the "rational" but unreasonable doubt that there is an external world. Wittgenstein's (1969) *On Certainty*, in particular, offers a sustained development of these issues. The way in which Wittgenstein treats the problem of belief and skepticism through our practices of assertion echoes Ramsey's view that there is a pervasive epistemic normativity of language that makes our speech acts trustworthy and reliable. A variety of standards are assumed in our conversations and our assertions are systematically associated with commonsensical assumptions that are required for collective action, and which must stay in place without being questioned.

There are special cases in which we can doubt that we have hands—G. E. Moore wrote a famous "proof" affirming the existence of his two hands against the skeptical doubt that there is no external world, and Wittgenstein discusses this issue in *On Certainty*. Such a doubt may emerge, for instance, in cases where there has been an accident or a surgical procedure. But in general, beliefs like "I believe I have two hands" cannot be seriously doubted without grotesquely distorting our communicative practices. If in a normal conversation someone says, "you cannot give me that book because you may not know that you have hands," the standards for asserting and communicating have been violated unreasonably, even if it is rational, in certain domains, such as Cartesian hyperbolic skepticism, to doubt that there is an external world. Shifting the standards of our communicative practices in this manner is, ultimately, a method for *eroding trust and becoming uncooperative*: "It's not a matter of *Moore's* knowing that there's a hand there, but rather we should not understand him if he were to say 'Of course I may be wrong about this.'" (Wittgenstein, 1969, 6e, 32) Our reaction should be: what could Moore *mean* by that assertion concerning his hands? What kind of mistake could it be? This issue concerning knowledge and assertion-standards is intimately related to the *limits of inquiry*, which is a central project of the *Tractatus*, and also to the distinction between what is reasonable, as opposed to merely rational, in Villoro's work. Wittgenstein writes:

> If someone is taught to calculate, is he also taught that he can rely on a calculation of his teacher's? But these explanations must after all sometime come to an end. Will he also be taught that he can trust his senses—since he is indeed told in many cases that in such and such a special case you *cannot* trust them?—Rule and exception.
>
> (1969, 6e, 34)

Our practices concerning the rules and standards for assertion are relevant to determine: a) what is acceptable evidence in a context in which we are communicating and cooperating; b) what are the meaningful reasons one can provide as justification; and c) what other epistemic practices might be salient for knowledge attribution, for the guidance of inquiry, and for reasonable doubt? The demand to provide epistemic grounds and justification must come to an end, but the end is not a certain proposition that strikes us as obviously and immediately true (Wittgenstein, 1969, 28e, 204). Consistent with the analysis offered earlier about pragmatism and attention, Wittgenstein says that it is not a kind of seeing or intellectual seeming on our part that ends doubt, but rather our *actions*, which constitute the "*bottom of the language-game*" (ibid.). This pragmatic approach shows that some beliefs must stay fixed and unquestioned for *any* kind of inquiry to proceed: "the *questions* that we raise and our *doubts* depend on the fact that some propositions are exempt from doubt, are as it were like hinges on which those turn" (1969, 44e, 341).

Addressing Moore's "proof" of the external world by also examining the proper limits of inquiry is a central goal of *On Certainty*. In this respect, the *Tractatus* is a *precedent* for *On Certainty*. Georg Henrik von Wright (1982, 175–6) goes further, arguing that the goal of delineating the limits of what is reasonable and sayable is the purpose of both the *Tractatus* and *On Certainty*. He writes:

> What Moore called 'common sense' [. . .] is very much the same thing as that which Wittgenstein in the Tractatus would have referred to as 'the limits of the world'. Wittgenstein's high appreciation of Moore's article must partly have stemmed from the fact that he recognized in Moore's efforts a strong similarity with his own. And his criticism of Moore in *On Certainty* we could, in the language of the *Tractatus*, characterize as a criticism of an attempt to say the unsayable.
>
> (von Wright, 1982, 176)

Moyal-Sharrock and Pritchard (2024) endorse this reading of *On Certainty*, and they explain why Wittgenstein's action-based examination of the beliefs that constitute bedrock was the foundation for the contemporary branch of the theory of knowledge called "hinge epistemology," which is also based on the work of Michael Williams on methodological necessities. What in the *Tractatus* is the boundary between nonsense and what is sayable, later becomes the "grammar" of what is meaningful and knowable. Comparing certainty with the hinges of the door of knowledge, Wittgenstein says: "If I want the door to turn, the hinges must stay put." (Wittgenstein, 1969, 44e, 343). About this image of knowledge and certainty as hinges on which inquiry turns, Moyal-Sharrock and Pritchard write:

> *Nonsense, the ineffable (or unsayable), grammar, knowledge, certainty*: these are the key notions that [. . .] Wittgenstein either modifies or relocates [. . .] We shall see that certainty becomes, in Wittgenstein's hands, a new animal: often called 'hinge certainty' and, less often, 'objective certainty', it is internally linked to nonsense, ineffability and grammar—all terms that Wittgenstein modifies or refines. As for *knowledge*, Wittgenstein relocates it. In fact, he effects a major shift in epistemology when he divests knowledge (more or less justified true belief) of its foundational status, which he attributes to *certainty*. Whereas the early Wittgenstein is concerned with understanding the

> limits of *sense*—what enables us to make or express sense and can therefore not itself be endowed with sense, the third Wittgenstein will be concerned with the limits or foundations of *knowledge*: what makes knowing possible and cannot therefore itself be an object of knowledge.
>
> (Moyal-Sharrock and Pritchard, 2024, 3)

Wittgenstein's strong notion of belief, discussed by Villoro in SCC, is clarified and expanded in *On Certainty*. The degrees of commitment, credence, and the different norms that apply to assertive expressions are tied to action. In this context, the distinction between background or bedrock beliefs and weaker or suppositional beliefs is more useful than the standard distinction between full beliefs and partial beliefs or degrees of credence. In a pragmatist theory of knowledge, updated with the psychology of attention, foundational reliability comes from attention capacities. Subjective states of certainty or doubt provide a comprehensive doxastic orientation where action and our communicative practices delineate what is certain or taken for granted and what we can doubt. But it all bottoms out in our practices of communication, which depend on attention and charity. Thus, the reevaluation of the *Tractatus* in *On Certainty* is deeply related to Villoro's exploration of the boundary between what is reasonable and unreasonable.

Villoro doesn't address Wittgenstein's *On Certainty* explicitly in SCC. But he is very interested in the role that strong beliefs play in epistemology and, in particular, in a theory of knowledge that is pragmatically inspired. Moreover, Villoro (1984) devotes a whole section of his book on the Spanish philosopher José Ortega y Gasset to the distinction between weak and strong belief. Like Wittgenstein, Ortega differentiates between a firm and strong notion of belief or bedrock and suppositional belief, where doubt is reasonable and where inquiry takes place.

Ortega calls subjectively rational opinions, opinions we are conscious and convinced of, "ideas." We try to justify ideas with reason and we judge them as probable or true. It seems that the JTB account of knowledge captures this notion of justification, of beliefs or degrees of credence that we judge as true or probable. Ortega says that ideas have fundamental presuppositions that can remain largely unconscious and which we rely on, without explicitly offering reasons for their justification. He calls these presuppositions "beliefs." Ortega says that we *have* ideas, but that we *exist* and *live* in our beliefs. Ideas are personal, while beliefs constitute our social heritage. They are collective convictions that we share without explicitly acknowledging them: we "face" them, rather than "accept" them. Villoro cites Ortega saying: "The tangible reality, to put it this way, of collective belief does not consist in my or your acceptance of it, but rather, it is she who, with our approval or not, imposes her reality and obliges us to rely on it." (Villoro, 2023, 185).

Beliefs belong to different kinds of activities, but they cannot be doubted if we are to act and hold on to something that allows us to confront concrete reality. Villoro gives as examples the belief in the existence of the street and the continuity of space beyond the room in which one is located. These bedrock assumptions play a vital role in our cognition. Villoro documents how Ortega's "image" or "figure of the word" is described as a vital *sensibility* or a "radical sensation toward life." This notion of vital sensibility associated with the image of the world, expressed in Ortega's earlier book *El tema de nuestro tiempo* (The theme of our times) is replaced in *Ideas y creencias* (Ideas and beliefs) with the notion of belief, along the lines of what Wittgenstein calls "certainty." Ortega's hinge epistemology is vitalist and, as Villoro says, Ortega is following an existentialist tradition here—the comparison that Villoro makes between Sartre and Wittgenstein, described in the previous chapter, comes to mind. Ortega's notions of *belief* and the *image of the world* not only resonate, but also seem deeply in line with Wittgenstein's notions of *certainty, forms of life,* and *language games.* Consider the following passage from Villoro:

The term "belief" in Ortega cannot be understood as separated from "world", or better, from the "interpretation of the world". Ortega's "beliefs" are the unmentioned presuppositions of all the rest of our beliefs, on which we erect the interpretation of the universe [. . .]. They establish the limits within which we can configure a world, for a collective, in an epoch. They constitute, therefore, what we could also call "the figure of the world" of an epoch.

(Villoro, 2023, 192)

As portrayed in the *Tractatus*, the figure of the world is the interpretation of the world *as a whole*, and the distinction between Ortega's ideas and beliefs delineates what in the *Tractatus* is the distinction between what is sayable and unsayable, reasonable and unreasonable. It is not surprising, then, that substantial similarities between Ortega and Wittgenstein have been identified in the literature. Both authors belong to the same generation, but they didn't interact with each other and come from very different philosophical traditions. Wittgenstein's early work was influenced by logical positivism and, through Ramsey, as Misak showed in her book, by pragmatism, particularly during the later stages of his work. Ortega was influenced by Marburg Neo-Kantianism, Nietzsche, Dilthey, and Husserl (Ariso and Wagner, 2016, 1).

Yet, there are strong similarities concerning their approach to rationality. Ortega's "ratiovitalism" aims at eliminating the tension between universal rationalism and relativism about truth. Ariso and Wagner write: "Taking the problem of truth as a reference point, he notices that relativism forgoes truth to bring life to the forefront, whilst rationalism relinquishes life to keep truth." (2016, 1–2) Ortega affirms that the central problem with rationalism is that it clings to a "fictitious reason" detached from life or any kind of vital function. Wittgenstein would also agree, in his later work, that the fictitious reason that seeks after absolute truths, rules, proofs of the external world, and so on, needs to be rejected in favor of a reasoning that is grounded in language games and forms of life. Wittgenstein declares in *On Certainty*: "My *life* consists in my being content to accept many things" (1969, 44e, 344). Villoro's distinction between reasonable and unreasonable rationality is clearly influenced by Ortega and Wittgenstein. Villoro's anticipation of how this distinction matters for social epistemology, its relation to ethics, and eventually politics and culture is highly original and ahead of his time. His pragmatic take on knowledge and belief remains insightful.

Western epistemology turned inwards: a diagnosis

A more radical claim can be made about Villoro's strand of pragmatism. The pragmatists opened the door to historically situated perspectives, but their analysis remained heavily focused on the two Cambridges. Villoro's pragmatism adapts to a Latin American perspective and develops distinctions in Spanish that have consequences for the relation between ethics and epistemology from within the philosophical traditions of analytic philosophy and phenomenology, which he eventually applies to political and legal issues. In this regard, it would seem initially plausible to associate Villoro's philosophy with Dewey's or even Rorty's strand of pragmatism. But as we have seen, Villoro deeply cared about the non-relativity of truth and was very much in line with the ideas of Peirce, Ramsey, and Wittgenstein. Yet, one must account somehow for the *anticolonial* character of Villoro's philosophy. For example, in writing about Ortega, he explicitly complains about "our proclivity to disdain philosophy written in Spanish" and to excessively value work produced in a major cultural metropolis (Villoro, 2023, 183).

A particularly innovative aspect of Villoro's philosophy is the centrality of practicing non-exclusion in concrete epistemic communities in order to achieve reasonable communication. This is essential for how Villoro conceives of the relation between epistemology and ethics. As mentioned earlier, his epistemology is explicitly designed to combat ideology and dogmatism, which are sources of colonial and oppressive thought. His pragmatic view of belief and knowledge are necessary elements of his anticolonial epistemology. But they are not sufficient for the full articulation of his philosophy. Ortega and Wittgenstein also opposed unreasonable views concerning the nature and extent of our knowledge. Skepticism and inattention can be an important source of colonial and ideological thought. What I am calling "the inward turn" of epistemology is the effort to build the theory knowledge on the basis of a weak, non-factive, and subjective state. Unsurprisingly, skepticism became a colossal challenge in Western philosophy, particularly after Descartes. This coincided with the rapid expansion of European colonial power, first with the Portuguese and the Spanish, and later with the French and the British empires. The transatlantic slave trade was paradoxically and grotesquely forged by societies that were embracing ideals of justice and equality in their most important legal documents.

Villoro was familiar with this kind of paradox, where knowledge does not lead to action or ethical evaluation. Everything becomes theatrical in this weakened and panicky epistemology. Hands and thoughts become divorced in an unfamiliar setting according to which one must have evidence from some higher place that the world, including *my own body*, really exists. Whole bodies of collective action become bracketed under the spell of withheld judgment. According to the internalist approach to the new evil demon problem, massive ignorance is compatible with perfectly and blamelessly justified belief. The route of justification can lead, therefore, to voluminous and unreasonable falsehood. The next chapter examines contemporary approaches to the thorny issue of how ethically and politically repulsive views can nonetheless be epistemically justified. We shall see that Villoro offered pioneering proposals for how to address this problem. But here it is important to stress that, for the pragmatist, this kind of divorce between thought and action is unacceptable and unreasonable.

Villoro understood that skepticism is a kind of epistemic escapism that helps justify ideological narratives. It diverts our attention from the world, including the world of ethics. Skepticism favors the kind of abstract rationality that the pragmatists repudiated: ideal conditions for eternal truth, propositions in a third realm, laws fixed by eternally true sentences, demon and dream scenarios, and so on. It also makes possible a kind of metaphysics that dispenses completely with human interests and actions—one could "rationally" doubt whether one has hands or whether the world existed 2 seconds ago. Villoro's definitions of belief and knowledge concern a subject that is poised for reliable action given concrete circumstances, determined by a sociopolitical community. He refers to the work of Gordon Allport on trait psychology and prejudice

(Villoro, 1982, 45–5), highlighting the importance of a hierarchical valence-structure for evaluations and consistent motivations. Villoro, like the pragmatists, rejects the "mental state" and "subjectivist" version of belief, partly because these internal and itemized states lead to skepticism and facilitate ideology. Following the pragmatist maxim that beliefs are habits of action, Villoro justifies empirically his account of belief by showing that motivations are consistently integrated into traits that dispose subjects to act in specific circumstances. These traits are not reducible to inner mental states in which abstract ideas are represented. Because of these characteristics, it is more appropriate to interpret the psychology that Villoro and the pragmatists appeal to in terms of the selective, reliable, and motivationally integrated functions of attention (see Fairweather and Montemayor, 2017).

The anchoring function of attention is actually indispensable to respond to the skeptic along the lines suggested by Ortega and Wittgenstein. If the knowledge that I have hands is challenged, the best I can do to answer such an unreasonable question is to point out that the circumstances are the usual ones. I can attend to them, move them, grab objects with them. This challenge would ultimately question the way I *live*. This type of unreasonable, but according to the skeptic, rational doubt, also questions my basic interactions with others, for instance by making possible statements like the one we examined before, presented by Wittgenstein: "this is my friend, she is not an automaton." These skeptically induced "assertions" are rational (they respond to a rationally framed doubt), yet they are deeply unreasonable. They are unreasonable and nonsensical expressions that make us escape from meaning and from the world into the "inner realm" of our ontologically detached heads. Thus, the escapism of skepticism is not merely epistemic, it also distorts the relation between epistemology and ethics.

The escapist mentality fostered by subjectivist skepticism makes possible unjust forms of inattention and ignorance that are considered as "blameless" by the skeptic, but which are clearly blameworthy. To counter this inward epistemic tendency, one must generate habits of discomfort regarding practices of inattentional injustice. Inspired by Ortega's view that our ignorance should make us feel uncomfortable, José Medina (2016) proposes an ethics and epistemology of discomfort centered on practices of resistance to systematic and operational ignorance regarding the exclusion or oppression of others, as well as insensitivity to injustice. He cites passages from Wittgenstein in which doubting our experiences of pain or other obvious aspects of daily life can only be achieved by a kind of self-blindness. Medina's proposal can naturally be understood as attention-based, with one caveat. Medina writes:

> Insensitivity is formed and maintained as a result of excessive self-trust and what is needed is not to energize the already overinflated will to believe, but rather, to redirect the will *not* to believe, so that it does not function outwards to eliminate or neutralize conflicting perspectives, but inwards to interrogate one's own perspective and to exercise critical self-distrust.
>
> (2016, 195)

Medina recommends solving inattentional blindness and active ignorance by turning inwards. This is contrary to the recommendation of Iris Murdoch (1971), who argues that what we need is to stop turning inwards, either by introspecting or by believing, so that we can genuinely *pay attention* to the world and its value. I will follow Murdoch in her criticism of inward reasoning, for reasons that will become clear in the next chapter. However, it is important to appreciate that the initial step that both Medina and Murdoch take is the same: we must move away from the escapist epistemology of belief if we are to succeed in improving our capacities for selection, thereby preventing epistemically and morally unjust blindness. This is not only compatible with Villoro's epistemology, but it is actually the required update his epistemology needs in order to effectively relate knowledge with freedom, epistemology and ethics. Regarding the anticolonial character of Villoro's philosophy, if the weak epistemology of inward skepticism is compatible with, or even supportive of, colonial thought, then Villoro's social epistemology is indeed deeply anticolonial.

References

Ariso, J. M. and Wagner, A. (2016), 'On Constraining Rationality and Revisiting the Logic of Beliefs: An Introduction', In Wagner, A. and Ariso, J. M. (eds.) (2016), *Rationality Reconsidered: Ortega y Gasset and Wittgenstein on Knowledge, Belief, and Practice*, Berlin Studies in Knowledge Research: De Gruyter (pp. 1–11).

Braithwaite, R. B. (1932–1933), The nature of believing, *Proceedings of the Aristotelian Society*, 33: 129–146.

Gettier, E. L. (1963), Is Justified True Belief Knowledge?, *Analysis*, 23(6): 121–3.

Greco, J. (2010), *Achieving Knowledge: A Virtue-Theoretic Account of Epistemic Normativity*, Cambridge: Cambridge University Press.

Hawthorne, J., Rothschild, D. and Spectre, L. (2016), Belief is weak, *Philosophical Studies*, 173(5): 1393–1404

Hurtado, G. (2003), ¿Saber sin verdad? Objeciones a un argumento de Villoro, *Crítica Revista Hispanoamericana de Filosofía*, 35(103): 121–134.

Hurtado, G. (2024), Una relectura de *Creer, saber, conocer*, *Diánoia*, 69(93): 233–246.

Lewis, C. I. (1946), *An Analysis of Knowledge and Valuation*, La Salle: Open Court.

Medina, J. (2016), 'On Refusing to Believe: Insensitivity and Self-Ignorance', In Wagner, A. and Ariso, J. M. (eds.) (2016), *Rationality Reconsidered: Ortega y Gasset and Wittgenstein on Knowledge, Belief, and Practice*, Berlin Studies in Knowledge Research: De Gruyter (pp. 187–200).

Moyal-Sharrock, D. and Pritchard, D. (2024), *Wittgenstein on Knowledge and Certainty*, Cambridge: Cambridge University Press.

Ornelas, J. (2017), 'Villoro, relativista malgré lui', In Stepanenko, P. (ed.), *Luis Villoro: conocimiento y emancipación. Homenaje póstumo en el Instituto de Investigaciones Filosóficas*, Mexico: UNAM.

Peirce, C. S. (1931), *The Collected Papers of Charles Sanders Peirce, eight vols*: *vols 1-6*, In C. Hartshorne and P. Weiss (eds.), Cambridge, Mass: Harvard University Press.

Schwitzgebel, E. (2002), A phenomenal, dispositional account of belief, *Noûs*, 36: 249–75.

Sosa, E. (2007), *Apt Belief and Reflective Knowledge, Volume 1: A Virtue Epistemology*, Oxford: Oxford University Press.

Sosa, E. (2009), *Apt Belief and Reflective Knowledge, Volume II: Reflective Knowledge*, Oxford: Oxford University Press.

Villoro, L. (1984), *José Ortega y Gasset*, Mexico: Fondo de Cultura Económica.

von Wright, G. H. (1982). *Wittgenstein*, Minneapolis: University of Minnesota Press.

Weinberg, J. M., Nichols, S. and Stich, S. (2001), Normativity and Epistemic Intuitions, *Philosophical Topics*, 29(1/2): 429–60.

Williamson, T. (2000), *Knowledge and its Limits*, Oxford: Oxford University Press.

Wittgenstein, L. (1969|1972), *On Certainty*, G. E. M. Anscombe and G. H. von Wright (eds.), G.E.M. Anscombe and D. Paul (trans.), New York: Harper.

6

The Figure and Mind of the World: Ideology and Collective Memory

Epistemology, ethics, and politics

To improve our attention to injustice and to the value of others, Medina and Murdoch advise reorienting our minds away from the solipsistic arrogance of belief. While their approaches seem incompatible, they have more in common than meets the eye. Murdoch, like Medina, is interested in moving away from belief and towards attentiveness, action, and discomfort in the presence of injustice. Murdoch understood that what constitutes the world and our capacity to navigate it is how our attention anchors us in it. She wrote that "our ability to act well 'when the time comes' depends partly, perhaps largely, upon the quality of our habitual objects of attention." (Murdoch, 1969, 56) According to Murdoch, attention imperceptibly "builds up the structures of value round about us." (Murdoch, 1964, 37). This *fabric of our being* is determined by our attention patterns.

But Murdoch, like Villoro, insists on "getting things right." Like Villoro, who requires an *objectively sufficient* condition for knowledge, Murdoch distinguishes attempt-attention from success-attention. Attempt-attention is an effort or intention to provide just and loving attention. Success-attention is the action of effectively displaying just and loving attention. One may see that something is wrong and still fail at displaying just and loving attention. There is a relation here not only to the reliability of a virtuous agent in displaying the right attention by looking at morally salient features, but also to meeting an objective standard for succeeding at this task by effectively displaying attention in action.

Just and loving attention is *externally driven*. One can be so self-absorbed and prejudiced that one fails completely to even see a morally significant feature in another person—their suffering or their isolation. Through habituation, one could become less self-absorbed and more able to see these features, but still be so inclined to judgment and belief in an inward fashion that one fails to genuinely appreciate them. But ultimately, one could succeed at genuinely appreciating and understanding the other person, and display a just and loving attention. Succeeding at loving attention, for Murdoch, should conduce to *action*: to doing the right thing. If I see someone in pain, and I start issuing judgments and beliefs about myself, I will not genuinely appreciate their situation and I will not act. Of course, the worst situation is when I am even incapable of seeing someone else's pain or distress. Attention anchors our reasoning and builds our capacities for acting in the right way, but we tend to blind ourselves to the reality of fellow human beings in a variety of ways. Belief and inward bias get in the way of just and loving attention, preventing us from unifying our epistemic and moral forces.

Since, as Murdoch says, "I can only choose within the world I can see," missing or ignoring morally salient features prevents us from even choosing between acting correctly or incorrectly—our freedom of choice is eliminated by blindness. But how can we become aware of these salient features if they are not even available to us because they are *imperceptible* to us? This is a central question in contemporary ethics and epistemology. From the first-person point of view it presents a monumental conundrum: I am blind to morally salient features, but all I have to go on is the way the world presents itself to me. So how could I be blamed for being blind to those features? Indeed, as the next section shows, a standard way of formulating internalism about epistemic justification affirms that I should be blameless for not seeing these features because all the evidence I can operate with depends on the world as seen by me.

To deal with this problem, Medina recommends resisting through experiencing discomfort about our own ignorance. This is an important attitudinal component that readjusts the way in which the subject sees the world, transforming blindness into sensitivity. But some external pressure seems to be necessary for this change to take place. In particular, without an objectively sufficient standard for the evaluation our own blindness, the prospect of adjusting our sensitivities to what is morally salient seems problematic. Thus, Medina's approach may turn out to be too subjectivist for Villoro and Murdoch. There must be something external and collective driving how the moral agent becomes disturbed. We will see that the key here is to *avoid turning inward*. However, an attitudinal adjustment is crucial for these three authors.

Since, for Villoro, the external pressures on our attentiveness cannot come from absolute truths and universal norms, we must appeal to concrete epistemic communities and their practices. Thus, a crucial part of the problem is that there is nothing beyond our practices and daily commitments that could cause discomfort on the basis of our ignorance, in good pragmatist fashion. Our attitudes and collective habits of inclusion or exclusion are the main source of what we end up seeing as salient or valuable. What we need to change, then, are our inward escapist routes, which keep us blind to injustices. According to Villoro's non-exclusion principle, we must change collective habits that constitute clear violations of epistemic and moral inclusion. The vitalistic element of experiencing discomfort when we are blind to moral salience can then be a kind of *attunement* with what we shouldn't ignore.

Collective belief can be one of the most powerful sources of exclusion and oppression. There is an inner pressure to conform to prevailing bodies of beliefs, for epistemic ease and also because of the social pressure to fit in. Villoro's epistemology is designed to combat ideology—collective belief that oppresses and maintains the status quo. In his book on belief and ideology (Villoro, 1985), *El concepto de ideología* (The concept of ideology), Villoro discusses Marx and Engel's notion of ideology, and then examines empirical evidence to explain the collective power of ideologies. Villoro highlights how motivational and doxastic attitudes are integrated, shaping the evaluative functions of our psychology, which generate an overall value-structure (Villoro, 1985, 101–6). He writes:

> These studies suffice to demonstrate the viability of our hypothesis: the concept of attitude can function as the intermediary link that allows for the connection of the social basis with collective systems of belief. Moreover, they provide the theoretical schema with a reference to observable facts, which allows for its confirmation or falsification [. . .]. The concept of *historical attitude* of a class or group would allow for the connection between the economic and social conditions and the ideologies of that group, thus providing a rational explanation to a historical process.
>
> (Villoro, 1985, 106–7)

As explained earlier, it is because of this attitudinal component of Villoro's epistemology that attention, in this case joint attention in the context of collective memory, is required to fully interpret its nature and scope. Ideologies clearly have an affective component. But their *purpose* is to keep a group blind with respect to certain facts, in order to exclude other groups. The rational explanations that ideologies provide turn inward, keeping the blind spots concerning moral salience firmly in place. A negative attitude produces collective blindness, a positive one produces engagement with what is morally salient. There is considerable friction and energy in this spectrum of collective negativity and positivity, manifesting in exclusion and inclusion. Collective ideological belief produces a *farce* that covers up and even justifies injustice.

Villoro has in mind a historical attitude central to Latin-American thought: the colonial rationale that explained and justified various forms of domination and exclusion throughout the continent. In the prologue to *The concept of ideology*, Villoro explains the thorny issue of how liberational movements in Latin America that challenged this colonial attitude, including Marxist ideologies, also fell into unreasonable justifications of violence. These counterbalancing historical attitudes are "unconscious gears of the same circle of irrationality that maintains oppression." (Villoro, 1985, 13) In Chapter 4, we characterized this phenomenon as the *invariance of structures of oppression across opposing ideologies*. Ideological thought is oppressive thought that excludes others in order to justify violence and injustice, rationalizing exclusion through structures of collective belief. Calling it libertarian, Marxist, or any other label, doesn't change the fact that the goal of collective ideological thought is to maintain the status quo and to keep the oppressed marginalized. Villoro writes,

> In both the violence of the dominators as well as in the most irrational forms of the forces of liberation we recognize the role of ideologies. Latin America is sick of ideological discourses. But the remedy is not the pure and simple negation of ideologies. To proclaim "the end of ideologies" when they still palpably dominate so many collective behaviors is the escape of an ostrich. The rational way is, on the contrary, to investigate what ideological thought consists in, in order to recognize it and clarify its function.
>
> (Villoro, 1985, 13)

One way of proclaiming the "end of ideologies" is by endorsing a universal theory of ethics and rationality according to eternal principles that must be followed so that the oppressed can be effectively liberated. Villoro's pragmatically driven philosophy criticizes this strategy, falling under what we now call a *non-ideal* theory, in epistemology, ethics, and political philosophy. To repeat a point made before, all we have to go on here are our practices of communication and recognition. We need to change ideological thought at this concrete and practical level. Otherwise, epistemic distortion can turn into collective psychosis. Inner bias and outer performance spin wildly into mutually supportive and *performative delusions*—a circle of irrationality that maintains oppression. The binary mind of belief-centered epistemology, *me* and *the world*, becomes dangerously theatrical. In extreme cases, this theatricality causes complete alienation. In his compelling analysis of the last years of the Soviet Union, Alexei Yurchak says,

> One common attempt to explain how ideological texts and rituals function in contexts dominated by unchallengeable authoritative

discourse whose meanings are not necessarily read literally is to assert
that citizens act "as if" they support these slogans and rituals in public,
while privately believing something different. Underlying this model
are theories of mimicry and simulation.

(Yurchak, 2006, 16)

In ideological contexts, honest assertions can only occur in complete
secrecy and privacy, if at all. Public assertions are highly choreographed,
and whether or not they are honest becomes *inconsequential*. Yurchak
opts for an alternative analysis in which subjects are not operating in
neatly circumscribed "spheres of action" but are rather interacting
in ways that make room for both the highly performative and the
incomplete or unpredictable. It is in the practices of the ideologically
oppressed, not in their heads, that one finds more nuanced explanations.
For example, by appealing to John Austin's analysis of *performatives*
we can analyze expressions that do something independently of the
intentions of the speakers—questions of sincerity and charity are, by
the very nature of this speech act, irrelevant. This is certainly a complex
issue, but the worst thing we can do in our analysis of ideology is to turn
inward. The ostrich buries its head in the sand of arrogant and solipsistic
belief. The price the anxious and skeptically driven epistemology of
belief pays for reflecting constantly on itself is to produce a theatrical
realm of political action governed by blind spots and biases that justify
ideological systems. Cooperative and reasonable communication
collapses under ideological thought.

The figure of the world and the mind of the world

Susanna Siegel's (2017) *The Rationality of Perception* defends a theory
of rationality that highlights the ideological role of collective belief.
Like Villoro's epistemology, Siegel's theory examines the role of valence
in epistemic states and attitudes. She analyses a problem for theories of
epistemic justification, which she calls "hijacked experience." To solve
this problem, she introduces the concept of *epistemic charge*, which

applies to experiences that can be positively or negatively impacted by inferential epistemic precursors. This allows Siegel to talk about processes that are very rarely discussed in the literature, such as those involved in epistemically downgraded or upgraded perceptual experiences, which prevent us from seeing salient features of the world—the kind of blindness that Murdoch and Medina also identify. This makes perception evaluative, and sensitive to features that are accentuated at the cost of others, making the whole world of perception a contested territory.

Like Villoro's approach, Siegel's proposal shows how epistemic justification is intimately related to social practices and evaluations. Although Villoro is more explicitly concerned with the task of combating epistemologies of domination, both Villoro and Siegel chart the social dimensions of the ethics of belief. The result, in Siegel's work, is that new conceptual possibilities are available. We can now talk about how *fearful seeing* forces us to ignore morally salient information, as well as evidence concerning basic perceptual features. Siegel describes the impact of negative or unjustified precursors on our conscious experiences, and on our epistemic capacities in general, as *farcical*. She writes,

> Whether it affects perception at the level of experience or not, an outlook can sustain itself through creating the appearances that the world is the way the outlook suggests it is. From the subject's point of view, her fear or suspicion is confirmed, or her desire satisfied, but this is a self-generated illusion [. . .]. A self-generated illusion of this kind is an epistemic problem. In theatrical terms, the problem is that perception becomes a farce, and the joke is on the perceiver.
>
> (Siegel, 2017, 4)

This farce is more powerful and crippling than the conscious belief that one is merely performing assertions one doesn't believe, as was practiced in the final years of the Soviet Union. But it has similar effects. One ends up in a theatrical situation in which unreliability or insincerity prevail. Siegel shows that applying a Bayesian approach to belief updates makes the farce pervasive (2017, 11). Again, the warning is that one must not turn inward. The solution to this problem cannot come from introspective insights because by their very nature, those insights are bound to reproduce the biases that keep creating and predicting outlooks that are farcical. The nature of evaluative perception demands an analysis of selection effects based on norms of attention (Siegel, 2017, 159). Ella Whitely (2024) has shown how discriminatory salience patterns of attention are *themselves* epistemically problematic. Collective patterns of attention based on farcical thought can have a powerful effect on the way the world appears to us.

Chapter 10 of Siegel's book focuses on what Villoro and philosophers from the Marxist tradition call *ideology*. Siegel's own terminology for ideology is "the problem of culturally normal belief" and she describes epistemic cultures as a kind of *mind of the world*. Villoro coins the term *figure of the world* in order to describe the kind of totality that Wittgenstein and Ortega identified with bedrock, hinge belief, or entrenched belief. Interestingly, Siegel's *mind of the world* is inspired by political sources, for example the writings of Frederick Douglass. She cites Douglass condemning the fact that on account of the instrumentalities of markets and bureaucracies that secured financial interests based on slavery, "they belittled our virtues and magnified our vices, and have made us odious in the eyes of the world." (Siegel, 2017, 195) The mind of the world is problematic because it entrenches belief regardless of whether it is epistemically justified or not. Siegel writes: "It became socially normal to believe that water from faucets was safe to drink, and it was socially normal under slavery to believe that blacks were only fit to be slaves. Social normality is a poor guide to well-foundedness." (Siegel, 2017, 195)

Beside the problem of hijacked experience, we also confront the problem of culturally entrenched belief. Since neither of these negative influences is evident through conscious introspection when we assess the evidential support for our beliefs, turning inward in search of a solution is hopeless. Siegel's important book makes this point abundantly clear. In the case of hijacked experiences, their negative charge reduces the epistemic value of the way we see the world from our conscious perspective. Culturally normal belief is even more insidious since it affects collective practices at all levels of societal organization. They are separate but mutually reinforcing pressures on our epistemic capacities. If turning inward is not a solution, then Villoro must be right in affirming that what we need to change is our concrete practices of communication through which we build epistemic and moral trust. This is as much a political problem as it is epistemic. The interface between individuals and their cultures is one that leaves a profound imprint in their doxastic attitudes, which from their perspective, is in no obvious way ill-founded. Siegel writes,

> There are important differences between the problem of hijacked experiences and the problem of culturally normal belief. In the case of hijacked experiences, the seemingly passive route to a hijacked experience turns out to be an irrational mental activity. In the case of culturally normal belief, in contrast, I've argued that the epistemically bad-making features are not located in the individual's mind. Instead, those features are located where the social frame puts them: in the factors that account for the normality of what's presumed.
>
> (Siegel, 2017, 196)

The factors that account for the normality of entrenched belief can be largely determined by epistemologies of oppression or domination. Siegel's analysis of hijacked experience is based on inference—an account of inferential cognition and rationality that is compatible with the view that attention plays key roles in shaping perception. Moreover, since inference occurs in an individual's mind, Siegel says that inference cannot explain the impact of the mind of the world on an individual. Attention at the individual and collective levels can provide a more thorough examination of these two negative influences and how they interface. Siegel's diagnosis of the problem is correct, and like Villoro, she emphasizes the importance of being constantly on guard against the pernicious influence of domination and exclusion. However, an analysis based on attention, rather than inference, allows for a deeper and more comprehensive theory of rationality, one in which Villoro's distinction between rationality and reasonableness is central. Regarding the oppressive role of ideologies, Villoro draws a useful distinction between the gnoseological and sociological aspects of belief in order to address the intricate problem of epistemic injustice produced by collective belief. In his discussion of ideology as an *instrument of domination*, Villoro writes,

> Thus far, the concept of ideology has referred to a basic false belief. But the same theory that demonstrates its falsehood should explain why we come to believe in it. [...] The explanation of ideological beliefs should be made in terms of their conditioning by the existing social relations, and by the social function they fulfill. In fact, on the one hand, our ideas are emanations or products of a social reality; on the other hand, they play a role in it. To the *gnoseological* connotation of ideology as false consciousness, we must add a *sociological* connotation. The latter cannot be derived from the former by simple logical analysis. Indeed, from the falsehood or lack of justification of a belief one cannot deduce anything about its relations with a society, and vice versa.
>
> (Villoro, 1985, 53–4)

Why fall into theatricality when the consequences are exclusion and oppression? How to explain the fact that many people believe in ideologies, even when confronted with evidence of their falsehood? Without an analysis of the role false or farcical belief plays in a society, the examination of ideologies, merely as false belief, is insufficient and inadequate. Through ideologies, domination is *imposed* in ways that leave epistemic agents with no viable options for resistance, and this imposition fundamentally includes, as will be discussed in the next section, our *linguistic practices*. There is also enormous pressure to conform, despite our best epistemic instincts. The social function ideologies fulfill is to exclude the vulnerable and privilege the dominant group—a valuable political goal for those in power. Once the farce is about how to impose exclusion through the threat of mental and physical harm, collective false belief takes on a different, non-epistemic dimension.

Epistemic domination causes a kind of *collective gaslighting* of our agency and autonomy. We cannot communicate in plain and sincere terms, we cannot assert and cooperate, we cannot trust each other, and we can only follow those that look like us or are like us. Worse, we permanently fall into a situation of doubt regarding our own capacities for communicating effectively and truthfully. A farcical existence of hopelessness takes hold of our lives, dominating our actions and speech. The collective energy of the public sphere dissipates into atomical fragments that can be easily controlled, commodified, and manipulated. The theater of communal ideological performances maintains structures of power. It is a dark kind of pretense, which unlike mere entertainment, deeply weakens our epistemic and moral agency. The gnoseological aspect of ideology concerns how you *orient* your epistemic life—badly, since you are being manipulated through falsehood. The sociological aspect concerns what ideology *does to you*—your agency becomes compromised and either you act immorally and erroneously because you perpetrate and enforce ideologies in your own interest, or you act theatrically because you are the victim of collective gaslighting.

However, ideologies have to be "true" enough, in order to convince people of their plausibility as guides for action. What could this mean, given the role that falsehood plays in justifying domination? Here, Villoro's analysis of Ortega proves useful. Ideologies become entrenched by turning belief that should be open for inquiry into a *bedrock of domination*. One feels powerless when confronted with such entrenched forms of collective oppression. We accept ideologies because they offer us a plausible way of navigating structures of domination, at least safely enough—one must distinguish their being *plausible* from their being *true*. Moreover, they present us with *rational*, albeit *unreasonable*, ways of structuring our beliefs. Legal systems that enforced slavery were rational, yet deeply unreasonable. Thus, Villoro's analysis of ideologies is very helpful in explaining their rational appeal as well. The sociological aspect of ideologies identified by Villoro escapes our inward capacities for reflection, and it is largely invisible to the conscious mind. Otherwise, it would be difficult to explain how ideologies get such a powerful grip on our minds. One of the most important sources of the strength of this grip is social conformity to political structures and to collective identities that shape ideologies.

Amia Srinivasan (2020) has lucidly examined this important aspect of ideology (what Villoro calls its *sociological conception*) in her criticism of epistemic internalism about justification. Srinivasan argues that internalism has deeply negative normative consequences for our moral and social reasoning, thus agreeing with Villoro's imploration to avoid turning inward in our epistemic assessments, in order to achieve reasonable rationality. Internalism is, roughly, the view that the conditions for justification are dependent exclusively on the conscious awareness or mental access to evidence by subjects. Externalists deny this claim. A key issue that Srinivasan explores is how the social cues that make salient structures and practices of oppression are largely unconscious. She calls our capacity to pay attention to these features, despite our consciously reflective limitations, a "subconscious sensitivity," which partly explains why externalism and standpoint epistemology are not only plausible alternatives to internalism, but also preferrable for normative reasons.

Srinivasan says that subjects who clearly *know* about socially salient features regarding oppression that they can identify reliably because of their position as oppressed in a social structure, depend on attention-like capacities that guide them through their social realities. In describing one of her examples concerning racism, she says that the subject has "no awareness, introspective or otherwise, of how her subconscious racism-detection mechanism works." Because of this, she "just knows" because her subconscious sensitivity allows her to know about these salient features of a situation of exclusion in a non-lucky way, attributable to her capacities as agent. She is *attuned* to the truth not by accident, but because of her abilities (Srinivasan, 2020, 396). On an internalist account, in contrast, the subject doesn't know, and she is not even justified in her belief concerning racism.

From an empirical point of view, our attentive and epistemic capacities can indeed be dissociated from our conscious awareness (Montemayor and Haladjian, 2015). Villoro's examination of the empirical literature on traits and attitude formation through habits of thought and sensitivities can be updated with these new insights. Villoro is interested in a pragmatic approach to this kind of positional externalist view. Thus, one can easily provide empirical support for a view like Srinivasan's. But is her view plausible from a *normative* point of view? How to reconcile these unconscious sensitivities with the freedom and agency of epistemic and moral subjects? Srinivasan endorses a Marxist view of standpoint epistemology. However, Villoro warns us about endorsing agendas, including Marxist ideological thought, that are imposed through social structures in a way that leaves ample room for practices of exclusion, such as the political situations of theatricality described above. Attentional sensitivities and attunement are critical for our linguistic practices to be successful and to help us coordinate our actions, toward liberation or oppression. Communication cannot depend on the endorsement of a specific political view about class or the oppressed—it requires a broader theoretical framework concerning the nature of our linguistic practices.

Independently of the debate between internalists and externalists, both Srinivasan's and Siegel's approaches are valuable examinations of the kind of ethical and epistemic issues that inform Villoro's social epistemology. Both of their approaches, like Villoro's own approach, would be better off and more complete with an explicit formulation of attention-based capacities involved in social attunement. Attention provides a powerful way of guaranteeing that our cognitive capacities do not merely turn inwards. The views of these two authors are the closest to Villoro's social epistemology, particularly his analysis of ideology, that one can find in contemporary analytic epistemology. The inward turn, toward conscious reflection, inference or belief, is erroneous and normatively problematic when confronting ideology. It can mischaracterize reality and foster arrogance. This issue, as we are about to see, extends all the way to how a specific language relates to a concrete community.

But not all kinds of internalism are incompatible with Villoro's approach. Zoë Johnson King's (2022) internalist interpretation of the cases presented by Srinivasan focuses on success conditions and entitlements, and is thus compatible with Villoro's pragmatic approach. The performance-normativity requirement that subjects should have a sense of their own *reliability* in their attempts at knowing and communicating fits well with the attitude-based and attentional understanding of the abilities and dispositions of epistemic agents articulated by Villoro. In both cases, members of an epistemic community must detect who is just lucky and who deserves credit. This "flagging" condition on good sources of evidence and information is the bread and butter of performance-normativity approaches, or virtue theories, in ethics and epistemology.

I agree with Johnson King that what we need is an achievement-based epistemology, and that endorsing it does not entail the acceptance of the structural and radical kind of externalism defended by Srinivasan. But such a virtue epistemic view is best articulated as a pragmatic one (Fairweather and Montemayor, 2017) like Villoro's, rather than a classically internalist one, with its assumptions about individual conscious reflection and supervenience conditions on mental content. Because of this, it is difficult to classify Villoro as either radically externalist or purely internalist. For Villoro, however, our practices for communication are what ultimately matters. So even if one applies an internalist gloss to what is basically a virtue epistemic or pragmatic account, Villoro's contribution to social epistemology is to firmly hold the view that our notions of knowledge and epistemic justification should reflect the pragmatic commitment to concrete social practices of non-exclusion. In this respect, the structural and Marxist view offered by Srinivasan fits better with the overall goal of Villoro's social epistemology, and illuminates Villoro's distinction between the gnoseological and sociological conceptions of ideology, with the caveat that Villoro would not endorse a Marxist framework. There is a tight relation between the figure of the world and the mind of the world. Systemic oppression depends on a negative collective outlook. Turning inward only reinforces it. Ideologies appeal to our worst attitudes—anger, frustration, and prompt-induced theatrical performance. We follow them by rote, and they create social dissonance: valuable goals are not prioritized while selfish and exclusionary agendas are strictly enforced.

Villoro, Rawls, and the politics of language

John Rawls's deeply influential work informs the political philosophy of Villoro. Rawls's theory of justice and his views on political philosophy loom large in Villoro's examination of justice, freedom, and human rights. In *Los retos de la sociedad por venir* (2007—one of Villoro's latest works) Villoro speaks highly of Rawls's theory, describing it as the best attempt at providing a deontological account of justice, as opposed to teleological views. Villoro even affirms that any contemporary analysis of justice must begin with a careful examination of Rawls's important theory (Villoro, 2007, 64). Previously, in *El Poder y el Valor* (Power and value) Villoro refers to Rawls's theory of justice as the "most accomplished attempt" at providing a neo-Kantian view of justice (Villoro, 1997, 224). We thus have interpretative and comparative motivations to examine the influence of Rawls on Villoro. We have an interpretative motivation because Villoro relies heavily on Rawls's ideas in developing his own view. We also have a contrastive reason to examine Rawls's influence on Villoro because it is useful to compare Villoro's non-ideal theory with the best-known ideal theory of justice in the English-speaking world.

Just as Villoro's epistemology is objectively constrained because he opposes views that dispense with content and truth (pragmatically understood), his ethics and political views aim at capturing *real values*, as opposed to *subjective states of mind* or emotions. In this, he is also a pragmatist. For instance, C. I. Lewis and John Dewey thought that the considerations that apply to the determination of truth concerning our best models to deal with the future also apply to justice and the good life—our ethical principles are also part of our overall strategy to cope with the future. But Villoro goes beyond pragmatism in his political and ethical views. I shall argue that he proposes a *capability approach* to justice that differs from Rawls's deontological account in key respects.

With Rawls, Villoro shares a strong interest in establishing normative standards that become generally accepted without becoming ideological or oppressive. The way in which Rawls proposes to achieve this goal is through the practice of reasoning through opposing views in order to achieve a reasonable and coherent perspective—the method of *reflective equilibrium*. In his theory of justice, Rawls postulates an epistemic state of ignorance designed to guarantee a kind of ethical neutrality, which allows us to agree on general principles with enough content to create a framework in which equality prevails. Central to Rawls's proposal is the view that ideological principles or agendas should be avoided in this process. Such a perspective can be interpreted as a *constructivist* approach:

> Rawls is a constructivist about justice. He held that a just society is one whose basic arrangements would be endorsed by persons in the Original Position. The Original Position is defined in terms of what such persons *do not know*. Roughly, they know general facts about the society they are in (such as the proportion of rich to poor) but they do not know particular facts about themselves (such as whether they are rich and talented or poor and prospectless).
>
> (Dancy, 2013, 746, my emphasis)

The Original Position (OP) is too abstract and general to accommodate Villoro's basic conditions of concreteness in circumstances and historical situations required for the negative route to justice and non-exclusion. But Villoro is keenly aware that any alternative to the OP, which allows for the clear formulation of general principles of justice, must be provided, such that there is no risk of falling into ideological thinking or moral relativism and skepticism. Rawls is also aware that an abstract condition concerning ignorance cannot provide the whole story of human morality and the search for justice. Subjects in the OP do not know if they belong to the powerful centers of knowledge production, or to the periphery, where exclusion prevails. A direct appeal to our rational and communicational capacities is needed here. Rawls proposes that, through reflective equilibrium, we must assess substantial views on the good life in all of their particularity and concreteness. This effort cannot, therefore, be interpreted in constructivist terms:

> Rawls is not a constructivist about the right and the wrong. His view seems to be that an action is wrong if it is forbidden by the best view we can come to about which sorts of actions are right and which wrong, that is, by the most defensible set of moral principles. The most defensible set of principles is that set which best fits our considered moral judgements about particular cases and any other general views and theories we might accept (e.g., in sociology and psychology). This is not a form of constructivism, as I see it, because it holds that an action is right if it is right according to the best overall view about which sorts of action are right. Rightness itself is not constructed here.
>
> (Dancy, 2013, 747)

We need not agree completely with this characterization of Rawls's nuanced theory in order to appreciate the importance of this distinction between the abstract standpoint of ignorance we assume to achieve consensus regarding principles of justice (the OP), and the particularity of the practices through which we engage each other in concrete situations (our substantive views on the good). Rawls eventually distinguished two senses of rationality involved in this distinction, calling them, as Villoro did, the *rational* and the *reasonable* (Rawls, 1980). Before examining the similarities and differences between Rawls's and Villoro's take on this distinction, it is important to appreciate the complexity that is at stake here, particularly concerning how rationality depends on specific mental capacities that must align with principles and values in a non-trivial way. The metaethical problem of how our rational capacities for choice and strategic reasoning become wider in scope and normative domain in order to arrive at principles of morality and justice is related to how we cognitively converge on the good. Historically, substantial views on value realism have been replaced by expressivist or non-cognitive views, and then back again in what seems to be an impasse. Jonathan Dancy contextualizes this issue as follows:

> The twentieth century began with what was a broadly intuitionistic consensus on meta-ethical issues. After the Second World War this was supplanted by forms of anti-realism, of which the most dominant was expressivist. Intuitionism managed eventually to claw its way back into the picture, but only as one among several live options, none of which enjoys any sort of dominance.
>
> (Dancy, 2013, 747)

Despite the back and forth between the opposite views of intuitionism and expressivism, Rawls's theory remains deeply influential, partly because the distinction between the reasonable and the rational provides a way of keeping the theory of justice robustly in place while changes in substantial views play out. Regardless of what one ends up saying about value and moral truth, rational principles must inform how justice is defined. The crucial relationship between truth and justice, as well as between rationality and freedom, should not completely depend on the cognitivist versus non-cognitivist views. Besides his constructivist account of justice and his formulation of a more substantial view of the good, Rawls's distinction between rational and reasonable, like Villoro's, addresses the profound differences that exist between abstract principles of rationality and the practices of cooperation that lead to consensus:

> To justify the design of the original position, Rawls reaches beyond the theory of rational choice to an argument from reflective equilibrium, claiming that our acceptance of the constraints of the original position coheres with our moral interests and our moral psychology [. . .]. The particular, political use of strategic rationality is justified not as itself strategically rational, but because that particular use is rational in a broader sense. In his later work, beginning with the Dewey Lectures, the term that Rawls uses for rationality in this broader sense is "the reasonable."
>
> (Krasnoff, 2014, 693)

Rawls expands on the notion of the reasonable by defining it as a conception of "the fair terms of cooperation," or terms that everyone may be reasonably expected to accept, in order to share burdens and benefits (Rawls, 1999, 316). As Larry Krasnoff points out, for this definition not to be circular, Rawls needed to define the reasonable as a quality of persons with a certain kind of *cooperative outlook*. Indeed, Rawls says in *Political Liberalism* that reasonable persons are not "moved by the general good as such but desire for its own sake a social world in which they, as free and equal, can cooperate with others on terms all accept" (Rawls, 1993a, 50). Because cooperation is the foundation of any kind of effort toward arriving at a specific set of principles for fairness, Rawls says that the reasonable presupposes and subordinates the rational (Rawls, 1999, 317). Rawls expresses his commitment to political liberalism by defining reasonable persons as cooperative without being moved by a specific and substantial view of the general good. Thus, Rawls came to reject the assumption that humans have a universal capacity for moral reasoning that leads them to accept reasonable principles, as a matter of human psychology, replacing it with his notion of an *overlapping consensus*. This issue is related to the linguistic analogy examined in Chapter 2, which Rawls suggested in *A Theory of Justice*. Interestingly, this debate about rationality, cooperation, and differences in ideology is currently playing itself out in philosophy of language, with deep implications for social epistemology, as I explain below.

More details are needed to get a full picture of the role of rationality in Rawls's legal and political philosophy, which would take us beyond the goals of this chapter. What is crucial to highlight here is that in our current ideological environment of polarization and identity politics, trust and cooperation cannot be taken for granted, let alone any overlap of agreement or consensus that is *genuine*, rather than theatrical. Inequality and injustice prevail in our society. The risk of abandoning the assumptions of the Rawlsian framework concerning rationality and reasonableness is that we fall into skepticism, despair, and choreographic outrage. Villoro starts with concrete inequalities and injustices, in accordance with his *negative route* approach. But he certainly wants to oppose, like Rawls, the political despair, polarization, and mistrust that skepticism and ideological thinking produce.

Richard Rorty (2007) proposed, on the basis of a comparison between the views of Rawls, Jürgen Habermas, and Annette Baier (among others), that justice should be understood as a larger kind of loyalty. What is relevant for our purposes regarding Rorty's proposal is his comparison of Rawls and Habermas in terms of their notions of *strategic* and *communicative* rationality, which resonate with the concepts of rationality and reasonableness. Both Rawls and Habermas insist on the importance of distinguishing a broader kind of rationality that serves as a condition for substantial exchanges among subjects, including the strategies they use in pursuing their interests. It is a kind of rationality that concerns procedure and cooperation, rather than substance:

> This definition of practical reason suggests that there may be only a verbal difference between Rawls' and Habermas' positions. For Habermas' own attempt to substitute "communicative reason" for "subject-centered reason" is itself a move toward substituting "how" for "what." Subject-centered reason is a source of truth, truth somehow coeval with the human mind. Communicative reason is not a source of anything, but simply the activity of justifying claims by offering arguments rather than threats.
>
> (Rorty, 2007, 51)

According to Rorty, Rawls and Habermas focus on "the difference between persuasion and force, rather than, as Plato and Kant did, on the difference between two parts of the human person – the good rational part and the dubious passionate or sensual part" (ibid.). They both abandon the notion of reason as *authority* and substitute the notion of rationality "as what is present whenever people communicate, whenever they try to justify their claims to one another, rather than threatening each other" (ibid.). This communication requirement for a theory of public reason is also fundamental, as we have seen, for Villoro's principle of non-exclusion in epistemology and ethics. Rorty explains how this emphasis on what Villoro calls reasonable communication and rationality, based on our practices for reason-giving, brings the perspectives of Rawls and Habermas closer together:

> The similarities between Rawls and Habermas seem even greater in the light of Rawls' endorsement of Thomas Scanlon's answer to the "fundamental question why anyone should care about morality at all", namely that "we have a basic desire to be able to justify our actions to others on grounds that they could not reasonably reject – reasonably, that is, given the desire to find principles that others similarly motivated could not reasonably reject.
>
> (ibid.)

Our practices for reason-giving are impossible without a robust convergence on what is true and what is just that depends on cooperation, rather than the arrogant authority of our individual reasoning. Otherwise, it would be impossible to justify our actions with reasons that others could not rationally reject. Rorty says parenthetically that Donald Davidson showed that any group of subjects that communicate through language share an enormous number of beliefs and desires, which guarantees a very substantial overlap among different cultures, making the idea that people can live in different silos or separate worlds incoherent (Rorty, 2007, 53). Rawls (1993a, 1993b), however, says that reasonable people would agree to conditions of communication and sociability that are roughly in accordance with the *basic rights* accepted in the West. Villoro agrees with Rawls in constraining political theory with human rights, but he would disagree, like Habermas (1993), with Rawls's ahistorical approach (this issue regarding historicism and value as defined by the West was the origin of Habermas's criticism of Rawls's notion of basic rights).

I think Rorty is right in mentioning Davidson's views on language in this context. Davidson's work is very useful in interpreting Villoro's notion of non-exclusion, as I argued in Chapter 2. It may also be useful to interpret the debate between Rawls and Habermas. In particular, a fresh look into Villoro's pragmatic approach to this issue may elucidate the way in which Rawls and Habermas rejected the conception of reason as a source of authority. In any case, there is clearly substantial agreement between Rawls and Villoro concerning the need to distinguish the rational and the reasonable, as a foundational distinction concerning the nature of rationality and the importance of genuine cooperation, as opposed to mere social coordination.

The first major point of disagreement between Rawls and Villoro concerns the character of the social dispositions and attunements that Villoro requires for his conception of a positively or negatively charged *attitude toward values*, which he uses in his work in epistemology and political philosophy. This notion is deeply related to the anchoring function of reason, examined in previous chapters. I argued that it is easier to interpret this notion as involving attention rather than merely beliefs and desires, so the overlapping consensus among subjects must be guaranteed through a more complex process than merely belief and desire "matching." A second and related difference between these authors is that Rawls's overlapping consensus is still too idealized for Villoro, partly because it is dependent on overlapping convictions among equals that are not equal in reality, and therefore, on conditions that may quickly turn ideological. Villoro avoids this problem with his negative route to justice. Injustices are always concrete, certainly concrete enough for those who suffer them, and they are visible to other subjects willing to attend to them. Villoro (1997) argues that a sufficiently objective criterion for the reality of what is valuable is *its absence*, which is felt differently by diverse groups and cultures across geographies and historical moments (the next chapter elaborates this criterion).

Villoro's original take on the rational and the reasonable through the negative route is explicitly historical and critical of the West as the sole model of enlightenment and basic rights that cannot be compromised. Appealing to Western standards in an abstract way, as if they were enshrined perpetually, still seems to operate under the assumption of rationality as the authority of the reasonable person who embraces, but also is allowed to enforce, Western values. Given the morally reprehensible past of the colonial West, clearly visible in Latin America, the notion of cooperation should not be framed exclusively in terms of the West and its abstract formulation of basic rights. Villoro's negative route to justice is designed to achieve this goal.

However, there is much in common between Villoro and Rawls. A crucial agreement among them is the centrality of sincerity, cooperation, and truth in ethical theory. This is an intricate issue, for instance, because Rawls's notion of a reasonable person is precisely one that never imposes the truth on those who disagree. But Rawls clearly has linguistic cooperation and trustworthy assertion in mind when he talks about reasonable social cooperation—his view about not imposing a group's perspective on another is not an endorsement of epistemic skepticism, but an invitation to eliminate sources of conflict and skepticism that impede social trust. This broader notion of rationality that reasonable persons must pursue, which is constitutive of *public reasoning*, becomes salient in John Harsanyi's views on utilitarianism and rational choice. Commenting on the limits of the utilitarian account, Harsanyi writes,

> I think the utilitarian theory I have described in principle covers all interpersonal aspects of morality. But I do not think it covers *all* morality. There are some very important moral obligations it fails to cover because they are matters of individual morality and of individual rationality. Perhaps the most important such obligation is that of intellectual honesty, that is, the duty to seek the truth and to accept the truth as far as it can be established—regardless of any possible positive or negative social utility this truth may have. (Telling the truth to others may be constrained by tact, respect for other people's feelings, or commitments to secrecy, etc. But admitting the truth to ourselves is not.)

(Harsanyi, 1982, 62)

Rawls and Villoro would characterize this obligation as our duty to engage in public reasoning, rather than an individual duty to oneself. But the main point Harsanyi is making here is perfectly compatible with Rawls's and Villoro's characterization of the reasonable as non-strategic and cooperative rationality, constrained by *public standards*. Honesty and sincerity are basic assumptions of public reasoning that cannot easily be taken for granted. Our collective efforts to communicate effectively are currently being challenged by the attention economy and social media. Publicly pursuing the truth is the only remedy we have against ideological and strategic thinking. The dangers of ideology are becoming worse with the radical polarization of our times. Instead of sincerity and solidarity we have created silos of information where the only thing that grows is suspicion and tribal thinking. According to Villoro, public reasoning is the opposite of ideological thinking. For him, the absence of truth is as corrosive to the social fabric as the absence of justice, and this absence is sufficiently objective to become the target of our collective efforts to eliminate injustice. Our practices of communication and public reasoning must be sincere and cooperative—ideological thinking is fueled by suspicion and skepticism, which fosters a lazy kind of dishonesty. Harsanyi writes,

> Intellectual honesty requires us to accept even very unpleasant truths rather than withdraw into a dream world or a fool's paradise based on self-deception. It also requires us to accept wholeheartedly the truth that we are not alone in this world but rather share a common human nature with many millions of others. Acceptance of this particular truth is, of course, not merely a matter of theoretical rationality; rather, it is also the intellectual basis of all social morality.
>
> (ibid.)

The basic conditions for sincere, cooperative, and truth-seeking communication are indeed the intellectual foundation of all morality. Commenting on the view that morality is a device for our mutual protection, Thomas Scanlon explains that for a contractualist view, the opposite is the case, because the idea of agreement is not a means of securing protection, but rather what we can reasonably agree on is what morality is *about* (Scanlon, 1982, 128). This of course, as we have seen, extends beyond the contractualist view to any view about the foundations of morality. These conditions are also behind the Rawlsian notion of *primary goods* as essential requirements for justice and rational cooperation. Primary goods include basic liberties like freedom of thought and consciousness, movement, choice of occupation, basic health, income, and wealth. Villoro articulates this notion of basic goods as fundamental *needs* that must be satisfied for individuals to be respected as persons, so that they can survive and flourish. Rawls explains why primary goods are not merely the theoretical consequences of a preference-based analysis or utility calculation, because they concern a foundational moral and practical problem that must be addressed by any theory of justice:

> The use of primary goods is not a makeshift which better theory can replace, but a reasonable social practice which we try to design so as to achieve the workable agreement required for effective and willing social cooperation among citizens whose understanding of social unity rests on a conception of justice.
>
> (Rawls, 1982, 185)

As it should be clear by now, there are substantial similarities between Rawls's and Villoro's political philosophies, including the constraint of pursuing primary goods in a communicational context of trust and cooperation. The similarities break down, however, when we consider the conditions for achieving consensus in each of their theories. For Rawls, these conditions are assumed to be those accepted by reasonable subjects, who converge on guaranteeing the set of freedoms labeled as "civil and political rights" in the West. For Villoro, by contrast, no such conditions can be assumed or taken for granted, and the only way to assure that there are conditions for reasonable consensus is to start with the elimination of concrete epistemic and ethical injustices (Villoro's negative route).

The nature of the conditions for consensus and communication is becoming a hotly debated issue in the philosophy of language, including the conditions underlying the very notion of propositional *content*, or neutral content, which requires speakers to non-luckily converge on a consensus about meanings for basic communication to take place. Evaluations of whether a proposition is true or false without qualifications seem impossible without the notion of neutral content.

Politics and attention are at the center of this debate, echoing the differences between ideal and non-ideal theories in ethics, as the views of Rawls and Villoro illustrate. Beaver and Stanley (2023) defend a revisionist theory of language that begins with conditions of asymmetry, where people have imperfect access to information and their capacities for cooperation are shaped by their political identities and group-oriented attention routines. Like Villoro, they use a negative and non-ideal methodological point as an initial assumption regarding speakers' concrete conditions.

It is indeed very rare to find ourselves in conditions of sincerity and symmetry in contemporary conversational settings. Commercialization, but also polarization, now prevail in our communicative exchanges, which have become notoriously strategic and manipulative. So there is considerable plausibility to this non-ideal approach to the philosophy of language. Beaver and Stanley argue, for instance, against the ideal assumptions underlying the Gricean maxims concerning truth, cooperation, symmetry, and sincerity, maintaining that communicative exchanges never take place in conditions of sincerity as a default. Similar to the view endorsed by non-ideal ethical theories that there cannot be a situation like the OP, Beaver and Stanley's non-ideal philosophy of language excludes idealized conditions for sincerity. In the spirit of Villoro's social epistemology and ethics, non-ideal theorists of communication must start from conditions of injustice and asymmetry. About the general contours of Beaver and Stanley's theory, Elisabeth Camp (2024) writes,

> When we step back, Beaver and Stanley's theory of meaning contrasts in provocative and productive ways with the orthodox theory. Meaning for them is *scalar* (defined in terms of degrees, as opposed to sharp categories); *perspectival* (defined in terms of holistic cognitive, affective, and behavioural associative networks, as opposed to discrete, truth-conditional, propositional information); *social* (defined in terms of collective states, as opposed to individual reflective beliefs); and *dynamic* (defined in terms of local and global context-change potentials, as opposed to static, abstract propositions).
>
> (Camp, 2024, 4)

The resemblance between this non-ideal approach to language and Villoro's social epistemology is striking, since these are all aspects that Villoro highlights about the essential conditions for reasonable action and communication. An *attentional* theory is needed here to explain these features. Similar to Villoro, the non-ideal approach does not make the achievement of reasonable communication dependent on sharp categories of universal truth or falsehood, access to abstract rules or meanings, or ideal conditions of symmetry. Rather, reasonable communication is achieved through the elimination of concrete impediments and asymmetries that are local and dependent on the perspective of speakers in a dynamic political environment.

However, there is a need for some notion of *correctness* in any theory of communication because a theory of meaning plays a *normative role* that cannot be explained by sensitivities and regularities alone. Here Villoro would strongly disagree with Beaver and Stanley's account, as would Ramsey and Wittgenstein. Camp writes: "As Wittgenstein taught us, any adequate theory of anything like meaning must explain how things can go *wrong*, understood not just as variation from a typical case but as a kind of failure," including cases where language is violent and harmful (Camp, 2024, 5). The advantage of Beaver and Stanely's approach is that it is value-laden, and it starts from a realistic and historically situated standpoint of asymmetry that acknowledges the pervasiveness of bias and injustice. Strategic and insincere habits of communication are indeed critical in shaping practices of oppression and injustice. We should not abandon this key insight by Beaver and Stanley. At the same time, a merely descriptive and causal analysis of the collective dynamics of attentional sensitivities, no matter how useful or accurate, cannot provide the conditions for correctness in reasonable communication, for either knowledge or justice, that Villoro demands:

> Beaver and Stanley's descriptions of these correlations, sensitivities, and behaviours are themselves highly abstracted and idealized. But they do not yet deliver a criterion of correctness, whether couched in terms of truth, utility, justice, or any other value.
>
> (Camp, 2024, 5)

Rational reconstructions like those required by the principle of charity are not mere idealizations, they are the foundation of our practices of mutual recognition and cooperation. Non-ideal theories must be compatible with reason-giving, as Rorty says. Non-ideal theories are indeed more realistic, and as Beaver and Stanley demonstrate, they can be given a solid scientific foundation. However, accounting for the normative component of non-ideal theories is one of the main reasons why attention is so fundamental. Attention must have correctness conditions: one must be able to distinguish ideological uses of collective attention from genuine uses of attentive cooperation. Therefore, a non-ideal approach to communication must be more explicitly based on attention habits, rather than statistical regularities, as Camp asserts. Crucially, attention can provide clear normative standards for correctness conditions in both epistemology and ethics, as I have argued. In this respect, Jessica Keiser's (2023) non-ideal theory of language based on *attention-direction*, on which Beaver and Stanley partly rely, is preferable. As she says, what we do when we communicate is, "first and foremost, to draw one another's attention to contents" (Keiser, 2023, 89). An attention-based view at the heart of the foundations of non-ideal communication avoids all the pitfalls concerning unreliability and mere statistical harmonization, and it can also provide a solid normative foundation, in terms of a virtue or performance-normativity approach (Fairweather and Montemayor, 2017).

Camp's point can be further developed through Villoro's distinction between the gnoseological and sociological aspects of ideology. We need normative criteria for the kinds of achievements or failures of linguistic agents and their attunements in conditions of cooperation. We also need normative constraints for the kind of social goals underlying communicative harmonization and political identification. Both require *non-lucky and attentive convergence* toward meanings (Fairweather and Montemayor, 2023) and social practices of inclusion or oppression grounded on such convergence. Rationality and neutral content must play a role in a non-ideal theory of communication. Neutral content depends on how we reliably converge on meaning, which can be understood as the gnoseological aspect of the fixation of beliefs in a communicational context and their influence on our epistemic outlook. The sociological aspect of this process concerns what this outlook entails in terms of social action, whether we cooperate with or manipulate others: who we trust and who we exclude. These are indeed situations of asymmetry, but these sociological components of ideology do not necessarily permeate the conditions governing the gnoseological aspects of communication, which are fundamental for determining correctness conditions. Consider here the distinction, based on the example by Silverstein examined in Chapter 4, between first- and second-order assertability.

Villoro's key insight is that the only way to connect freedom with knowledge is through reason-giving practices of communication, with mutual cooperation as the paradigm of reasonable communication, even if this paradigmatic situation is rarely achieved in practice. Neutral content in conditions of cooperation helps us distinguish lies and manipulative information from genuine cooperation and sincerity. We cannot eliminate this from a theory of language. Unlike Stanley and Beaver, Villoro assumes that truthful and cooperative communication plays a primordial role in the eradication of injustice. This is similar to Rawls. It is about *how* we get to achieve consensus and public reason through shared meaning where Rawls and Villoro differ.

Collective memory and collective attention

Since, according to Villoro, concrete contexts, relations, and structures of asymmetry determine the sources of injustice that must be eliminated, then a proper appreciation of the history of these sources of injustice is an important aspect of the systematic application of the principle of non-exclusion to our societies. Moreover, an explanation of the sociological aspect of ideologies fundamentally depends on a historical approach. What manipulative and false systems of belief do to us socially—where they locate us, how they force us into certain groups—

is largely shaped by historical processes that determine these manipulative practices across time. The kind of resonance and attention-based theory that is now becoming popular in philosophy of language appeals explicitly to these historical determinants of group-identity and social salience. Since social salience depends on collective sensitivities, Villoro's strand of historicism also appeals to collective forms of attention and responsibility.

For Villoro, the methodologies required to pursue a negative route to ethical and epistemic justice require a non-idealized, yet anti-skeptical version of what is reasonable. In particular, the historicity of non-idealized contexts of action implies the interconnection and articulation of *multiple identities* or cultures of engagement. Overlapping ideologies can powerfully articulate a cultural bedrock of domination. Reasonable, as opposed to rational, communication demands encountering "the other," no matter how alien we might find them, on their own terms. As Rawls proposed, we can assume that there will be enough commonality for the cooperation needed to identify areas of overlapping consensus. But, for Villoro, this assumption should never be interpreted as a guarantee that *our standards* of rationality will, or should, universalize as the paradigm of "the reasonable person."

Villoro turned to Zapatismo and, more generally, to the multi-ethnicity of Latin-American cultures, with vibrant indigenous communities, in an attempt to begin a national effort in reasonable communication that would engage substantially with collective memory and history. Chapter 1 narrated how Villoro's philosophical interests concerning Zapatista culture were in line with his earliest work on indigenous people and cultural identity, converging toward the later part of his life with his political activism. In an article on Latin-American identity, Villoro (2022) argues that art is frequently contested territory, a place where a powerful group imposes its standards of practice for creation and appreciation at the cost of alternative cultural traditions. However, even under domination, art is a source of cultural and political identity and *resistance*, where the dominated can still express oppressed practices of culture transmission and ancestral knowledge.

Villoro argues that there are three key factors when we search for our identity, independently of how we are positioned in the social hierarchy: our tradition, our concrete historical situation, and our life projects (Villoro, 2022, 39). Culture is deeply tied to collective identity and to how it is structured in the larger frame created by the history of oppression. The risk is that culture, as Beaver and Stanley point out, is a source of ideology. It is because of this that history is so important in framing cultural identities. However, history is also contentious territory. Narratives of domination are preserved even after they become subsumed in a narrative in which the oppressor becomes oppressed (Villoro mentions the status of Spain as an example, from colonial force to occupied territory under the French). Historical narratives preserve a set of commitments, resonances, and appreciations. In this respect, they are a very powerful source of attentional attunement and alignment. Herein lies a conundrum: *how to distinguish culture from ideology?*

Villoro was interested in this question since *Grandes Momentos*.[1] How could a spiritual tradition of forgiveness and liberation turn ideological, violently oppressing indigenous peoples? How could a group of revolutionaries create a national culture with distinct practices without becoming oppressive? A genealogy of power and practices becomes relevant here. Interestingly, there is recent work on Michel Foucault's pragmatist commitments that might help inform Villoro's own take on the question of culture and ideology. In a recent book review, Colin Koopman mentions Foucault's distinction between *savoir*

---

[1] This claim is further developed in Chapter 1. The Villoro archive at UNAM contains extensive documentation supporting Villoro's continuous commitment to creating a non-ideological dialogue with the indigenous world until the end of his life, from his lifelong interest in history, sociology, and anthropology to his engaged participation with the EZLN. To give one example, Box 9, File 46 of the archive contains documents on collective memory and collective forms of attention relevant to cultural appreciation; the importance of human rights and legal philosophy in creating a framework for a reasonable dialogue; and a moving set of documents on the "mesas de diálogo" where enormous effort was put into the creation of contexts of dialogue that could teach the Mexican government how to "govern by obeying" (a famous slogan of the EZLN).

and *connaissance*, which correspond to the Spanish *saber* and *conocer*, and then relates them to two notions of power:

> Just as Foucault's archaeology relied on a contrast between the everyday knowledge of *connaissance* and the implicit system of rules of *savoir*, Foucault's genealogy should be understood as involving a similar contrast between the everyday operations of force in the sense of *puissance* and the implicit system of rules for power that he referred to with his signature concept of *pouvoir* (which can roughly be summarized as referring to the "depth" conditions of the exercise of power).
>
> (Koopman, 2025)

Culture is a crucial interface between bedrock and open inquiry. Cultures of cooperation are the antidote to ideological cultures—in the next chapter, I call these cultures of cooperation a *bureaucracy of intimacy* because only a large, well organized, and transmissible kind of culture against ideology can become a collective path toward liberation. For liberation to succeed, knowledge and freedom need to have an impact on bedrock, in its epistemic and ethical dimensions. Tradition is, according to Villoro, a life-style or form of life that transcends geographies and material conditions. Our historical situation, by contrast, is the concrete manifestation of culture given our material conditions, which might be quite unfavorable—think of indigenous art during colonial Spanish rule in the Americas, which was for the most part forbidden and had to take on a Catholic or Spanish character to survive. Despite this forced performance, indigenous art transcended oppression.

Villoro relies on the historicity of our concrete social situation to articulate his non-ideal approach to justice. He explains how a rational conception of justice starts from a concrete experience of injustice, perceived as one's own exclusion from epistemic and moral communities. The dissident and excluded member of society need not be "normal" to create a genuine political identity (Villoro, 2022, 86). Villoro says that his non-ideal route to justice is not innocuous, because it situates the search for justice within a historical process with real people, in concrete situations that challenge a given understanding of morality in order to improve their situation (Villoro, 2022, 87).

Our cultural identity determines our capacity to perceive asymmetries in social status. The erasure of our ethnic and social identity in favor of universal norms was a major goal of the Enlightenment, with various positive results, including the foundation of contemporary democracies. However, the official erasure of our cultural differences, for example in favor of a homogenous situation like the OP or the social contract, also caused profound injustices. We are not detached from our conditions of existence, which are never homogenous. If our genealogies and cultural identities are erased, then genocide and barbarity can be brushed away as contingencies of our political goals, all of which are idealized and hypostasized as political strategy. Erasing history is a tool to justify oppression. Public reason and communication cannot be reasonable if our principles of rationality are mere abstractions that avoid history. The practice of ignoring history and flagging certain identities as irrelevant or peripheral is deeply antithetical to the pursuit of justice.

For Villoro, a truly just society must be multi-ethnic. Families, societies, and epistemic collectives frame our interactions through shared memories. As in the case of individual memory, two epistemic functions are critical here. One concerns the reliability of sources of information, the other the sense of shared experience that amalgamates the group and shapes how it imagines itself in the future. We could extend Villoro's distinction concerning ideologies and refer to these functions as the *gnoseological and sociological aspects of collective memory*, which correspond to the conditions required for the articulation of *puissance* and *pouvoir*. These epistemic issues concerning collective memory thus take on an ethical and political dimension. Because of the importance of collective memories for our cultural identity, they do so much more rapidly than individual memories. Imposing or denying a collective narrative is dangerous, even if based on evidence or rational principles, and it may harm those with alternative accounts of historical events.

Memory consolidation at the collective level is deeply political, and collective forgetting can be a powerful tool of domination.

The victims of crimes, particularly war crimes, often see the process of forgetting the occurrence of these unjust events as explicit denials of their dignity, through the erasure of the most salient of their collective memories. Collective memory erasure is a cruel form of epistemic and moral injustice. Truth and reconciliation panels and courts play the two essential roles of finding the truth and framing a narrative that includes the silenced and oppressed. Forgetting the horrors of traumatic experiences may be important for reconciliation to occur, but when peace is imposed through memory erasure, forgetting becomes the enemy of justice. Most of the vast number of colonized peoples were silenced by both erasing their history and by framing their identity through the lens of the interests of the oppressor.

Even when the facts are uncontroversial, the way in which collective memories are formed, or imposed upon historical narratives, is typically a heated topic of political debate. Answering questions like "which events count as the most relevant," or "which battles were the decisive ones," determines which culture is portrayed as dominant. For instance, the competing national memories of the Second World War cause both pride and indignation because of the moral and political cost of the war. According to experimental evidence, these memories have been proven to be highly *ethnocentric* (Roediger and Zerr, 2022), and therefore, unreasonable. From an epistemic point of view, there is a crucial asymmetry between individual and collective memory here concerning injustices against entire groups of peoples. Villoro's distinction between the gnoseological and sociological aspects of ideology is useful in examining this asymmetry. Sociopolitical selection, collective attention, and the historical record create a social narrative. But because the costs of injustice are much higher, collective imagination cannot play the more substantial role that imagination plays in personal memory consolidation and reconsolidation—the formation and updating of memories. The asymmetry is that the possibilities of reshaping and imaginatively reconstructing collective memories should be smaller, in the spirit of unifying, as Villoro wants, knowledge and freedom. And yet, collective imagination clearly must play some role, opening the door for ideological thinking.

Unsurprisingly, cooperation and reasonable communication are critical to address this difficulty. Confronting past brutality and collective silence seems to require indirect uses of imagination that are more capable of conveying traumatic memories with compassion and depth than a cold consultation of the archival record. Merely recollecting horrific events does not produce the required understanding necessary for recollecting our past in order to cope with the future. This is why the Zapatista movement was never interested in a mere revision of the history of Mexico, but rather, in a comprehensive movement about how to rethink indigenous forms of life and, more importantly, *a call to action* to engage each other more reasonably. The next chapter shows how this is an important lesson regarding the relation between culture and history, which informs Villoro's capability approach.

References

Beaver, D. and Stanley, J. (2023), *The Politics of Language*, Princeton: Princeton University Press.

Camp, E. (2024), *The Politics of Language*, by David Beaver and Jason Stanley, *Mind*.

Dancy, J. (2013), 'Meta-ethics in the twentieth century', In M. Beaney (ed.), *The Oxford Handbook of the History of Analytic Philosophy*, Oxford: Oxford University Press (pp. 729–49).

Habermas, J. (1993), *Justification and Application: Remarks on Discourse Ethics*, C. Cronin (trans.), (Studies in Contemporary German Social Thought), Cambridge, MA: MIT Press.

Harsanyi, J. (1982), 'Morality and the theory of rational behaviour', In A. Sen and B. Williams (eds.), *Utilitarianism and beyond*, Cambridge University Press (pp. 39–62).

Keiser, J. (2023), *Non-Ideal Foundations of Language*, New York: Routledge.

Koopman, C. (2025), Review of *Power and Freedom in the Space of Reasons:*

Elaborating Foucault's Pragmatism, Notre Dame Philosophical Reviews (online).

Krasnoff, L. (2014), 'The reasonable and the rational' In Mandle, J. and Reidy, D. A. (eds.), *The Cambridge Rawls Lexicon*, Cambridge: Cambridge University Press (pp. 692–7).

Montemayor, C. and Haladjian, H. H. (2015), *Consciousness, Attention, and Conscious Attention*, Cambridge, MA: MIT Press.

Murdoch, I. (1969), "On 'God' and 'Good'", In M. Grene (ed.), *The Anatomy of Knowledge; Papers Presented to the Study Group on Foundations of Cultural Unity, Bowdoin College, 1965 and 1966*, Amherst, MA: University of Massachusetts Press (pp. 46–76).

Murdoch, I. (1964), The Idea of Perfection, *The Yale Review*, 53(3), reprinted in Murdoch (1971).

Rawls, J. (1980|1999), Kantian Constructivism in Moral Theory, *The Journal of Philosophy*, 77(9): 515–72. Reprinted in Rawls, J. (1999), *Collected Papers*, In S. Freeman (ed.), Cambridge, MA: Harvard University Press (pp. 303–58).

Rawls, J. (1982), 'Social unity and primary goods' In A. Sen and B. Williams (eds.), *Utilitarianism and beyond*, Cambridge University Press (pp. 159–86).

Rawls, J. (1993a), *Political Liberalism*, New York: Columbia University Press.

Rawls, J. (1993b), The Law of Peoples, *Critical Inquiry*, 20(1): 36–68.

Roediger, H. L. 3rd, Zerr C. L. (2022), "Who won World War II? Conflicting narratives among the allies", *Progress in Brain Research*, 274(1):129–47.

Rorty, R. (2007), 'Justice as a larger loyalty', In R. Rorty (ed.), *Philosophy as Cultural Politics, Philosophical Papers, Vol. 4*. Cambridge University Press (pp. 42–55).

Scanlon, T. M. (1982), 'Contractualism and utilitarianism', In A. Sen and B. Williams (eds.), *Utilitarianism and beyond*, Cambridge University Press (pp. 103–28).

Villoro, L. (2022), 'La búsqueda de la identidad cultural latinoamericana', In J. Villoro and G. Hurtado (eds.), *La Identidad Múltiple*, Mexico: El Colegio Nacional.

Whitely, E. (2024), Order-Based Salience Patterns in Language: What They Are and Why They Matter, *Ergo: An Open Access Journal of Philosophy*, 11(26): 689–715.

Yurchak, A. (2006), *Everything Was Forever, Until It Was No More: The Last Soviet Generation*, Princeton: Princeton University Press.

7

True Revolutions: A Bureaucracy of Intimacy

Intellectual upheavals and the importance of clarity in opposing ideology

Villoro is a key figure in Latin American analytic philosophy. As we have seen, much of his most influential philosophical work engages explicitly with many of the major figures of analytic philosophy from the last century. Since Villoro was a devoted political activist who joined an armed group representing indigenous people, it is pertinent to ask what attracted Villoro to analytic philosophy? Typical analytic philosophers are dramatically different from Villoro. They almost never become as politically involved and see things at a safe distance. It would have made much more sense for Villoro to join his Marxist colleagues in Latin America, many of whom repudiated analytic philosophy as a kind of intellectual anesthetic, imposed by English-speaking centers of academic power onto the rest of the world to keep their philosophical views subdued. In fact, it might have been the case that because of his political activism, Villoro was under a fair amount of pressure not to embrace analytic philosophy as openly as he did. In his engagement with it, as in other aspects of his life, he proved to be insightful and courageous.

The solution to the apparent contradiction between his left-wing activism and his engagement with a tradition that is suspect in anticolonial circles is that Villoro appreciated the *anti-ideological* commitments of analytic philosophy, manifest in its emphasis on rigor and clarity. He particularly valued analytic philosophy's determination that philosophers should not appeal to authority or tradition, which characterized other movements, including Marxism.

A terrible consequence of analytic philosophy's commitment to clarity by not appealing to tradition is that some practitioners thought it authorized doing philosophy without knowing any of its history and ancient traditions. Some of them thought, remarkably, that ignorance of philosophical traditions is compatible with rigorous thinking. Obviously, this is a very superficial kind of rigor that constitutes a type of epistemic injustice against non-dominant philosophical traditions. Villoro did not make this mistake and, as we have seen, he engaged with and knew many philosophical traditions very well—phenomenology, existentialism, Marxism, and the history of philosophy at large. Many of the courses he taught at UNAM were on ancient Greek philosophy and philosophy of religion, relying directly on texts from the major spiritual traditions.[1] He learned from, and openly appealed to, Zapatismo as a philosophical approach to culture and politics. However, he did admire analytic philosophy and became a prominent exponent of it in Mexico. It is instructive to see why analytic philosophy is indeed anti-ideological by examining the history of analytic philosophy itself. This brief exposition will illuminate Villoro's conceptions of philosophy and intellectual revolution.

Condemning ideology is essential for disruptive and revolutionary thinking. The Marxist tradition provides a clear example of why disruption must be accompanied by clarity of thought and anti-authoritarianism. Marxism in Latin America was deeply politicized and became very ideological, with many factions fighting against each other and, in some cases, employing cruel forms of violence as their modus operandi. In Peru, for example, a strand of Marxist thought became the ideology behind *Shining Path*, a violent group that terrorized Peru for decades, and whose leader, Abimael Guzmán, was a philosophy professor prior to joining the movement. Many revolutionary groups throughout Latin America found inspiration in Marxism, the Soviet

---

[1]   For instance, Files 13–17 of box 3 of the Villoro archive contain documents about the Renaissance and middle ages that Villoro used for some of his classes. They include class notes on canonical texts on theology, magic, spirituality, nature, and politics.

Union, and Communist China. The tendency toward ideological alignment in the left was very strong. Villoro resisted this tendency by opposing the ideology that dominated much of the political discourse of anti-imperial and socialist narratives. Ironically, Marxism became ideological, but Villoro was deeply sympathetic with the essence of Marxism as a challenge to oppression. He saw in analytic philosophy a better way of taking on this commitment.

Analytic philosophy was a reaction to unclear and manipulative thought. It became obsessed with resisting ideologies and doctrines based on authority. Philosophy should not be based on the acceptance of dogmas or entail any allegiance to a school of thought. One of the key commitments of analytic philosophy is to always present the argument one defends as clearly as possible, without appealing to tradition or the thoughts of others, and to examine its merits in its own right. In its best rendition, analytic philosophy is an exercise in honest, clear, and anti-authoritarian thinking. It became influential during dangerous and dark times, when science was attacked and reframed in ideological terms—for instance, the Nazis called the work of Einstein on relativity and the entire new field of quantum mechanics "Jewish science." Many intellectual debates were drowned in arcane terminology. Appealing to authority was a common practice. Two of the founders of analytic philosophy, Bertrand Russell and G. E. Moore, argued against British idealism with the aim of stopping this way of doing philosophy. Russell and Moore would be surprised by how contemporary analytic philosophers have created sub-areas that are equally mired in arcane terminology and siloed from one another.

A common misconception of analytic philosophy is that it is a movement that initiated and developed primarily in the English-speaking world. This is, at best, only partially true. Three of its founders and key exponents were German (Rudolf Carnap, Carl Gustav Hempel, and Hans Reichenbach). And of course, one of the main sources of the movement was the work of Gottlob Frege, who was also German. This is not surprising given that Germany was, before the Second World War and for at least a century before, a major, if not the most important, center of knowledge production in the world. However, analytic philosophy also involved Austrian thinkers, chiefly Wittgenstein. With the establishment of the Vienna circle, analytic philosophy developed into a dominant force in philosophy, first in Europe under the guise of the "linguistic turn" and then in the United States through the intellectual exodus created by the war, where it took the familiar shape we recognize today.

The founders of analytic philosophy intended to launch what Villoro would call a "revolution" or "reform" of intelligence. Many of them, unlike most of their contemporaries, thought this meant that the new philosophy needed to be fully informed by science, its findings and methods. Eventually, this initial motivation pushed forward mostly by the German members of the movement (mainly Carnap and Reichenbach) collapsed into the sub-area now known as *philosophy of science*. The revolution that Carnap, Reichenbach, and other members of the Vienna circle had in mind was supposed to reform philosophy by dropping arcane and dogmatic *methods*, particularly the use of introspection and intuition as the sole source of the authority of reason. The revolution had Kant as one of its main targets, although because of its emphasis on method, it opposed many philosophical views. Much more can be said, but it suffices to focus on one example: Reichenbach's work on the philosophy of space and time, which defends the theory and methods of Einstein against Kant.

Kant's Copernican revolution aimed at establishing the limits of reason in a way that inverted the traditional search for truth from arbitrary, dogmatic, or hypostatic claims to the conditions for reasoning that our cognition imposes on inquiry. This revolution regarding the limits of reason has had an enormous impact on philosophy to this day. In various areas of philosophical inquiry, we are still coping with Kant's audacious reform of intelligence. A revolution like Kant's is more profound than the kind of scientific revolution that Kuhn had in mind, because it concerns the very foundations and limits of reasoning. It is this kind of revolution that the science-oriented exponents of early analytic philosophy had in mind.

Against Kant's conscious *intuition-based* conditions for our knowledge of space and time, Reichenbach (1958) argued that intuition or phenomenology has no authority over our *knowledge* of spacetime. Appealing to what he calls "Einstein's epistemology," Reichenbach explains the development of the theory of relativity at various stages, all of which involve the abandonment of intuition in favor of experiment and innovation. A crucial stage concerns the revolution in geometry that showed that Euclidean geometry—the only one conceived of as possible and intuitive—was only one case of a coherent geometry with zero curvature. This expanded the limits of what was a reasonable axiomatization of space, because there were perfectly conceivable and coherent geometries that violated the axiom of the parallels. This led to the key question that Einstein focused on: which of these geometries is *empirically adequate*—an empirical or a posteriori issue, in opposition to Kant's a priori transcendental aesthetics.

Another factor about Einstein's epistemology that Reichenbach emphasizes is his use of new forms of visualization that challenge the traditional view of space and time. Einstein asked what would happen in a situation that could eventually be experimentally tested, even if it is highly counterintuitive. Instead of taking the rate of time to be uniform across the universe as a matter of a priori truth, Einstein visualized highly accelerated frames of reference and clocks, rather than an assumed God's eye "timekeeper." The point of this brief explanation of Reichenbach's work is that the original intent of the pioneers of analytic philosophy was not merely to explain a scientific revolution, but rather to initiate an intellectual reform that resembled Kant's own Copernican revolution—a reform that tested and expanded the limits of reason. As we saw previously, this is also the kind of project that interested Villoro.

In a historical twist, Kantianism and intuition-based philosophy more generally has regained its position as a powerful movement within recent analytic philosophy, both in epistemology (for example, internalist normativism and evidentialism) and ethics (notably, the influential work of Rawls). One would think that this is a recent comeback, given the anti-Kantianism of some of the early proponents of analytic philosophy, like Reichenbach. Yet, Analytic Kantianism is now more than 50 years old, starting with the work of Peter F. Strawson at the end of the 1950s (Beaney, 2013, 5).Today, against the initial scientific approach that eventually was labeled as "naturalism," we find the comeback of intuition-based methodology in most sub-areas of philosophy (and a resistance against this methodology by the "experimental philosophy" movement). Analytic Hegelianism is more recent, but it is also flourishing, and there is also now a strand of analytic phenomenology (ibid.), themes that would be considered as anathema by the early proponents.

With all these developments, one wonders what the term "analytic philosophy" really refers to. For our purposes, analytic philosophy is, as an intellectual project, a thorough revision of the methods and goals of philosophy so as to achieve clarity and oppose ideological or dogmatic thought. Defined in this way, this project is fully consistent with Villoro's philosophical outlook. However, what did analytic philosophy mean in Latin America? The answer to this question is not as positive as its characterization as a reform of intelligence. Even when analytic philosophers from Latin America are very rigorous and original, they are still perceived as subsidiary thinkers at best, and most of them remain ignored and underappreciated. Most analytic philosophers in Latin America are destined to be promoters of the views of those who publish in the dominant centers of knowledge in the English-speaking world—a sad situation of intellectual colonialism. Villoro himself is largely ignored in the English-speaking world, where the dominant trends in analytic philosophy are produced. Why shouldn't the adherence to analytic philosophy in Latin America count as ideological, given this asymmetry?[2]

For Villoro, analytic philosophy provided a refreshing way of doing philosophy, one that allowed him to articulate his own brand of

---

[2]   Latin American thinkers have always valued their unity, based on their peoples' struggle against oppression across the Americas, as a distinctive aspect of their cultures, philosophies, and revolutionary movements. Condemning dominant cultures is part of this struggle and for many, this means rejecting philosophies produced in the centers of power. For instance, see Mariátegui (1925).

pragmatism in a way that incorporates key features of the political realities of Latin America, including its colonial past. So he was not merely parroting the style of the metropolis or engaging in the promotion of others' ideas through subordinate-thinking. The asymmetry in intellectual power between the English-speaking world and Latin America is bigger than analytic philosophy, and there was nothing Villoro could do about it. What he could do, he excelled at, namely, producing original and important work that mattered for Latin America's struggle against oppression and ideology.

The possibility of cooperative and non-exclusive communication is key to Villoro's normative account. In his engagement with analytic philosophers, Villoro's work anticipates some of the trends of recent analytic philosophy, such as moral and pragmatic encroachment, as well as non-ideal views about epistemology, ethics, and philosophy of language. Intellectual revolutions require clear and anti-ideological thinking. They require a discipline of thought. Analytic philosophy is inspired by this goal. Villoro is very much interested in bringing to light the political dimensions of our search for the limits of reason in concrete contexts of communication where any space for reasoning is contested, rather than in abstract realms of ultimate truth and scientific enlightenment. However, Reichenbach's search for clarity is one that Villoro finds crucial in any kind of genuine intellectual revolution, in thought and in action.

True revolutions: politics and culture

The goal of arriving at ultimate truths and principles through a perfect language, promised by the "linguistic turn" and the early exponents of analytic philosophy, never came to fruition. Carnap's *Aufbau* proved to be an idealization that was unrealistic and problematic—the main critic of Carnap's program was the pragmatist Willard van Orman Quine. Indeed, the pragmatists warned us that these were unreasonable goals. Nevertheless, Villoro shares the vision of the early analytic philosophers in conceiving philosophy as revolutionary and deeply anti-dogmatic. As mentioned, Villoro is also interested in cultural revolutions, like the Renaissance, which changed the contours of the figure of the world. Revolutions that reform intelligence require disciplined and careful thinking. But they also require cooperation, solidarity, and engagement. As we saw before, Wittgenstein is frequently interpreted as raising issues concerning meta-philosophical questions, such as the limits of reason and the purpose of philosophy. In a paper on Wittgenstein, Rorty writes,

> Admirers of Dewey like myself think that the point of reading philosophy books is not self-transformation but rather cultural change. It is not to find a way of altering one's inner state, but rather to find better ways of helping us overcome the past in order to create a better human future.

(Rorty, 2007, 169)

If one adopts a "therapeutic" reading of Wittgenstein, the therapeutic effect of philosophy cannot be equivalent, according to Rorty, to personal epiphany. Villoro very much agrees with this point, unsurprisingly, given his other pragmatic commitments. In his formulation of the pragmatic understanding of Wittgenstein, Rorty compares the goals of the logical empiricists of the Vienna circle to those of the pragmatists. Their mutual interests in rigor and clarity must be conceived of as a collective pursuit of truth and the proper *guidance of inquiry*. Rorty writes,

> Despite their disagreements with Dewey, the positivists shared his conception of philosophy as a form of cultural politics. Carnap and Ayer thought that they might be able to make society more rational by formulating the rules that govern our language. They believed themselves to have acquired a superior grasp of those rules, thanks to their familiarity with symbolic logic. By spelling out those rules, they hoped to get undisciplined thinkers back on the rails. Their understanding of the "logical syntax of language" would enable them to draw a clear line between the cognitively meaningful and the cognitively meaningless.

(ibid.)

As we saw previously, the Vienna circle didn't deliver the perfect language for rationality that they promised to humanity, partly because they did not pay enough attention to the warning of the pragmatists that we should not look beyond our communicative practices and ways of living in our search for the truth. Yet, the unfeasibility of their project does not mean that their intention wasn't the right one. It is how they executed it that created the problem. Rorty says that the actual practices of communication of these analytic philosophers were impatient and unreasonable, because they were trying to force upon our communication practices an abstract idealization that could not possibly accommodate the entirety or complexity of human affairs. However, the idealistic project of the Vienna circle still enjoys a lot of appeal. One can find echoes of it in early cybernetic projects concerning the automatization and optimization of bureaucracies and now in the current development of general artificial intelligence.

The warning from the pragmatists is as prescient as ever: what makes rationality *reasonable* is our practices of communication and the democratization of knowledge. Given that the current development of artificial intelligence is monopolizing both knowledge production and access to informational resources, our ideal "problem solver" has the potential of destroying our communicative and democratic practices (see Morozov, 2013; Montemayor, 2023b). By relying on technologies that create more inequality, we are distancing ourselves from reasonable practices, turning the world into an unfamiliar place where decision making is always delegated to corporations that operate strictly under the guidance of strategic, rather than reasonable, rationality (a point made earlier, but with a different emphasis, in Chapter 3).

Surrendering to technologically imposed strategic reasoning amounts to the capitulation of the philosophical project. Clarity of thought and purpose depend on an articulation of reason in which reasonableness is never replaced by instrumental rationality. Villoro defines philosophy as the disruptive activity of reason that delineates the limits and purpose of all scientific reasoning—it delineates the limits of reason. Philosophy is the opposite of strategic reasoning, which depends on specific agendas, tasks, and partial interests without focusing on the very conditions for communication and cooperation.

Scientism, even if well intentioned, as was the case with the members of the Vienna circle, is inadequate as a reform of intelligence. We need to abandon projects where idealizations and bodies of "perfectly rational" beliefs are imposed on epistemic communities. No real revolution—that is, no reasonable reform of intelligence, can simply be a "takeover" even if it is done through the best versions of instrumental reasoning. Expertise is very important, but it cannot replace reasonable communication. Real revolutionary changes in science that move humanity forward transform the figure of the world. These are profound changes in our habits and dispositions for joint attention and cooperation, never merely changes in sets of bodies of belief, as if social transformation depended on a sort of "reshuffling" of axioms, norms, and systems of belief. What transforms humanity are the practices that increase our capacities for joint attention, solidarity, and cultural transmission.

In the long term, any real intellectual or philosophical revolution becomes a *cultural transformation*. In a letter to his brother, the writer Henry James, William James says that pragmatism has the potential for producing radical cultural change, comparable to the transformation produced by the Protestant Reformation in Europe (cited by Rorty, x). A transformation of attention brings with it a new field of action that revolutionizes what is and is not salient, and what is relevant and worth our effort. It is our best hope for the kind of radical cultural reformation that Rorty and other pragmatists had in mind, including Villoro. This understanding of ethical and social transformation is a point where ideal theories like Rawls's, and non-ideal theories like Villoro's disagree.

Concrete conditions for development and effective agency are important for both authors, but only for Villoro must they be the starting point—the OP abstracts away from these conditions, putting participants in a state of ignorance. Rawls explains that the intuitive strength of the precedence of liberty, which the OP is meant to guarantee as a condition for justice, is that people would not exchange their liberty for economic advantages once "a certain level of wealth has been attained" (Rawls, 1971, 542). He says that the denial of equal liberty can only be accepted "if it is necessary to enhance the quality of civilization so that in due course the equal freedoms can be enjoyed by all" (ibid.). But despite this concrete, situational qualification of the precedence of liberty, Rawls postulates the OP as the conceptual point of departure in our deliberations about justice. There is also an assumption that we converge on our capacities for rationality, and that we have a largely homogeneous underlying moral psychology. These are assumptions concerning the symmetry of individuals in a political organization. But our capacities also depend on concrete conditions, access to resources, and historically imposed patterns of domination. These are highly asymmetric conditions across individuals and communities. Non-ideal theories start from these asymmetries in their analysis of justice.

For Villoro, the conditions of inequality that constitute our point of departure in moral theory (the methodology of the negative route) can only be exposed through our capacities for joint attention, which are not symmetrically aligned. In Villoro's pluralist and multi-ethnic approach, the "other," in its full concreteness and theoretical inconvenience, should not be eliminated through ignorance. Rather, we must open ourselves attentively and patiently to the value of the other, without judging and inserting our beliefs about them, turning them either "less other" because they fit our conceptions, or irrelevant, because they are incomprehensible and untrustworthy. Discomfort is part of this process. But it is only through this negative route that we can then achieve a shared acquaintance with the concrete forms of exclusion and injustice that organize our political lives. Attentiveness reshapes our figure of the world.

Villoro's engagement with Wittgenstein, as explained in earlier chapters, is quite significant to understand why, although Villoro agrees with Rawls on many substantial issues, he cannot accept the OP as the departing point of ethical inquiry. Ignoring the concrete situation of others invites conceptions of them in which we describe them as mere theoretical postulates or worse, as statistical items, as if they were a phenomenon or a fact, potentially reducing them to strategic reasoning. Villoro fully agrees with Rawls's claim regarding the precedent of liberty. For Rawls, the unconditional precedence of liberty needs to be an axiom of ethics and political philosophy, and this means that the other can never be treated strategically or as a mere fact. However, for Villoro, this condition should never be interpreted as a license to *ignore* the other. In fact, if we ignore the other, postulating her axiomatically, as symmetrically positioned with us in a formal equation for justice, we risk engaging in ideological thinking.

This is why being clear and rigorous in our philosophical outlook requires the discomforts of patient attention and even *silence*, understood as the effort to *not turn inward* toward our inner voice that incessantly tries to explain everything, sometimes by explaining it away. We must make the world salient in a way that is not framed exclusively by our convictions and biases—a principle regarding our actions, not just our axioms and descriptions. If we ignore the other, the inner voice of the authority of reason can prevent us from achieving knowledge, forcing us into a theatrical existence in which the contents of our axiomatizations are never realized, as was the case in societies that embraced universal equality in their legal documents while enforcing slavery. Attentive engagement is important in moral theory and epistemology because it prevents us from treating others as mere facts or items in an abstract axiomatization of norms. It guides our cognition in a way that clears the path toward knowledge and freedom. Being clear and rigorous about this important issue makes us more cooperative and charitable, bringing *energy* into our epistemic and ethical communities.

Ideal theories have the advantage of providing firm foundations to normative systems, similarly to an axiomatic system in which some truths are held as self-evident—a model of human rights that became crucial in Constitutional law. This model has not proven to be efficient either in domestic or international law. Injustice and inequality are rampant, despite various efforts to ameliorate our conditions of asymmetry. In this critical respect, Villoro's point of departure is not only more realistic, but also more demanding. Instead of appealing to our capacities to arrive at a point of stasis and abstract equilibrium, it forces us to jointly attend to the multiple injustices and inequalities that we created, so as to think through, one by one, the kind of considerations about rationality, reasonableness, and justice that occupied Rawls, particularly in his later thought.

Another key aspect of Villoro's view is that it focuses on cultural transformation as a way of *reenergizing* the public sphere and the social fabric, in somewhat the same way as the proposals of his pragmatist predecessors, particularly Dewey. The apex of ethical reasoning is not an idealization, but a kind of intimacy and solidarity that keeps growing and expanding—a practice of mutual attention. I call this a *bureaucracy of intimacy*, because it requires a significant degree of organization and social planning. Cultural transformations reenergize our sentiments and sensitivities, and they make us better by strengthening our capacities for joint attention. This renewal occurs within a concrete historical process, which depends on the material conditions imposed by being the biological organisms that we are, and by our educational practices and modes of engagement—what Wittgenstein calls "forms of life."[3] Earlier, we discussed the notion of charge—positive and negative attentional dispositions in Villoro's attitudinal epistemology and ethics, as well as Siegel's notion of positive and negative epistemic charge for perceptual experiences, based on inferential precursors. The psychology of these approaches is not one that requires the rational introspection of norms and equilibria. It is, rather, a psychology of degrees of attachment to various kinds of value, grounded and anchored in social practices.

---

[3] In this respect, Villoro's view is consistent with other philosophical accounts that aim at decolonizing epistemology and ethics. In particular, his emphasis on material conditions as essentially life-involving is in line with Enrique Dussel's ethics of liberation, especially Dussel's material *principle of life*. Dussel (2013, 92) explicitly says that human life is the *mode of reality* of the ethical subject. For an examination of this principle that contrasts it with discourse ethics, see Zúñiga (2021, 121–2). For a broader defense of a philosophy of liberation and anticolonialism informed by this principle see Dussel (2015).

By combining Villoro's insights with an attention-based psychology of our attitudes and sensitivities, we can conceive of the revitalization of epistemic and moral charge through joint attention as a powerful kind of *cultural energy*. We are already paying collective attention to highly commodified contents on social media. This type of collective yet passive and even subordinate or addictive attention can be deeply alienating because it forces us to commodify our interactions rigidly within an instrumental kind of rationality. This kind of joint attention harms our cognitive capacities and because it alienates us from one another it negatively charges our communication and interactions. According to Dewey and other pragmatists, democracies are not merely strategic institutions for market-like competitiveness, electoral results, and mere consensus making. They are mainly the result of practices that seek equality in the public sphere through education and cooperation—positively charged kinds of joint attention. Democracy requires an educated public that has a fair degree of independence from commercial forces and political ideologies. A public sphere shaped by knowledge and freedom should be a space of *resistance* to ideological and commercial impositions on our collective attention.

How to understand charge and energy, positive or negative, in cases of cultural collective attention in which neither truth nor justice seem to be at stake? Although our current version of the public sphere through social media is a mixed bag of attention to monetized status-seeking and ideological bias in highly commercialized communities, some cases of leisure-oriented cultural attention are interesting to explore in this context. Sports are a big source of income for those who sell media advertisements and products based on them. Millions of people enjoy sports around the world for their own sake. The amount of time, money, and energy people are willing to spend on sports simply for enjoyment and entertainment is considerable. The collective attention fans put into sports has a high degree of energy and even if it is manipulated for commercial reasons, it retains some of the purity of a *disinterested* kind of attention, similar to the attention we give each other in a personal conversation, or when we see something beautiful.

If only this kind of energy could be oriented towards cooperation and solidarity, our societies would become fairer and our communication would be less dominated by ideology.

This kind of cultural energy in social exchanges is very rarely examined in contemporary epistemology or philosophy of mind, but it is clearly Villoro's main focus in his analysis of cultural identity in relation to the sociological aspect of ideology. We have focused too much on the *gnoseology of cognition*, largely centered on the mental states of individuals, at the cost of ignoring the essential vitality and nature of our social energy. Charge as positive cultural energy, rather than positive *justification*, is good for cooperation, but it is neither *intrinsically* good nor necessarily *normatively adequate*. Gladiatorial events in Rome and mass executions during the Second World War are examples of socially energetic cooperation that are deeply immoral and epistemically corrupt. Energetic cooperation, as opposed to collective apathy, has clear social benefits, such as rapid social transformation and an expedite reallocation of resources. For this kind of cultural energy to emerge, we need to be in concrete situations and contexts in which we can *identify* with groups—the opposite of Rawls's OP. Social energy doesn't come from mere consensus or egalitarian symmetry in the abstract, but from social bonds that develop through joint attention to concrete and quite specific realities, including collective memories, which can become deeply ideological.

We can now use the conceptual apparatus provided by Villoro to see why conspiracy theories are good for the *sociological* purpose of creating bonds and trust among the conspirators. However, they are bad for *gnoseological* purposes, because they are negatively charged with respect to epistemic and moral justification—they concern falsehood and exclusion. Thus, *cultural energy is orthogonal to epistemic and moral charge*. Radical transformations that use accelerated forms of social reshaping can turn into the terror that came after the French Revolution, and under Nazi Germany and Stalinist Russia. Ironically, once the new bureaucracies of power are imposed by these highly energetic but negatively charged revolutions, their effect is oppression, injustice, and the sense of a lack of autonomy—a socially depressed and apathic culture. This is why, under Villoro's interpretation, these revolutions do not count as *real* revolutions of intelligence that truly benefit humanity as a whole, like the Renaissance in Europe or the flourishing of contemplative traditions in Asia—radical and accelerated movements that were positively charged culturally and normatively. The energy of ideological revolutions creates the momentary appearance of unity and transformation. But this energy quickly withers and collapses into tyranny and ideological thinking. What looks initially as a powerful way of reshaping the figure of the world becomes instead an accelerated devastation of the social fabric.

Conspiracy theories and ideologies create strong bonds, but their social purpose is to manipulate people and exclude other groups. They provide the fastest and easiest forms of group exclusion by *othering* all outside members. The ones with the new vision must dominate the others—new revolutionaries quickly turn into tyrants. This appearance of novelty is what makes them so alluring; they seem to present a new vision that produces rapid and substantial cultural energy. Unfortunately, since they are negatively charged with respect to justification, only insiders benefit and the energy of their group is quickly oriented towards exclusion. Ideologies seem to present us with new figures of the world but, in fact, they are the continuation of the same ugly sociopolitical exclusion that has shaped human injustices throughout our history. By rapidly excluding other groups as the realization of their vision, they erode the public sphere and destroy the possibility for reasonable communication. By definition, ideological movements cannot meet Villoro's criterion for knowledge and freedom: compliance with our best standards for determining what is sufficiently objective and for appreciating what is valuable through reasonable communication in the most *inclusive* way possible. These are standards concerning reality and concrete situations. If a conspiracy theory becomes aggressively exclusive by silencing others, then it will harm both groups, the excluded and the included, by preventing them from knowing the truth according to our best standards and practices. It will also harm them *socially* by dividing them into an oppressing dominant group and an opposing oppressed group that is now targeted as "the other."

Cultural identity became a major theme in Villoro's late work, where he engaged in a series of conversations with Subcomandante Marcos. However, from the beginning of his career, Villoro had a strong interest in cultural identity and its development in Mexico. In fact, Mexican identity was the main concern of the Grupo Hiperión. What happens in this later period is that Villoro's analysis of ideology in relation to cultural identity becomes clearer and more encompassing. The othering of indigenous Mexico is clarified from the perspective of Mexico's accelerated projects of cultural rationality, like the Spanish imposition of Christianity and the modernization of Mexico. When we use our group identity to cancel and silence others as irrational, even if we are justified from a *rational* perspective, legal or theoretical, we are still *unreasonable*. Non-ideological social energy must produce cooperation, rather than exclusion. Many of our current forms of rationality lead to exclusion, and the automatization of decision making will exacerbate exclusion.

Thus, according to Villoro, there are *four dimensions* of energy and charge for collective attention and communication. Since this classification applies to both epistemic and moral evaluation, their interaction creates a complex social structure with eight dimensions defining the interaction between knowledge and freedom. The epistemic domain has positive and negative *gnoseological charge* concerning justification, and also positive and negative *sociological energy* concerning either trust and cooperation or distrust and apathy. These distinctions can be applied to epistemic communities, as well as individuals, creating various degrees of epistemic engagement. Enfeebled collective attention leads to public apathy. But mere positive energy is catastrophic without the safeguards provided by positive gnoseological charge. The same is true of the ethical domain, but here, as I am about to explain, the standard for sufficient objectivity needs to be complemented with Villoro's account of *value*. Notice that while these are distinct aspects of communication among groups, they all need to integrate into a single structure that shapes communicative practices and political arrangements. Therefore, the theoretical usefulness of these distinctions does not entail that we can neatly separate the epistemic from the moral domain, or the sociological from the gnoseological, as they unfold in concrete practices of communication. Besides being a multidimensional perspective on cultural energy and charge, Villoro's account allows for a range of degrees of engagement, rather than binary clear-cuts.

The entire perspective of collectives and their figure of the world can also become active or passive along these different degrees of involvement, from social boredom to cultural rapture. There is a lot of potential here for an analysis of the politics of attention and the study of political movements. Like attention in individuals, collectives can be in a state of flow or immersion in which everything goes smoothly without much monitoring or intervention, or they can choke and become paralyzed because of too much reflection on norms and principles. As we saw, entire nations can participate in a theatrical and epistemically enfeebled performative charade, or they can actively engage in rapid sociocultural transformation, for good and for bad. The range of action involved here goes from the pure passivity of being picked up to get to a destination to risking one's own life. The vitality of our responses as individuals and as members of groups comes with a sense of urgency, which *also comes in degrees*, and which matters to epistemic and ethical communities. Too much acceleration is disruptive. Too much reflection and deliberation is boring and stifling. Bureaucracies are useful because they can operate at different rhythms, like the different rhythms of legal systems and markets. They also provide a stabilizing character that brings cohesion to a diverse group of people with multiple and frequently opposite interests. The next section expands on this notion.

Before explaining Villoro's account of positively charged joint attention to ethical injustice, we need to appeal to his notion of *absence of value* as objective criterion for evaluations of moral and social harm. As part of his negative route, according to which we shall not assume abstract symmetries concerning epistemic and moral equality and justice, but rather begin with concrete injustices, Villoro introduces the notion that the absence of what is valuable provides a standard of evaluation that is equivalent to the requirement for *sufficiently objective justification*, that knowledge must comply with. The value of essential goods to satisfy our needs is patently and urgently experienced by those who are deprived of these goods. Villoro argues that the needs we share as vulnerable biological and social creatures can serve as an evidential basis for objectively, rather than subjectively, valuable goods—their absence is as powerfully experienced as any other concrete reality. Using an analogy with health, Villoro says that not satisfying what is needed to maintain health harms an individual in a way that is obvious to that person and everyone else (Villoro, 1997, 16).[4] Villoro refers in this context to a popular saying about value in Spanish, which is the equivalent of "you don't know what you have until you lose it."

El Poder y el Valor (Power and value) puts forward ideas about needs and value that Villoro was planning to incorporate in his unified account of knowledge and freedom. Villoro argues for his need-based account of value as a response to David Hume's naturalistic fallacy (1997, 48), or the problem that it is invalid to deduce what we should do from what is objectively the case. Villoro's view, which I shall interpret as a version of the capability approach, is also consistent with his pragmatic and normative commitments, examined earlier. There are deep continuities between his ethics of belief and his political theory. For instance, like the distinction between the gnoseological and the sociological aspects of ideological belief, Villoro distinguishes the value we perceive subjectively as beneficial or harmful to us from the objective value it really has (Villoro, 1997, 55–70). The first can be illusory and a source of ideological belief. The second is crucial in organizing societies and structuring a fair system of government. Villoro explicitly says that "what satisfies a need has objective value to the extent that such a need

---

4   I thank Guillermo Hurtado for bringing Villoro's account of the absence of value as objective criterion to my attention.

is verifiable." (1997, 52) The distinction, then, is between what we think we need and what we really need. A real need can be verified as a real deficiency, something that harms us if we don't have it, making us not only experience, but also confront, the absence of something very valuable, an absence that is thwarting our development or flourishing.

Needs can serve as the foundation of a capability approach that also explains the foundational nature of human rights (Montemayor, 2023b). The real value of needs we must satisfy so as to develop and be capable of having a dignified and autonomous life constitute objective aspects of our concrete situation that should count as basic goods. It is no coincidence that towards the end of his career, Villoro became keenly interested in legal philosophy and human rights. No instrumental or strategic reasoning can replace the real value of satisfying our essential needs—needs are *non-fungible*. In fact, appealing only to what we subjectively experience as a need in order to compete for vulnerability is a destructive kind of calculation in which there is no room for reasonable attention practices. Protecting human rights must always be on the horizon of philosophical preoccupations, as part of disruptive thinking. In accordance with Villoro's pragmatic perspective, human rights are not static or eternal truths. Villoro views them more like constant calls for action, demands on our collective attention that should constantly guide our communities. Moral value and human rights have *need-based* conditions. Protecting them is a constant project that requires expansion, cooperation, and constant work.

Villoro's unfinished unified account of ethics and epistemology, which I articulate here with an updated view of the epistemology and ethics of attention in the light of the capability approach, can now be completed. To summarize its main features, there are two normative dimensions to the degrees of positivity and negativity of charge and energy: the epistemic and ethical domains. There is positive and negative *energy*: the cultural force a community uses to collaborate and develop its own identity. There is also the positive and negative *charge* of our practices, or their degree of justification, which is specified by *sufficiently objective* standards for knowledge and value concerning our epistemic and moral evaluations. Energy with negative charge is a major source of ideological thinking, but when it is combined with a positive charge, energy is a foundation of reasonable rationality that makes possible an *attentive public* seeking to address injustices. Unfortunately, the allure of identity politics has repeatedly shown that ideological thinking can be more powerful than reasonable communication. Villoro's normative perspective is unique in this regard. It acknowledges that cooperation of any kind has a positive component that needs to be evaluated sociologically. This positive component can become ideological if it is not justified. Cultural energy depends on the combination of these key factors, which should be guided by reasonable communication.

A bureaucracy of intimacy: Villoro's capability approach

As we saw in Chapter 4, Villoro's view allows us to explain the invariance of structures of oppression across various ideologies, even if they contradict one another. This explains why there can be a *pendulum effect* in politics: people in power, from far left to far right, leave systems of domination largely untouched. Villoro understood that this is why more profound changes, like those he sought concerning multiculturalism and Zapatismo, required legal reform.[5] But even legal reform is not enough. What is needed is a reform of intelligence and reasoning. The strategic reasoning involved in ideological thought explains the invariance of oppression across ideologies as a pernicious practical problem. The structures of power are based on rational idealizations, the best we can come up with. If the poor remain poor

---

[5]   Moisés Vaca (2017) argues that Villoro's multiculturalism should be conceived as a framework for the international legal effort to protect ethnic groups, cultures, and nations, comparing Villoro's proposals with Will Kymlicka's. For a philosophical analysis of similar issues centered on discourse ethics and sociology see Nino (1994, 168–99).

and the oppressed excluded, then a better implementation of those perfect rationalizations is needed. But that is very difficult.

Rationalizations prevent us from attending to the real absence of what is needed to make a better world. Ideological thinking is based on the conviction that we are acting perfectly rationally, so we turn inward to identify the gap between our rationality and our sad concrete realities. But the gap is in our attentive capacities, rather than in our thinking: we are blind to what we must be jointly attending to. We need to attend, rather than think and explain ceaselessly. However, because ideologies are an important source of social energy, they have a powerful grip on our imagination, making us feel like justice is being served through our righteous rationalizations. This is why, as Villoro's philosophy requires, it is crucial to have objective standards based on real needs to appreciate how injustices stay the same across the opposing rationalizations of rival ideologies. The capability approach is consistent with this point, and it provides a fruitful way to understand Villoro's comprehensive normative view.

What is the capability approach? Amartya Sen defines the capability approach as: "an intellectual discipline that gives a central role to the evaluation of a person's achievements and freedoms in terms of his or her actual ability to do the different things a person has reason to value doing or being" (Sen, 2009, 16). Although there have been many refinements and clarifications of this view, Sen's definition captures its core features. Villoro's views in *Power and value* clearly align with Sen's definition, particularly regarding the centrality of actual capacities to pursue what one values in concrete, rather than abstract conditions. Satisfying real, rather than merely subjective needs, is also essential to the capability approach. The key question in all the areas of application in which the capability approach has been productively put to work is: *"What are people really able to do and what kind of person are they able to be?"* (Robeyns, 2017, 9).

In economics, the capability approach has provided more reliable measures to identify poverty and oppression. Sen, the original proponent of the capability approach, received the Nobel prize in economics for his contributions to welfare economics and the economic analysis of well-being. But as Ingrid Robeyns says, the capability approach is flexible enough to produce much more than a rigorous framework for welfare economics. It has been a very productive approach to public health, development ethics, environmental policy, and technology studies (Robeyns, 2017, 9), to name a few. It has also been useful in constructing influential theories of justice (Anderson, 1999; Nussbaum, 2006). In line with Villoro, the capability approach provides a more structural, contextual, and historical explanation of injustices by focusing, unlike alternatives, on real circumstances concerning oppression and exclusion, rather than the mere accumulation of material resources or the mental states of people. Villoro's view draws a similar contrast between the strictly subjective and potentially ideological appreciation of value and the real value of being able to freely act in the world and not be treated as inferior.

The capability approach shares insights with utilitarian and Kantian perspectives, but without the emphasis on rules or the evaluation of actions one at a time. In this respect, it adopts a pragmatic perspective, because a central concern of the capability approach is how people can live a dignified life, with an emphasis on their actual actions and practices. For this reason, it is also deeply compatible with virtue views, both in ethics and epistemology. These key analogies between Villoro's ethics and the core commitments of the capability approach justify interpreting Villoro's view as a version of the capability approach that has a strong emphasis on issues concerning social epistemology.

Villoro wrote that ethics needs to move forward from neo-Kantian accounts (like Rawls's) and neo-Hegelian views (like Sandel's) by embracing a revolutionary and disruptive standpoint. He explains this standpoint in terms of concrete motivations, real values, and objective standards for the improvement of societies (1997, 224–5). His version of the capability view focuses on a hierarchy of real needs and the capabilities required to satisfy them. The absence of opportunities is evident to those who lack them, limiting their capacity to have social, moral, epistemic, and effective legal standing. Optimizing and calculating is important, for instance, by preventing corruption and bureaucratic waste. But whatever strategy we follow in becoming a more just society, the real needs of the excluded must be at the center of analysis.

Revolutionary cooperation and the disruption of ideology through philosophy are central themes in Villoro's late work. But "revolution" doesn't here mean violence—Villoro dedicated several texts and presentations to the idea that real revolutions do not necessitate violence, and that violence is just a moment of social disturbance and upheaval that is not essential to revolutions. A revolution of attention is what is required, because it is transformative, moving us collectively toward the needs of those who suffer from a diminished social standing. The binders containing Villoro's latest work at UNAM's archive are about Zapatismo. He saw in Zapatismo the possibility of disruptive thinking grounded in real and historical needs, including how we attend to and communicate with one another.

The capability approach requires constant vigilance to how we attend to the real needs of others. It asks us to change our strategic standpoints to prevent their actual exclusion from epistemic and ethical communities, thereby forbidding us to treat them as inferior and unworthy of our consideration, independently of our ideological rationalizations. In Villoro's account, this requirement helps transform our societies into more reasonable contexts of communication. Doing so does not create an environment of competition in which we are trying to gain attention by exposing our vulnerabilities. This is the kind of strategic and commodified reasoning that Villoro and the capability theorists reject. A society where people are competing to be the most vulnerable is as ideological and broken as one in which people are assumed to be equal when in fact they are grotesquely different in their social standings because of asymmetries in power and wealth.

A disruptive kind of rationality centered on capacities and reasonable communication must move beyond social disruption, including violence. For lack of a better word, we can call this type of disruptive order a "bureaucracy of intimacy." The idea is that, like a bureaucracy, a revolution of attention must reverse the hyper-instrumental and strategic rational schemes that dominate government and commerce into reasonable communication. Only a very large bureaucratic effort can do this. Villoro was inspired by the organization of Zapatista groups, which followed the principle of "governing by obeying" through active and engaged participation. But clearly, other types of efforts are possible. Whatever shape it takes, this reorganization of our attention and attitudes should be transportable, given the urgency of our current predicaments—it should be compatible with great variations in cultures so as to unify them against ideological thought imposed through instrumental reasoning.

It should also be bureaucratic, resembling current strategically rational and efficacious bureaucracies—one cannot live today without paying taxes or registering vehicles, independently of whether one lives in fascist or liberal regimes. Transportability is one of its essential features, but not the only one. The other has to do with energy and charge—*both* need to be positive. Some organizations that have tried to liberate humanity through a combination of transportability, energy, and charge, with very mixed results, include Soviet revolutionary groups, Freemasonry, and almost all organized religions. The constant threat of falling into ideological thinking is what makes the capability approach so useful in framing alternative organizations that truly help people without promoting the exclusion of others.

For Villoro, the "others" of Mexico, the original inhabitants of the continent, fall under the vast category of "others" in the West. The attempts of Zapatistas at creating a bureaucracy of intimacy among themselves that could oppose other dominant groups outside Mexico constituted, in Villoro's mind, the best effort against colonialism, done *reasonably*. "Reasonable" means here, as in Rorty's account of justice, capable of expanding our loyalties to those who are not enough "like us." Seeing "the other" as trustworthy, and more importantly, as having similar needs and abilities, allows us to cooperate with them. What needs to be reversed is the permanent lens of greed and commodification that our contemporary bureaucracies of information and unequal distribution of wealth have imposed on us.

This sounds very utopian, but my goal is to emphasize that Villoro's philosophy asks for *concrete social organization*—the "regulative idea" of his philosophy is to look for concrete areas of social asymmetry in which disruptive thinking is needed to produce real change toward justice. Like the capability approach, it is an empirically informed proposal. It is aimed, like Zapatismo, at institutions and communicators of *cultural transmission*, including families as well as educational or spiritual associations, that have been affected by techno-commercialized bureaucracies that are highly centralized, hegemonic, and homogenous. These powerful strategic processes are fast-moving parts of our strategic reasoning that seem like necessities—like our gluttony for consumption and the constant replacement of goods which seem now to be completely out of the deliberative control of societies. Disruptive practices must culturally transmit the resistance to ideologies of exclusion and oppression that we assume now as bedrock belief.

The rapidity of our automation and technification needs to be countered by slower communities of care and attention. We seem to be trapped in a *global Cassandra puzzle* (based on the Greek mythological character): we know a lot about the future collapse of ecosystems, military tensions, and increasing political polarization, and we know that there are ways to prevent these problems. Yet, we seem incapable of acting, and refuse to take any measures because we are immersed in political ideologies, agendas, and strategic reasoning. Unlike the Greek myth, this is not because no one believes these terrible things are imminent. Rather, it is because we are not prioritizing these threats as the most salient aspects of the world we need to pay attention to. We are constantly turned inwards, toward our most cherished ideologies, full of righteous rationalizations that prevent us from acting, thinking that "the other" will take advantage of our willingness to be more cooperative. At the same time, we are helplessly surrendering our deliberative capacities to strategic reasoning, which is increasingly out of our hands and falling in the hands of corporations that only care about profit. Strategic reasoning is a fine aspect of rationality, but it can be, and nowadays systematically is, unreasonable.

Mere silence and shutting down our screens won't liberate us from epistemic slavery and moral catastrophe. Villoro cared, for Wittgensteinian reasons, about the role of silence in framing our actions, and felt deeply moved by the kind of silence and peace produced by spiritual experiences—his text on the Blue Mosque is particularly relevant in this regard.[6] But even silence needs to be reasonable. The amount of energy that we are collectively wasting in our ideological obsessions has reached tragic proportions. Villoro's philosophy has a lot to offer in our search for remedies that could make our lives better. Silence, for Villoro, is never just *retreat*—as the analogy he made between Sartre and Wittgenstein, mentioned in Chapter 4, shows. Even silence can help us organize, if it is reasonable: we need to temper down our ideological and excessive "inner chatting." Our communities and our planet cannot sustain the dominant and institutionalized strategic reasoning that shapes our contemporary world. If we do not start the Villorian project of creating bureaucracies of intimacy and care, we do so at our own peril.

References

Anderson, E. (1999), What Is the Point of Equality? *Ethics*, 109(2): 287–337.

Beaney, M. (2013), 'What is analytic philosophy?', In M. Beaney (ed.), *The Oxford Handbook of the History of Analytic Philosophy*, Oxford: Oxford University Press (pp. 3–29).

Dussel, E. (2013), *Ethics of Liberation: In the Age of Globalization and Exclusion*, Durham, NC: Duke University Press.

Dussel, E. (2015), *Filosofías del Sur: Descolonización y Transmodernidad*, Madrid, España: Ediciones Akal.

Mariátegui, J. C. (1925|2011), 'The Unity of Indo-Hispanic America', In H. E. Vanden and M. Becker (eds.), *José Carlos Mariátegui: An Anthology*, New York: Monthly Review Press (pp. 445–50).

---

6   For a discussion of the role of silence and the sacred in the work of Villoro concerning the religious and epistemic senses of "silence," including Villoro's interpretation of Wittgenstein, see Stepanenko (2022).

Morozov, E. (2013), *To Save Everything Click Here: The Folly of Technological Solutionism*, New York: Public Affairs.

Nino, C. (1994), *Derecho, Moral y Política: Una Revisión de la Teoría General del Derecho*, Buenos Aires, Argentina: Siglo XXI Editores.

Nussbaum, M. (2006), *Frontiers of Justice*, Cambridge, MA: Belknap, Harvard University Press.

Rawls, J. (1971), *A Theory of Justice*, Cambridge, MA: Belknap, Harvard University Press.

Reichenbach, H. (1958), *The Philosophy of Space and Time*, New York: Dover.

Robeyns, I. (2017), *Wellbeing, Freedom and Social Justice: The Capability Approach Re-Examined*, Cambridge, UK: Open Book Publishers.

Rorty, R. (2007), 'Preface', In R. Rorty (ed.), *Philosophy as Cultural Politics, Philosophical Papers, Vol. 4*. Cambridge University Press (pp. ix–x).

Rorty, R. (2007), 'Wittgenstein and the linguistic turn', In R. Rorty (ed.), *Philosophy as Cultural Politics, Philosophical Papers, Vol. 4*. Cambridge University Press (pp. 160–75).

Sen, A. (2009), 'Capability: Reach and Limit', In E. Chiappero-Martinetti and J. M. Roche (eds.), *Debating Global Society: Reach and Limits of the Capability Approach*, Milan: Fondazione Giangiacomo Feltrinelli (pp. 15–28).

Stepanenko, P. (2022), 'El Silencio en Luis Villoro y Ramón Xirau', In C. Tame Domínguez and J. L. López López (eds.), *Reflexiones Críticas Sobre la Filosofía de Luis Villoro*, Puebla, Mexico: BUAP.

Vaca, M. (2017), 'El Multiculturalismo de Luis Villoro', In P. Stepanenko (ed.), *Luis Villoro: Conocimiento y Emancipación*, Mexico: IIF, UNAM (pp. 303–24).

Zúñiga, M. J. (2021), 'Ethics of Liberation and Discourse Ethics: On Grounding the Material Principle of Life', In A. Allen and E. Mendieta (eds.), *Decolonizing Ethics: The Critical Theory of Enrique Dussel*, Pennsylvania: Pennsylvania State University Press (pp. 107–26).

Index